LIFECYCLE INVESTING

To Chris,

Hope its not too
late for us,

warmly,

Barry

LIFECYCLE INVESTING

A New, Safe, and Audacious Way
to Improve the Performance of
Your Retirement Portfolio

IAN AYRES AND **BARRY NALEBUFF**

BASIC
BOOKS

A Member of the Perseus Books Group
New York

Published by Basic Books,
A Member of the Perseus Books Group

Designed by Brent Wilcox

Library of Congress Cataloging-in-Publication Data
Ayres, Ian.
    Lifecycle investing : a new, safe, and audacious way to improve the performance of your retirement portfolio / Ian Ayres and Barry Nalebuff.
        p.   cm.
    Includes bibliographical references and index.
    ISBN 978-0-465-01829-1 (alk. paper)
    1. Retirement income—Planning.   2. Investments.   3. Portfolio management.
I. Nalebuff, Barry, 1958-   II. Title.
    HG179.A994 2009
    332.6—dc22
                                                            2009042543

10 9 8 7 6 5 4 3 2 1

To our teacher,
Paul Samuelson (1915–2009)

CONTENTS

Introduction

IN 1986, YALE was in financial turmoil. Its buildings were in serious disrepair, and incoming president Benno Schmidt went so far as to propose closing the Sociology Department as a way to save money.

Back then Yale's endowment stood at $1 billion. It was led by a new endowment manager named David Swensen. He was a surprising choice. Swensen came with an economics Ph.D. (from Yale), but no previous experience in endowment management. As a result, he didn't start with any prejudices as to how the money should be invested. He found that half the endowment was in U.S. equities, another 40 percent was in U.S. treasuries and corporate debt, and less than 10 percent was elsewhere. To his mind, that didn't make much sense.

There were two problems. First, since equities historically outperform debt—at least in the long run—it seemed that the portfolio was far too light in terms of equities. Second, the portfolio was undiversified. It was 90 percent domestic and had little exposure to commodities, real estate, venture capital, or anything international.

While economists are fond of saying there's no such thing as a free lunch, Swensen followed the advice of Nobel Prize–winner Harry Markowitz: Diversification is a free lunch. By doing a better job of spreading risks across different investments, you can earn the same return with lower risk. Or you can get a much higher return for the same amount of risk. Swensen took the latter approach.

Twenty-two years later, under Swensen's management, Yale's endowment had grown to $22 billion. Even after the market collapse of 2008, it is still safely over $16 billion. To put that in perspective, if Yale had stayed with a traditional equity allocation, the endowment would have been only $6 billion. Swensen managed to deliver a stunning 11.8 percent annual return over the past decade—double the return on bonds—without increasing the long-term risk.[1] Yale has two new residential colleges in the works, and we think at least one should be named after him: No one has contributed more money to Yale (or any other school) than David Swensen.

The goal of this book is to help you achieve something similar for your retirement portfolio. Over the last 138 years, stocks have outperformed bonds—not every year, but for every generation. On average, stocks have outperformed bonds by 5 percent. Even if this equity premium isn't as high going forward, stocks are still the better bet over the long run. By helping you achieve better diversification, we can help increase your exposure to stocks and improve your total return, all without increasing your risk.

Where's the free lunch?

Swensen helped Yale do a much better job diversifying across asset classes. That meant investing internationally, in timber, in start-ups, in real estate. We hope that you are already doing some of this. There are index funds that can give you broad exposure to the world's equity markets, to commodities, and to real estate.*

Our plan takes diversification a step further. Just as Swensen helped Yale achieve better diversification across asset classes, we aim to help you do a better job diversifying your investments across time.

---

*Putting your money in a well-diversified index fund means that you don't have to pay attention to the markets or quarterly earnings or pretty much anything else. To get maximum diversification you should ensure that the index fund includes foreign as well as domestic equities. Almost 60 percent of the total world's share value comes from stocks traded outside the United States. In terms of which mutual fund to go for, fees matter. The low-fee index funds consistently outperform the high-fee ones. Thus the ultralow-fee Fidelity Spartan and Vanguard index funds fit the bill. Of course, low fees also mean low ad budgets. If you see a firm spending loads of money trying to convince you to invest with them, you should realize that it will be your money that's paying for the ads.

Diversifying Time

In its simplest form, diversification across time is an intuitive idea that's a lot like asset diversification. Just as it would be a mistake to invest all your savings in a single stock, it would be reckless to concentrate all your exposure to the stock market into a single year. If you did that and the market happened to nosedive just then, you'd be toast. You're much safer spreading your stock investments across decades.

But most people don't do a good job of spreading. In terms of raw dollars, they invest very little in the market when they're young compared to when they're old. Even after accounting for inflation, a typical investor has twenty or even fifty times more invested in stock in his early sixties than he had invested in his late twenties. A few thousand dollars of stock exposure in your twenties doesn't provide much diversification when you have so much more invested later on. From a temporal diversification perspective, it's as if your twenties and thirties didn't really exist. Instead of investing $50,000 in the market when you're young and $1 million when you're older, it would be better to invest $100,000 when you're young and $950,000 when you're older. The total market exposure is the same, but it is better spread out across time. As an empirical matter, most people are missing out on twenty years of potential exposure to the stock market where they could be diversifying risk. Instead of spreading their risk over forty years, they concentrate it in the last ten or twenty years of their working lives.

To solve this problem, we offer a simple but radical idea:

Use leverage to buy stocks when you're young.

Spreading your investments better across time means investing more when you're young. But there's a good reason why you (and pretty much everyone else) don't invest more then: You don't have the money. That's where leverage comes in. The main point of this book is to show that it's prudent to make leveraged investments when you're young. You can hold your lifetime exposure to the stock market constant and reduce risk by having more exposure when you're young and less when you're older.

The Free Lunch

We'll show that better diversifying across time can reduce portfolio risk by 21 percent. Here's what that means in terms of dollars and cents. In our simulations, a traditional investment strategy leads to a nest egg of $749,000.* But the average belies the potential risk. There's a wide range of outcomes in the data.

A good way to measure risk is by the range of outcomes that you'll see 95 percent of the time. That gives you a sense of how good or bad things can be. Under the traditional investment strategy that range is $490,000 up or down.

With our lifecycle strategy, you can get the same average result, $749,000, but reduce the range by 21 percent, or $105,000, either way. At the top of the range you make $105,000 less, but in the worse case, you end up with $105,000 more. The worst case is when this really counts, since under the traditional strategy you only had $259,000. Now you can have $364,000 and greater peace of mind. This gain can be seen in Figure Intro.1.

Whether you think that a 21 percent improvement is big or small, that's just our starting point. The power in discovering a new diversification tool is that it lets you make new trade-offs between risk and return. Once you have a new method for controlling stock risk, you can safely hold more stock over the course of your life. We'll show you a way to increase your return by 50 percent without increasing your risk.

These results almost sound too good to be true. But this isn't a late-night TV commercial that promises you'll make millions buying distressed property WITH NO MONEY DOWN! There are no operators standing by. Our strategy is a straightforward application of research done by Nobel laureates Paul Samuelson and Robert Merton. (We explain this connection in the next chapter.) That said, at the end of the day, you shouldn't believe

---

*This result, of course, depends on the savings rule, investment allocation, and much more. We lay out all the assumptions in Chapter 3. But one thing it *doesn't* depend on is the premium that stocks earn over bonds. The total stock exposure is the same, and so the gains are all coming from improved diversification.

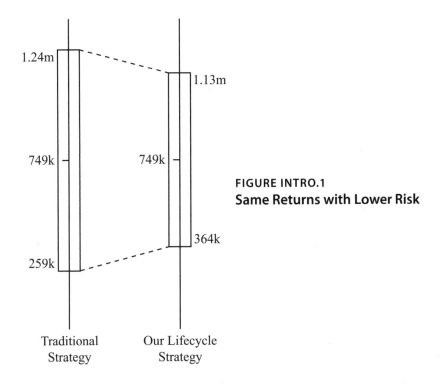

FIGURE INTRO.1
Same Returns with Lower Risk

us or anyone else because of who we are or what the distinguished blurbists say on the cover. You should follow our advice because it makes sense and because historical and simulation data confirm it. *Trust, but verify*. When it comes to something as important as your retirement savings, you can't rely on theory or common sense alone, no matter how sensible it seems at first blush and no matter how many people say it's the thing to do. Demand to see the data!

We have tested our approach using stock market data back to 1871. In each and every case—including the great crash of 1929 and the almost great crash of 2008—our diversifying strategy did better than a traditional investment strategy. It also worked better on the Nikkei and FTSE stock data and in Monte Carlo simulations with alternative stock return distributions. Chapters 3 through 5 provide the details, and all our data and estimates are available online at www.lifecycleinvesting.net.

The crash of 2008 was a nerve-wracking time for investors. The S&P 500 ended down 38 percent, and the day-to-day gyrations were at historic highs. In these uncertain times, temporal diversification becomes all the more important. The larger the volatility, the more important it is to diversify. Our simulations show that the leveraged lifecycle strategy—even in today's market—still beats traditional strategies for those who would have just retired and for those who are close to retirement. As for those just out of college, while it is a challenge to start off with a loss, the stakes are still very small. A greater exposure to the market when you're young allows you to reduce exposure right before retirement, and that would have been a propitious move in 2008.

Two Cheers for Home Ownership

Temporal diversification is one reason why buying a home is a smart long-term investment. People have been doing with housing something very close to what they should be doing with regard to their retirement investments. You buy a home with borrowed money (though not too much borrowed money), and the leverage declines as you pay off the loan. Housing investment is naturally diversified across time because it exposes you to the same investment in the housing market year after year. Even in your twenties, with $25,000 down, you can buy a $250,000 house or apartment. Although the bank "owns" your home, you still have full $250,000 exposure to the market. With homeownership, you keep a relatively constant exposure throughout the course of your life.

The reason why people make so much money on real estate over their lifetime is because they've had a lifetime of substantial exposure to the real-estate market. Homeownership is one of the very few ways that people have been willing to diversify across time. This is a huge, hidden benefit of buying a home. It's not a coincidence that the home often becomes the biggest single retirement asset.

The problem with homeownership is that it sacrifices asset diversification. Homeowners are nicely diversified across time, but all their housing risk is invested in a single property, a single housing stock if you will. It's better to diversify across time and across assets. Our leveraged stock strategy does just that—you're diversified across assets because you invest in a diversified portfolio of stocks, while at the same time keeping that exposure a lot more even as you age.

While people are comfortable investing in a home on a 10:1 leveraged basis, they have not been able to bring themselves to invest on even a 2:1 basis in stock. If people bought houses the way they bought stocks, they'd wait until they'd saved enough to pay cash for the whole house. They'd be lucky to buy a house before their fiftieth birthday. All we are proposing is to make stock purchases a little bit more like buying a house.

Of course, as the recent housing collapse has dramatically demonstrated, housing prices don't just move upwards. Just because buying a home with 5:1 or even 10:1 leverage is a prudent way to invest for retirement, that doesn't mean that it's prudent to buy real estate with 20:1 or 100:1 leverage or to take out a mortgage that's more than you can afford to carry (hoping that prices will shoot upwards so that you can refinance). Excess leverage or debt leads to excess risk. But that doesn't imply that we should eliminate leverage and mortgages with it. Both too much and too little leverage lead to poor outcomes.

We are not proposing something extreme like buying stocks with 5 percent or 10 percent down—just buying stocks with a 50 percent down payment when you're young. Even a small amount of leverage when you're young makes a huge difference because the effects get compounded over many years. According to Einstein, the most powerful force in the universe is compound interest. (The quote is likely apocryphal, but the claim is likely true.) The fact that people mostly miss out on investing in the market for the first twenty years of their working lives is what so substantially shrinks their ultimate nest egg.

If the key to buying real estate is location, location, location, the key to buying stocks is diversification, diversification, diversification. Without using leverage, you won't be diversified over time. While it may seem paradoxical, exposing yourself to more market risk by leveraging stocks early on actually reduces your overall investment risk. You can increase your expected retirement savings by 50 percent while reducing the risk of a bad outcome. Buying stocks with leverage will ultimately *reduce* your investment risk.

When we first made this proposal in our *Forbes* column, we got hate mail.[2] Readers wrote in accusing us of reckless financial endangerment. This isn't something the investment gurus advise or practice. Suze Orman, for example, invests less than 10 percent of her wealth in stocks. At most the gurus suggest investing 85 percent of savings in stock when you're young and ramping down from there. That's generally bad advice. (We explain the exceptions in Chapter 6.) Those in their twenties and thirties would do better to invest more than 100 percent of their retirement savings in stock. Ideally they should be at 200 percent stock.

There are only two dimensions on which investments can be diversified. You can diversify across assets, and you can diversify across time. Harry Markowitz, along with John C. Bogle, led the first diversification revolution. Markowitz won a Nobel Prize for showing people how to optimally diversify the assets in their portfolios. Bogle, the founder of Vanguard, brought asset diversification to the masses by creating low-cost index funds.

Until now, investors have not appreciated the potential value of temporal diversification. The gains from diversifying across time are even more important than the gains from diversifying across assets—for the simple reason that the returns in different years are less correlated than the returns in different stocks. This book seeks to foster a second diversification revolution. Better diversification across time leads to reduced risk. And reduced risk allows for increased market exposure and higher returns.

We appreciate that this book may take you out of your comfort zone. In the good old days, you didn't have to worry about how to invest for retirement. Employers offered defined benefit plans that provided a pension based on your final salary. This was great on several counts. You could know exactly where you'd be. You didn't have to worry about inflation. (To the extent that your salary went up with overall prices, your pension would be indexed, at least until the point at which you retired.) And you didn't have to worry about how to invest your savings.

Unfortunately, the world has changed. Defined benefit plans have been replaced by defined contribution—with employer matching if you're lucky. That means you're the one responsible for planning and investing for retirement. And you only get one chance to get it right.

To finance your retirement, you need to save right *and* invest right. Many people are having trouble saving enough. They only compound the problem when they invest their savings far too conservatively. A smarter allocation can improve your nest egg by 50 percent. That's a lot easier than increasing your savings by 50 percent. Through the process of improved diversification you can get this increase without more risk.

Our Plan

The plan of the book is straightforward. In Chapter 1 we lay out the life-cycle view of investing. This provides the intuition for why leverage when you're young leads to lower risk. Then in Chapter 2 we explain just how the strategy works. Chapter 3 presents the empirical results. The proof of the pudding is in the reading. We show that our strategy would have significantly increased retirement wealth in the past, even for people who lived through the Great Depression or retired in 2009.

In Chapter 4 we beat what we hope is by then a dead horse. If you still have doubts about the advantage of our leverage strategy, we show you that it works not just for U.S. stocks but also for stocks around the world. We show that the results remain true even if the future returns on stocks aren't as good as they have been in the past. We show that the strategy still works even if borrowing is more costly. We fully expect that some skeptics will remain. For those who want to try their own hand with the data, you will find it all online at www.lifecycleinvesting.net. Please share with us what you find.

Assuming we have you convinced at that point, Chapter 5 is designed to help those of you who are late starters. What good is knowing all this now if it is too late to act? In addition to helping prepare your kids, it turns out that there is much you can still do even in your forties and fifties.

In Chapter 6, we apply the brakes. Before you go ahead and follow our advice, you should read this chapter. A leveraged lifecycle isn't right for everyone, and we provide six reasons why it might not be right for you. For example, before you invest in stocks, first pay off all your student loans and credit card debts. If you have a 401(k) plan with an employer match, put your savings there first. You won't be able to invest with leverage (at least not at present), but the employer match is even better than leverage. Our goal is to help you get more exposure to equities when you're young. Some people are already heavily invested in the stock markets through their jobs. If you work on Wall Street, you don't need any more exposure to equities.

Chapter 7 tells you how to pick the strategy that's right for you. We help you tailor the equity allocation to your own tolerance for risk and your own views about prospective risk and return. We also help forecast what you'll need to afford your retirement. You can use these guides to work backwards and figure out how much you'll have to save along the way to get there.

Chapter 8 then lays out some step-by-step instructions for how to implement the lifecycle strategy. This includes what option contracts to purchase, how much you'll pay in implied interest, and what bonds to buy. We also consider the alternative strategies of investing in leveraged mutual funds or buying stocks on margin.

Finally, in Chapter 9 we confront the worry that we might become too successful and as a result no longer be giving good advice. Does our approach still work even if everyone does it? Fortunately, the answer is yes, and we explain why in this, our concluding chapter.

CHAPTER 1

A Leap of Faith

ON JANUARY 7, 2009, Andrew Verstein, then a third-year law student, did something that would scare the daylights out of most of us. Andrew took most of his hard-earned retirement savings, $4,770 of it, and took a leap of faith—by buying a LEAP, a December 2011 option to buy 100 shares of an index based on the S&P 500.

Many of you will instinctively think that Andrew was acting recklessly, but we hope to show you that just the opposite is true. Andrew has it right—he stands a good chance of retiring with 50 percent more savings than he'd expect using conventional strategies, while significantly reducing his risk.

Before deciding whether Andrew was reckless or brilliant, let's pause to explain just what he did. LEAP is the acronym for Long-term Equity AnticiPation, which is a fancy way of saying a long-term stock option. Andrew's option gave him the ability to buy 100 shares in the SPDR (pronounced Spider), a fund designed to mimic the performance of the S&P 500 index. A SPDR share is just like one-tenth of the S&P 500 index.* Andrew's option allows him to buy SPDR shares at $45. That's like an option to buy the SPDR shares at half price. Of course, the option wasn't free. He paid $47.70 a share or $4,770 in total for that privilege.

For Andrew to make money, the SPDR price has to be more than $47.70 above $45 a share, or $92.70. To the extent the market goes above 92.70, Andrew will make money—at double the rate he would if he had

---

*On January 7, the index opened at 927.45, while the SPDR opened at 92.00.

just invested his $4,770 in the S&P directly. His $4,770 would only have bought 52 shares directly; with the option, he has exposure to 100 shares. But if the market goes down, Andrew loses money twice as fast, too. If the index ends up being worth less than $45, he will have lost his entire head start on retirement savings.

Gambling His Retirement?

Andrew is remarkably thrifty, perhaps to a fault. Before law school he worked for a year as a paralegal, and the job took him to Paris, Milan, and Mexico City. As a result, most of his living expenses were taken care of, allowing him to save a prodigious amount even on a modest salary. He probably should have enjoyed more of the local color, cappuccinos at the street cafés, but that isn't his style.

So why is Andrew taking this gamble with his retirement? The short answer is he was convinced that buying the LEAP is a prudent investment—not because he was sure the stock market is going up and wanted to make a short-term killing. In fact, after the volatile stock swings of 2008, Andrew's not sure at all about whether stocks will increase or decrease over the life of his option. But he sees this purchase as part of a conservative, long-term strategy to invest for his retirement. Andrew read an early draft of an academic article we wrote on diversification across time, and he followed up by asking how it would be possible for him to put the article's theory into practice. We wrote this book to let you in on that conversation.

To get the long answer, we go back to work done in the 1960s by Paul Samuelson and Robert Merton. In their groundbreaking articles, they ask how someone who had all of his or her retirement savings up front in cash would choose to allocate it between stocks and bonds.[1] Imagine for a moment that you are twenty-five and inherit a $500,000 trust fund that can only be spent when you reach retirement age. How would you invest it today between stocks and bonds?

Your answer would obviously depend on your tolerance for risk and the expected returns on stocks and bonds. For the sake of argument, let's say that your allocation is 60:40, 60 percent in stocks and 40 percent in bonds. Now we have to translate this situation back to the real world, where, alas, no one has left you with such an inheritance.

Put yourself in Andrew's shoes. You're twenty-five, soon to be a newly minted JD, and you've saved $5,000 for retirement in your IRA. How would you invest that money between stocks and bonds?

If your answer is 60:40—put $3,000 in stocks and $2,000 in bonds—you've fallen into the trap. This is the mistake that most people make. This fails to consider that Andrew's future salary is much like a bond. The average starting salary at New York law firms is above $150,000. On that salary, Andrew plans to put away at least $10,000 a year into a 401(k) plan. And the amount saved will go up with promotions and inflation. Those savings contributions are like mortgage payments, though he hasn't borrowed any money. Instead, his 401(k) plan is like the bank, collecting payments that are worth $500,000 from today's perspective.

Here is Paul Samuelson's investment advice for someone just like Andrew:

> If you are a young professional with future [earnings that] cannot be efficiently capitalized or borrowed on, to keep your equities at their proper fraction of *true total wealth,* you should early in life put a larger fraction of your liquid wealth in common stocks.[2]

Most of Andrew's true total wealth is tied up in his human capital and over time this will be converted to financial capital. In theory, Andrew could go out and sell his future savings contributions to someone who would give him $500,000 today in return. In practice, no such markets exist. Just like the trust fund kid, Andrew has something worth $500,000 today that he doesn't have access to. His anticipated future savings is like owning a half-million bond that is stuck in his portfolio. Fortunately, money is fungible and so Andrew can compensate by overinvesting the parts over which he does have control.

If he were to invest his current $5,000 savings 60 percent in stocks and 40 percent in bonds, then it would be as if he had $3,000 in stocks and $502,000 in bonds. Were he to invest all $5,000 in stocks, he would still be below 1 percent in stocks. Even if he were to leverage his $5,000 investment at a 2:1 ratio, so that he has exposure to $10,000 of the market, he would be 2 percent in stocks, far below his desired ratio of 60 percent. Investing with leverage won't get him to 60:40, but it moves him in the right direction. Viewed from this perspective, we hope you can see that what Andrew did in exposing himself to $10,000 of stock risk isn't at all radical. From a more holistic perspective, he put less than 2 percent of his true savings at risk.

Andrew knows that he is just starting out. He wants to learn what he is doing when the stakes are $5,000, not $100,000 or $500,000. As Andrew explained to us: "When I wanted to learn something about sports, I decided to make some small bets. That way I had a real incentive to learn about the players and the game. When it comes to stocks, this is giving me a chance to learn while the stakes are still small."

Andrew played a bit of poker in college. He was even good enough to win some small tournaments. But he's not a gambler. Those tournaments had buy-ins of $2, and Andrew walked away with $100. If he were to get better at playing poker, Andrew knew he'd have to raise the stakes, and that isn't how he wanted to spend his time. In the case of investing for retirement, however, he couldn't afford just to sit on the sidelines and watch.

When it comes to financial investments, diversification is essential. Andrew took this gamble in order to better diversify his portfolio. His investment was already well diversified in one way: He bought options on an index of stocks rather than any one stock. That's the smart, if boring, thing to do. Jim Cramer wouldn't have much to shout about if the average investor was like Andrew and just bought stock market indices. Andrew knows that his job is to be a lawyer, not a stock picker. In law school, he didn't have time to figure out which stocks would outperform and which ones wouldn't. Even if he did have time, he is smart enough to know that he isn't likely to beat the average.

Later in life, Andrew can do even more in terms of diversifying his portfolio. He can add foreign stocks, commodities, and real estate to the mix. But for now, spreading his investments across the 500 stocks in the Standard and Poor's index is a good start.

Total Dollar Years

To see how Andrew's investing strategy reduces his risk, we calculate a new measure of stock market exposure, something we call "Total Dollar Years." Total dollar years is the sum of dollars you have invested in stock each year. If Andrew were to invest $5,000 in year 1, $10,000 in year 2, and $15,000 in year 3, he would have invested a total of $30,000 "dollar years." Andrew is much better diversified against temporal fluctuations in the stock market when he invests the total dollar years more evenly across time, here $10,000 in each of three years. The total dollar years are the same, but they are better spread out. Of course, Andrew didn't have $10,000 to invest in year 1 and that's why it made sense for him to buy the LEAP.

You should think of every year of your life as a distinct investment opportunity. Diversification tells us that you shouldn't put 80 percent of your stock investment into just 10 stocks. You do better to spread your bets across a broader portfolio.

The same idea of equal allocation applies to investment periods. People make the mistake of putting 80 percent of their stock investments in just ten years. This can have disastrous consequences if those ten years happen to end badly. In fact, as we write this in the summer of 2009, the S&P stands at its 1997 level. People close to retirement who invested the bulk of their stock money in this lost decade will not have done well. You are better off spreading your stock investments across several decades. Keep the total dollar years the same, but spread them out over more years.

Use Leverage

The naysayers respond that this kind of temporal diversification just isn't possible because young people don't have more money to invest. You can't invest what you don't have. But that's flat wrong. When it comes to housing, people invest what they don't have all the time. You save for a down payment, and then go out and buy a house or condo worth ten times as much by borrowing the difference. Lenders are willing to lend the money because the house serves as collateral.

The same holds true for stock investments. You can take what you've saved and combine that with borrowed money to purchase more stock than your total savings. Federal law limits the amount you can borrow— it can't be more than you put up. So if you have $4,000 to invest, you can borrow another $4,000 from your stockbroker in order to buy $8,000 of stock. This is called buying stock on "margin."

Buying stock on margin increases your exposure and hence your short-term risk. It's called a "leveraged" position because, like Archimedes' lever, a small movement in the market can produce a large movement in port-folio value.[3] If you buy a $500,000 house with a $450,000 mortgage and a $50,000 down payment, then you are leveraged 10:1. A 10 percent in-crease in the house value translates into a 100 percent increase in your equity ($550,000 – $450,000 mortgage = $100,000). Of course, if hous-ing prices fall 10 percent, your portfolio would have lost all of its value. The more leverage, the more short-term risk.

The same leveraged effect applies to stock bought on margin. If you buy $8,000 of stock using $4,000 of margin and the stocks go up 10 per-cent, to $8,800, then you've made 20 percent on your $4,000 investment. You get twice the return on the market, whether it goes up or it goes down.

Our point is not to encourage risk taking—quite the contrary. Buying stock on margin when you're young reduces long-term risk because it al-lows you to do a better job evening out your otherwise lopsided exposure to the market. If you have $4,000 of market exposure when you're twenty-five and $200,000 when you're sixty-five, it would be better to bring the initial exposure up to $8,000 and reduce the final exposure to $196,000.

While buying stock on margin helps in terms of diversification, it cre-ates some other problems. If stocks fall enough, you can be asked to put up more collateral. If you don't meet this margin call, then your portfolio will be liquidated, whether you like it or not. Since you didn't have more money to invest in the first place, you probably won't have the money to put up in the event of a margin call. A second issue is that many (but not all) brokers charge high interest rates for a margin loan. The cost of this interest can more than offset all the gains from diversification. From our perspective, buying stocks on margin has too many drawbacks to make it an effective tool.

Fortunately, there's more than one way to skin a cat. You can get effectively the same amount of leverage through buying a call option. The advantage of the option is that there aren't any margin calls. Whether the market goes up or down, you won't be called on to put in more money. A second advantage is that call options allow you to double your exposure to the market at a very low cost. In Chapter 8, we show that in recent years the implied interest rate associated with long-term call options that provide 2:1 leverage was only 4 percent.

This is why Andrew invested in LEAPs as his way of better diversifying his portfolio. Andrew spent $4,770 to get an option to buy the SPDR for $45. If stocks go up 10 percent from where they were when he started (from 92 to 101.2), Andrew will make $850 on his $4,770 investment, which is an 18 percent return. If stocks fall by 10 percent, then he will lose $990, or 21 percent.* He has the same leverage as if he bought stocks using a margin loan, but he doesn't have to worry about getting a margin call or paying usurious interest.

Proposing leverage often sets off red flags. Recent events highlight the issue. Young investors who followed our advice would have lost 64 percent of their savings in 2008. What does that say about our strategy?

While losing 64 percent of your investments is never fun, it is much better to do so when you're twenty-five than when you are sixty-five. This is true for two reasons. First, you have a lot more time to adjust in response. Over the next forty years, you can work harder, save more, or consume less. Second, even following our advice, you'll have a lot less money in the market when you are twenty-five compared to when you are sixty-five. If Andrew ends up losing 64 percent of his initial investment, he'll be

---

*The reason why the up and the down aren't completely symmetrical is that the LEAP price includes some implicit interest on the part of the shares Andrew hasn't yet purchased. These calculations are provided in Chapter 7.

down a little over $3,000. That's painful, but not crippling. If he loses 64 percent of his nest egg when he's sixty-five, that's a major problem.

Remember that our advice isn't just for twenty-five-year-olds today. There is the corresponding advice for sixty-five-year-olds: Namely, buy a little less stock. If we had written this book forty years ago and an older version of Andrew had been following our advice all along, then he would have been less invested in the market in 2008 and thus lost less. We've done the simulations and found that he would have come out 7 percent ahead overall compared to following the traditional approach.*

Because we propose investing more when young and less when old, you'll obviously come out ahead if the market performs better when you're young and worse when you're old. And you'll do worse if the market does poorly when you're young and booms when you are near retirement. But that's not a fair test for evaluating our strategy. Our goal is to reduce risk. That means giving up some of the highs in return for missing some of the lows. We can't eliminate all the risk, but by diversifying time we can reduce it substantially.

Of course, Andrew got off to a bad start. January 2009 was the worst January in the history of the Dow Jones Industrial Average, all the way back to 1896.[4] As of May 2009, he was back in the black. There will be more ups and downs along the way. We can't tell you how things will turn out for Andrew. That will take another forty years. But we don't ask you to take our word on faith. In Chapter 3, we tell you what would have happened over the last 138 years if you had followed our advice, including what would have happened to those who just retired at the end of 2008.

(Dis)counting Your Chickens Before They Hatch

The diversifying benefits of leverage are possible whenever you know you're going to have a substantial amount of savings in the future. Gener-

---

*The traditional approach landed at $635,000, while our lifecycle strategy ended up at $679,000. Both were down significantly from 2007, but our approach fell less.

ally speaking, this is due to a rising income. But there are some other ways this might happen.

This is the second book we've written together. In 2000, we signed a contract to write *Why Not?*, a book on creativity for Harvard Business School Press. We knew we were going to get a sizable advance in a year's time and that we were going to invest almost all that money in the stock market as soon as we got it. The question we failed to ask at the time was: Why wait two years before exposing any of that money to the benefits of market risk? One answer is that we didn't have the money in hand to invest.

But that's a poor argument. To explain why, we'll use some round numbers for the sake of illustration. Let's say that we each started with $160,000 invested in stocks and $40,000 invested in bonds. Our desired allocation prior to getting the book advance was to be 80 percent in equities, 20 percent in bonds, as illustrated in Figure 1.1.

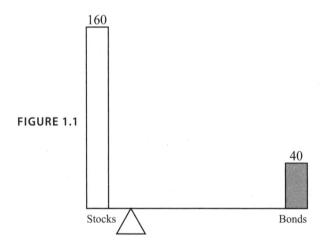

FIGURE 1.1

Sticking to round numbers, our book advance was roughly $150,000, which translated to about $45,000 each after taxes. We each planned to spend $5,000 of that amount and put the other $40,000 into our retirement savings. (Okay, we're not much fun now, but we'll have enough money saved to still have some fun when we're old.)

Remember that our goal was to be 80 percent invested in stocks, which implies that when we got the advance we'd put $40,000 into our retirement account, of which $32,000 would go into stocks and $8,000 into bonds.

That's all fine for the future, but why wait? There was nothing stopping us from taking the $40,000 we already had in bonds and putting $32,000 into stocks right away. If you are thinking that was increasing our allocation to stocks, you have it backwards. Doing this was required to keep our allocation 80/20.

Say we did nothing. Then our portfolio would become tilted more toward bonds, as in Figure 1.2 below. We had the $40,000 in regular bonds, plus the book advance. The promissory note from our publisher wasn't exactly like a regular Treasury bill. (Although given the size of Harvard's endowment, we're not sure which is the worse credit risk.) And we'd actually have to write the book to get the check. We were pretty confident, though, that we would get the book done.

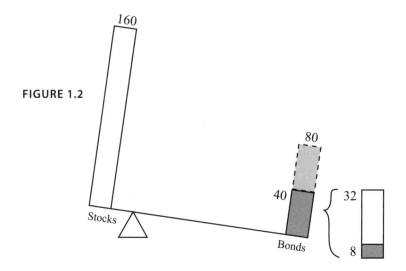

FIGURE 1.2

To rebalance the scales, all we had to do was move $32,000 from bonds over to stocks as in Figure 1.3. Although it may then look as if we only had $8,000 invested in bonds, the forthcoming advance checks are much like a bond. We knew the amount and when we'd get it, and we could figure out how much would be left over after tax. Thus our true bond holdings were really the $8,000 in government bonds plus the $40,000 note from our book.

To do this calculation right, there's one more step to take. Since we wouldn't get the bulk of the money for a year, we should discount the

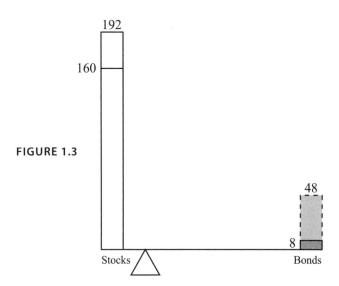

FIGURE 1.3

$40,000 to take this into account. We could get $40,000 in a year by buy-ing a $38,000 zero-coupon bond. That implies that the true incremental amount we have in bonds isn't $40,000, but only $38,000. We should have treated the $40,000 in a year as like $38,000 today and chosen to in-vest 80 percent of that amount, or $30,400.

While a book advance might seem like a special or esoteric situation, there is a general lesson here that is the key intuition underlying our whole strategy. Your future salary is a lot like our book advance. You can predict, more or less, how much you will make in the future and what you will do with that money. Our main point is that you should figure out how you would invest that money if you had it today and then try to achieve that outcome. You won't be able to do this perfectly, but getting close counts.

There are two steps here. The big step is to realize that (if you are like most people) your future salary is like a bond and therefore you are prob-ably much more heavily weighted in bonds than you realize. The second step is to discount that bond back to today. Because that money comes in the future, it isn't quite as valuable as if you had it today.

We were all taught as children not to count our chickens before they hatch. And we agree. But you should discount your chickens before they hatch. Instead of ignoring your future retirement savings, you should cal-culate the present value of expected saving contributions and start investing some of those contributions in the stock market today. The "present value" of future dollars is the amount of cash in hand today that would make you just as happy. The present value of a future dollar is always less than a dollar, but it isn't zero—and your optimal investment today should take it into account.

The central mistake that young investors make is to ignore their expected future savings. Earlier we estimated that the present value of Andrew's future savings was over $500,000. But even if Andrew is less confident—he is taking a year off to volunteer in China before starting at a law firm—it is hard to envision a world where the present value of his savings wouldn't be at least $200,000. To avoid bunching all his investments into his fifties and sixties, Andrew needs to expose some of that present value to the market now.

Discounting Your Income

Think of it this way. If you are thirty, earning a steady $100,000 per year, and putting aside $5,000 then, mathematically, it is as if you have $120,000 invested in bonds. Your future savings contributions of $5,000 a year over the next thirty-six years are worth $120,000 today. Thus if you have $50,000 in current savings and 90 percent of that invested in stocks, it isn't the case that you have 90 percent of your assets in stocks. A more accurate picture is that you have $45,000 in stocks and $125,000 in bonds ($5,000 from current savings plus $120,000 future savings). Only 26 percent of your true total savings portfolio is in stocks. Investing a little more in stocks when young isn't as risky as you may have thought.

Actually, the percent in stock is far lower than 26 percent. If you earn $100,000, you can expect that Social Security will replace about 25 percent of your income upon retirement. That replacement income is even more valuable because it is indexed to inflation. To buy an annuity that provides the same terms would cost roughly $500,000 at the time of your retirement, or about $190,000 today. Thus your total bond holdings are closer to $315,000. That means your $45,000 in stocks is only 13 percent of your portfolio. Here you were thinking that 90 percent was a high percentage to put in the market. But when you think of how much of your wealth is already in bonds, even putting 200 percent in stocks only brings you up to 28 percent overall.

The Status Quo

The mistake that we made with regard to our first book advance is small compared to the mistake that just about everybody makes in investing for retirement. If you are like most people, you follow one of two strategies when it comes to investing the money in your 401(k) plan.

Option 1: Set a fixed allocation rule—say 75 percent into stocks, 25 percent into bonds—and forget about it. The allocation is the same today as when you first joined the plan and filled out the forms. If it is any comfort, that's where we were before starting out to write this book.

Option 2: Put all your money in a target-date fund based on your expected retirement age. Thus if you expect to retire in 2050, you would invest in the "2050 Fund." Target-date funds essentially automate the birthday-rule advice: Hold stocks in proportion to 110 minus your age. Thus at age twenty-five, they invest 85 percent of your portfolio in stocks, while at sixty, they invest 50 percent in stocks. A 2050 fund follows the birthday rule for someone who is presumed to be age sixty-five in 2050.

Target-date funds are one of the most important financial innovations in recent times. The first such funds were introduced to the market in 1993 by Barclays Global Investors. Now most mutual fund companies offer them. By 2008, they had grown to over $200 billion in assets.

The advantage of this approach is that the fund automatically does all the rebalancing for you. Each year it shifts more of your money from equities into bonds. In addition, the fund also rebalances when there is a shift in the relative value of the two components. Thus after the stock crash in 2008, the stock portfolio would have fallen below the targeted percentage and thus the fund reallocated toward equities.

While both these options are simple and popular, it turns out there are problems with each one. The constant percentage rule is much like a broken clock that's right twice a day. Sometimes, the rule is close to being right, but other times it is way off. When you're young, the allocation is almost surely too low in equities, and when you're older, too much. It also doesn't take into account market movements that should lead you to rebalance your portfolio.

The big problem is that any constant allocation rule leads to a lopsided allocation across time. Say you put aside $4,000 each year into your 401(k), of which 75 percent goes into stocks. That means you'll be putting $3,000 into stocks each year. Roughly speaking, you'll have $3,000 in the market for year 1, $6,000 in year 2, and $9,000 in year 3. You'll have three times the market exposure in year 3 than you had in year 1. You'll have ten times the market exposure in year 10 compared to year 1.

In practice, the ratios are even more extreme. Contributions to 401(k) plans generally go up over time with an increase in salary. Moreover, the stocks in the portfolio will (hopefully) grow in value. Our simulations show that the typical birthday-rule investor has about twenty times more invested in the market in year 10 compared to year 1 and three times more invested in year 20 than year 10.

What that means is that you are implicitly placing much bigger bets on some stock years over others. If you were temporally diversified, then you'd have a much more constant amount invested in the market each year.

Target-date funds do a better job diversifying than the constant percentage rule, but still suffer from two problems: high fees and a flawed strategy. Many charge too much—way too much. One of the worse offenders is Franklin Templeton. They charge 5.75 percent for the privilege of paying 2.99 percent in annual fees on their 2035 fund. (If you want to avoid upfront fees, then their C class shares lift the annual fee up to 3.69 percent.) Over twenty years these fees come out to a staggering $739,000 based on a $300,000 initial investment. This amount combines the $356,500 in direct fees you pay and another $382,500 in lost earnings on those fees.[5] The fees come out to more than what you'd expect to take home after fees, namely $659,000.[6]

Not everyone fails the fee test. Vanguard gets kudos for getting it right.[7] Their target-date funds invest in a collection of index funds. In terms of the allocation between stocks and bonds, everything is automated. The end result is that their total all-in fees are under 19 basis points (a basis point is one-hundredth of a percent). The same investor putting $300,000 in the low-fee Vanguard target fund would pay only $49,486 in fees and end up with $1,349,000, more than double the amount from Templeton.

There's no good reason to pay high fees. A computer program can do a perfect job of allocating your money between equities and bonds. The equities could be put in a worldwide market index fund. Essentially that is what Vanguard does and why it is able to charge so little.

Even with Vanguard, you still face the second problem: The allocation rule is flawed. The standard lifecycle fund holds stocks roughly in proportion to 110 minus the investor's age.[8] Thus a twenty-year-old might be 90:10 in stocks versus bonds, while a sixty-year-old would be 50:50. Understanding diversification across time tells us that 90 percent as an early asset allocation is far too conservative.

Target funds help you diversify across time by ramping down each year. That's the right idea. But because they start at 90 percent and go down from there, the cost of the ramp down is that your overall exposure to equities is reduced. You might think that the average between 90 percent and 50 percent is 70 percent, but remember that much less money is invested at 90 percent. When weighted by dollars, your average equity exposure is only 60 percent.

Beating the Status Quo

Reading this book may help convince you that 60 percent is too conservative. Of course, taking on more exposure also means taking on more risk. Here's where the improved diversification comes into play. The improved diversification allows you to get significantly more market exposure while maintaining the same level of downside risk. Instead of taking the gain in the form of reduced risk, you can get a much higher return.

The strategies that get you there are very different than either investing a constant percentage of your savings or following the birthday rule. To diversify across time requires investing far more in stocks when you are young—not 90 percent, not even 100 percent, but up to 200 percent. With the improved diversification, you can then safely aim for more exposure to stocks across your whole investment life. The increased exposure is what boosts your returns, while the better allocation across time is what keeps the risk under control.

Our mean-improving strategy matches the risk profile of the birthday rule but provides a 50 percent higher return on average. We can also match the risk profile of the constant allocation rule and provide a 60 percent higher average return. You can have a much bigger upside while still protecting your downside.

These gains are especially important as lifespans continue to increase with improvements in medicine. You can't just save for fifteen or twenty years of retirement. There's a good chance you'll make it well past age ninety.

That's the motivation behind Andrew's plan. If he sticks to his guns and follows the strategy laid out in the next chapter, we estimate that he could retire six years earlier and still afford the same retirement spending. Or he could afford to pay for fifteen more years of retirement without outspending his savings. We hope he enjoys every minute.

We hope to help you the reader in the same way. We believe this book has the potential to have a profound impact on your life. If you follow our advice, you really can look forward to your retirement.

CHAPTER 2

The Plan

WE NOW EXPLAIN how to use leverage to temporally diversify your retirement savings. As we do so, it will help to think of the analogy of a child trying to reach a cookie jar on the kitchen counter. The evolution of this process is very much like how you should invest over time.

The Cookie Jar

Initially, the child is short, too short to get his hands on the counter, so he jumps up as high as he can. For a long time, even when jumping, he still can't reach the counter. But he keeps trying. Over time, he grows and gets closer and closer. This is phase 1.

As the child grows taller, he eventually reaches the counter and jar. For the first time, he has reached his goal. This is the start of phase two. He continues to grow in phase two. Although taller, he still has to jump but doesn't have to jump as high as he can. So long as he is jumping, he remains in phase 2.

Eventually the child grows tall enough to reach the jar without jumping at all. Indeed, at full adult height, he is taller than the counter and can even reach down and get what he needs. This is the third and final phase.

Our strategy's three phases of equity allocation correspond to the child trying to reach the counter. When young, you don't have enough saved to reach your target level of market exposure. Even if you jump as high as you can, you still fall short. In this case, "jumping" means you use leverage to increase your exposure. As we discuss below, "high as you can" means doubling your exposure, or 2:1 leverage. Even 2:1 leverage won't initially get you to the target, but you'll get closer as the portfolio grows.

Phase one lasts until your portfolio grows to the point that 2:1 leverage gets you to the target allocation. This leads into phase two. Here you still have to use some leverage to reach the target but don't have to jump all the way. As your portfolio grows, both through contributions and appreciation, you can reach the target with reduced leverage. (If the market declines, you may need to go back and increase your leverage for a while.)

Eventually, you will reach the target without using any leverage at all. This initiates phase three. You begin this phase at 100 percent stock, and as your assets grow, you reduce the exposure until you hit your target allocation.

Two Numbers

While it may seem a bit complicated, our lifecycle strategy really comes down to just two numbers:

(1) The present value of your lifetime savings
(2) Your "Samuelson share"

The present value of your lifetime savings is the cash value of your current savings plus the present value of your future savings contributions. This present value is the total amount you should think about allocating. With Andrew, even though he only had $5,000 of savings in cash, he had a present value of expected lifetime savings of at least half a million dollars.

What percentage of this present value do you want to invest in the stock market? The easiest way to answer this question is to imagine that someone gave you access to all of your lifetime savings today. Say you actually had $500,000 in cash (like the trust-fund kid in Chapter 1), but all locked up in your IRA. You can't spend it or even borrow against it. All you can do is choose how to allocate the money between stocks (including international stocks, real estate, and commodities) and bonds. Your target allocation is what fraction you would put into stocks.

We call this central target allocation your "Samuelson share" in honor of our teacher, Paul Samuelson. Samuelson showed that for a plausible type of risk preference, individuals would want to allocate a constant percentage in the stock market year after year, regardless of what happened to the value of stock. Samuelson's model crucially assumed that you had all your savings in cash at the beginning of your life. This entire book is, in some ways, just a simple extension of the Samuelson idea. When some of your savings contributions will be received in the future, you should still try to invest a constant percentage of your savings—where savings is measured as the present value of what you have now and what you will have later.

The Samuelson insight leads to a simple investment rule. Every year of your working life your investment target is the product of your Samuelson share multiplied by the present value of your lifetime savings. If Andrew's Samuelson share is 60 percent, and if at the beginning of a particular year the present value of his lifetime savings is $500,000, then Andrew should try to invest $300,000 in stocks (and a diversified portfolio of other risky assets). We emphasize that this is merely a target. When Andrew is just starting out, he will not, even with leverage, be able to hit his target. But we will show that moving toward the Samuelson target pays big diversification dividends.

We can't tell you what your Samuelson share is. (But Chapter 7 will help you discover your own answer.) Your answer to the allocation question depends on two factors, one of which is the same for everyone and one of which is personal to you. Because of this individual aspect, the target allocation number will be different for each person.

The first, universal, factor is the return and risk associated with stocks and how this compares to bond returns. The higher the return on stocks and the lower their risk, the more you will want to allocate to stocks.

The second, individualized, factor is your attitude toward or tolerance for risk. The more risk averse you are, the less you will want to invest in stocks, whatever their predicted return. The word *predicted* is important. While the actual return on stocks will be the same for all investors, the problem is that this return isn't known. Thus you have to make investment decisions based on your expectation or prediction of the risk and return. These expectations will differ across people, and so there is an idiosyncratic element to the first factor as well.

Three Phases

Following the Samuelson target naturally gives rise to a lifecycle strategy with three distinct life phases.

> Phase 1: In the first phase—which typically lasts for the first ten years of your working life—retirement savings are leveraged at 2:1.
>
> Phase 2: In the second phase—which typically lasts until your mid-fifties—investments are partially leveraged, more than 100 percent but less than 200 percent.
>
> Phase 3: In the final phase—which lasts until retirement—investments are fully unleveraged, and your portfolio includes corporate and government bonds along with stocks.

Consider, for example, Ian's nephew, Orus. At thirty-one, Orus is a former Air Force captain who recently began working for a property/casualty insurer. He and his wife earn about $200,000 a year and are putting aside more than 10 percent annually. Added up, the lifetime value of his future savings is around $400,000 today. To that amount we add what he has saved up so far; in Orus's case, that's about $60,000. All together, the present value of his total lifetime savings is thus $460,000. That gives us our first number, and we are halfway there.

Orus has inspected his own tolerance for risk and his expectations about future stock returns to determine that his Samuelson share is a rather conservative 40 percent. That means if he were given all of his lifetime savings today in cash, he would invest just 40 percent in stock and the rest (60 percent) in government bonds.

His target is to invest 40 percent of the full $460,000 of savings in stock. That comes to $184,000. Even if he were to invest all of the $60,000 available today, that would be only 13 percent of his total—present and future—savings. Investing at 2:1 leverage will get him up $120,000—closer but still far from the $184,000 goal.

You might think that Orus will be in phase 1 until he has $92,000 saved. At that point, investing at 2:1 leverage will give him the target $184,000 exposure to the market. That's not quite right. Over time Orus's total savings will change and with it his desired level of market exposure. The $184,000 exposure is just right only if his total savings are still $460,000. When Orus has $92,000 saved up, the value of his future savings will most likely have fallen, as there are fewer years left to contribute (although it might rise if he's had a big promotion). If the value just happens to fall from $400,000 to $368,000, then the total will still be $460,000, and so his target will remain at $184,000. But we don't expect things will work out this neatly. The value of current savings depends on how much the market goes up or down, and so the two numbers generally won't even out. If the value of Orus's future savings is $378,000 when his stock portfolio is worth $92,000, then his total savings add up to $470,000. That means his target would grow to $188,000, and he would still be in phase 1.

When Orus's current savings exceed 20 percent of his total savings, he enters phase 2. For example, if his IRA has $100,000 and his expected future savings contributions remain at $400,000, then total present and future savings is $500,000, and his current $100,000 invested at 2:1 leverage will get him to $200,000, or 40 percent of the total.

As his savings continue to rise (as a result of market returns and additional contributions), he can start to delever. For example, when his retirement savings grow to $150,000 and his future savings add another $318,000, then his target is 40 percent of $468,000, or $187,000. He can invest his available $150,000 with about 5:4 leverage and get to $187,000. He is still more than 100 percent invested, but at 125 percent, not 200 percent.

Orus stays in phase 2 until his current savings hit 40 percent of the total. At that point, he can hit the desired level of market exposure without using any leverage. This is phase 3. Say that his savings have grown to $275,000, while the value of his future contributions has fallen to $300,000. The sum of his lifetime savings is thus $575,000, and so the desired market exposure is $230,000, or five-sixths of his liquid savings.

He ends up with 84 percent of his current savings invested in the market, which is how he gets to 40 percent of his lifetime savings invested. As the market rises or falls, Orus adjusts to keep his exposure at the desired 40 percent level. His savings are large enough that leverage is no longer required.

Together, these three phases represent a new kind of lifecycle investing. While traditional target date funds start at investing 90 percent of current savings in stock and ramp down to 50 percent stock allocation, our leveraged lifecycle starts at 200 percent of current savings before ramping down ultimately, in Orus's example, to just 40 percent of current savings in stock. The ending stock allocation—just before you retire—will be exactly equal to your Samuelson share because at that point you will no longer have any future expected savings. So if you are trying to invest 40 percent of your present and future discounted savings, that will be just the same as investing 40 percent of your present savings.

Figure 2.1 compares the stock allocation under the birthday rule to our lifecycle strategy. The allocations you see are based on historical simulations (that you'll learn a lot more about in the next chapter). In pursuing a 40 percent Samuelson share, the typical investor will remain in phase 1, investing 200 percent of her current savings, for about ten years. This makes things easy for people like Andrew or Orus: Their initial strategy doesn't depend on the target.

When you're just starting out, it's hard to know what life has in store. Will you make partner? Will you be promoted or laid off? But a lot of uncertainty is resolved over time. It's a lot easier to estimate your lifetime savings when you're thirty than when you're twenty-three. Another way to think about this is even if you make really, really conservative estimates about the present value of your future savings—including the chance that you may not have any—you still are going to want to invest 200 percent of your current savings in stock.

As you look at this picture, also keep in mind that the 200 percent at the start is applied to a much smaller amount than the 40 percent at the end. Thus in terms of actual dollars invested, the two strategies come close

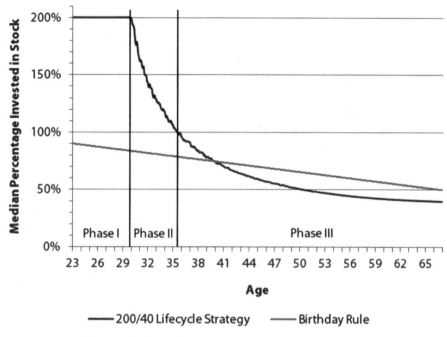

FIGURE 2.1 **Phases of Lifecycle Strategy**

to having the same total dollar years exposure. In fact, the birthday rule provides a slightly larger total stock exposure than the lifecycle strategy that aims for a final stock allocation of 40 percent.*

Social Security

There is one more significant part of savings that we need to consider: Social Security. Having Social Security is like owning a giant bond that starts paying off at retirement age. Thus, even at retirement, Orus will have substantial expected future savings in addition to whatever he has saved up in his retirement accounts. For many retirees, the present value of Social Security on the day they retire can often equal the savings that they've accumulated over the course of their lifetimes. For example,

---

*The two allocations come out the same when the Samuelson share is 41.7 percent.

imagine that Orus has $300,000 saved and that his Social Security payments are worth another $300,000. If his goal is to be 40 percent in stock, then the 40 percent should apply to the $600,000 total. In other words, Orus should have $240,000 in stock, which is 80 percent of his non–Social Security assets.

Ignoring Social Security highlights a big mistake most people make. You might think that Orus is being cautious when he aims for a 40 percent Samuelson share. But the way most people put the rule into practice, the 40 percent only applies to money in their retirement accounts. Thus they put 40 percent of $300,000 in stocks, which is only 20 percent of their true portfolio. Most investors inadvertently end up being far too cautious. This costs them dearly in terms of their returns.

The value of Social Security as part of your savings portfolio is something to consider at every age, not just right before retirement. Taking this into account leads to an even bigger gain from following our strategy. The reason is that you are even more in bonds than you thought you were.

In the next chapter, we first provide the empirical results without taking Social Security into account. We do this for several reasons. We want you to see that our leveraged lifecycle can produce big gains even without considering Social Security. A second reason is that the replacement income provided by Social Security depends on your income. The Social Security bond is worth less as a percentage of income as your wages rise. This complicates all the calculations, as it means we can no longer simply scale everything up or down with income. A last complication with Social Security is that its future is uncertain. While we expect Social Security will continue to exist, the benefits may look different than they do today.

That said, the theory is clear: Social Security is truly part of your lifetime savings, typically a very large part. Therefore you should take it into account when considering your portfolio allocation. And we will.

At this point, you can see flaws with the allocation rule employed by target-date funds. The birthday rule only looks at the money in your account, not your whole portfolio. As a result, it allocates far too little to stocks when you are starting out. Even 90 percent of your savings is a tiny fraction of your assets. That's why we employ leverage.

The target-date funds also allocate too little at the end. We think Orus is cautious but reasonable in wanting to hit a 40 percent target. But taking Social Security into account means that, when Orus is near retirement, he would need to put close to 80 percent of his non–Social Security savings in stock in order to achieve 40 percent exposure in his overall portfolio.

Why Stop at 2:1?

As you contemplate employing leverage, you may be wondering why you should stop at 2:1. Can't you do even better with 4:1 or 10:1? The kid jumping up to the counter was jumping as high as he could. He might have been limited in terms of how high he could jump, but you are not so constrained when it comes to leverage. Thus it might seem you could hit your goal sooner if you employed more than 2:1 leverage.

Our recommending 2:1 leverage doesn't mean 10:1 or 20:1 is better. Two ibuprofen will get rid of your headache; taking the whole bottle can kill you. The same thing is true with leverage: 2:1 leverage can reduce your risk, while 10:1, or even 4:1, leverage can make things worse. Excessive leverage is what got our economy into the financial mess of 2008.

One problem with increasing leverage is that it greatly increases the risk of a wipeout along the way. A second issue is that the interest rate on the money you borrow goes up. If you try to gain more leverage via stock index futures, we've found that the implied borrowing cost for leverage beyond 2:1 quickly exceeds the expected returns. In other words, more leverage gets expensive quickly.

We've read on the web how one person seriously misinterpreted our advice. If his posts are to be believed, this (now) poor fellow invested using 20:1 leverage and borrowed on credit cards to do so. Just so there will be no doubt: We do not advise going above 2:1 leverage. And if you are even considering borrowing on your credit card to buy stock, don't. Along with taking on too much risk, you will almost surely pay far more in interest that you can make with the stocks.*

Now that we've highlighted the dangers of excess leverage, don't go too far to the other extreme. Our cautions shouldn't be taken to mean that any amount of leverage is a bad idea. A couple ibuprofen can work wonders, and a bit of salt can really improve the flavor—just don't go overboard.

We expect that you may have more questions, and we hope to answer them in later chapters. But now that we've explained the basic idea behind our retirement investment strategy, we should spend some time demonstrating that it actually works. Thus we turn to the data.

---

*In fact, before you buy any stocks, you should first pay off your credit card debt. Paying off your debt is much like investing in a bond, one that pays you the same interest rate that you were paying on your credit card. Thus if you are paying 18 percent on your credit card, then paying off this debt is like buying a bond that pays 18 percent. Even better, it is like getting 18 percent tax-free. While stocks generally outperform bonds, they don't outperform the interest rate on credit cards.

CHAPTER 3

Historical Performance

THEORY IS NICE, but to convince you that diversifying time can make a real difference in your life, we want to begin by showing that it would have helped people in the past. To do this, imagine that we had written this book in 1871 and that, ever since, people have followed our advice. How well would they have done? We look across the ninety-six generations (we call them cohorts) of people who could have taken our advice and evaluate how much money they would have retired with.[1] We look at each case individually, along with the average, the top 10 percent, the bottom 10 percent, and the worst-case scenario. When even the worst-case scenario does better, you should have confidence that our gains come with reduced risk.

Our initial analysis is based on what happened in the U.S. stock market from 1871 through mid-2009.[2] If you think the last 138 years were an anomaly in the U.S. markets, later on we redo the calculations to show that the advantages apply even with a much lower equity premium. Even if the U.S. markets were a statistical fluke, the benefits of diversifying over time were not. We show that the advantages of our investment strategy apply to the historical performance of stocks trading in London and Tokyo as well.

To demonstrate the value of our advice, we create a contest between three different investment strategies:

a constant percentage rule,
a target-date rule,
and our leveraged lifecycle strategy.

In the right corner, wearing the blue shorts, is the constant percentage rule. It invests 75 percent of its savings in stocks and the remaining 25 percent in government bonds. While it may sound too simple, this comes closest to what many of us do with our retirement money—sign up for automatic payroll deposits into a mix of mutual funds and bonds, and then let things ride. Inertia is a powerful force.

Of course, different people use different proportions. A 75:25 split is aggressive by traditional standards. Most people come closer to splitting their savings 60:40 between stocks and bonds. The reason we focus on the 75:25 split is because when it gets soundly beat, you'll know that the fault wasn't for its lack of being aggressive enough. (A 60:40 allocation rule gets beat just as soundly.)

In the left corner, wearing the red shorts, is the defending champion: the target-date rule. It is used, with some minor variations, by Fidelity, Vanguard, and most financial service firms. These funds allocate assets based on the investor's age. At age twenty-three, 90 percent of assets are invested in stocks, ramping down to 50 percent in stocks by age sixty-seven. The target-date strategy is just a fancy name for the birthday rule—the percentage invested in stocks roughly equals 110 minus your age. Target-date funds automate the adjustment process. This is a great convenience, since it requires a lot of work to constantly rebalance your portfolio based on your age and recent stock performance. With target-date funds, you sign up and forget about it. That part works great. The only problem is that these portfolios don't come anywhere close to the optimal dynamic strategy, and many of them charge high fees. We will cut them a break and pretend that they don't charge any fees at all. That way, we can highlight that the fault lies with the strategy, not the fees.

The challenger is our very own leveraged lifecycle strategy. This is a diversified strategy that aims to invest a constant Samuelson share of lifetime savings in stocks. As emphasized in Chapter 2, the word *lifetime* is the key differentiating feature of our approach. Investment allocations aren't based just on your present savings but on the discounted value of all future savings. We call the allocation goal a "target" percentage because in the early years, investors don't have enough cash to reach their investment goals, even using leverage, but they can still aim for it.

For our initial demonstration, we imagine an investor choosing a fairly conservative Samuelson share strategy of 50 percent—trying to expose 50 percent of lifetime savings to the market. Since 50 percent of lifetime savings is well more than anyone's initial savings, that means the person must use leverage or margin starting out. We cap the amount of leverage at 2:1, or 200 percent. In practice, this means that investors start out in phase 1 investing 200 percent of their current savings in stock, but, as they age, they gradually stop investing with leverage and end up with 50 percent of their savings in stock just before retirement.

As shorthand, we refer to these strategies by the stock allocations at the beginning and end of a person's work life. The constant percentage strategy is the 75/75 strategy. The target-date strategy is the 90/50 strategy. And our preferred lifecycle strategy is the 200/50 strategy.*

To make it a fair contest, we hold everything except the investment strategy constant. Our model investor saves 4 percent of her earnings each year and has an income profile that reaches $100,000 at retirement.[3] Over her lifetime, this comes to a total savings of $194,573. While the total amount saved is important to your retirement account, it isn't important to our results. If you save twice as much each year, or ten times as much, then you will have twice or ten times as much when you retire, whatever strategy you follow. The relative ranking isn't changed by the size of the investments.

Eureka

The breakthrough for us came when we simply compared the historic performance of the 75/75 strategy to our diversifying 200/50 strategy. Before this book, no one would have thought that leveraging your savings 2:1 for the first decade of your work life and then ramping down to 50 percent would be safer than investing 75 percent of your savings in stocks

---

*Unlike the birthday rule, our strategy doesn't fall in a linear path from 200 percent to 50 percent.

and 25 percent in government bonds. We're so used to seeing leverage as inherently risky that every financial advisor would run screaming from such a strategy.

When we first delivered these leveraged results at Yale, our no-nonsense colleague (and expert in all things ERISA) John Langbein was unconvinced. He thought the result was driven by the aggressiveness of the leveraged strategy rather than by any diversification advantage.

It's a reasonable concern. There is a sense in which being more aggressive does provide a kind of worst-case protection. The stock market's returns have been so much higher than those of government bonds that merely throwing more money into stocks can end up bailing you out. If you just roll the dice on stock enough times, you are almost bound to come out a winner. That's why traditional stock investment strategies—like the birthday rule or the 75/75 strategy—usually beat the bejabbers out of a strategy which keeps all of your money in government bonds. Even though bonds are much less volatile, they expose you to a near certainty of a low outcome because their mean return is so low. Langbein thought we might be running a similar game with regard to leveraged stock strategy.

It may seem at first that a 200/50 strategy is more aggressive than the 75/75 strategy. Overall, our diversifying lifecycle has more years where the stock allocation exceeds the constant 75 percent. However, the initial leveraged years are the years where the current savings are smallest. In fact, the two strategies are equally aggressive, and historically they produced identical average returns. When we hold savings constant (for a hypothetical person with a $100,000 salary at retirement) and apply the two investment strategies to historic returns for ninety-six different lifetimes, we find that they both produce the same average retirement accumulation of $749,000.

Our "aha" moment came when we compared the distribution of returns. We found that the 200/50 strategy reduced risk by more than 20 percent. Over the ninety-six different historic simulations, its standard deviation is 21.4 percent less than the standard deviation of the traditional 75/75 strategy.

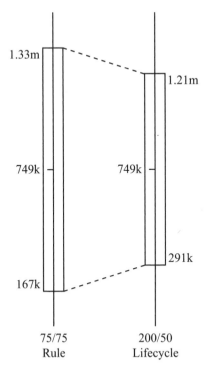

1.33m

1.21m

749k   749k

FIGURE 3.1
Same Returns with Lower Risk

291k

167k

75/75   200/50
Rule   Lifecycle

Based on historical market volatility, there's a 99 percent chance that the constant 75/75 rule will lead you to end up with something more than $167,000.* And there's a 99 percent chance you'll end up with something less than $1.33 million. That's the range you see on the left side of Figure 3.1. Under the 200/50 path, you will still end up with $749,000 on average, but now the range is reduced to $291,000, to $1.21 million.

When we saw this figure, we knew we were on to something. The diversifying lifecycle isn't reducing risk because it is throwing more money into the stock market. It has to be exposing the same amount of money to stock, since it ends up with the same average return. It is reducing risk because it spreads the stock exposure across more years. This result doesn't

---

*In the introduction, we presented the numbers for two standard deviations, a range that covers 95 percent of the potential outcome. Here we are being even more conservative. We are looking at the 98 percent range of outcomes, so that there's only a 1 percent chance of ending up below the bottom level.

depend at all on how much stocks outperform bonds. We knew we had a pure diversification play.

Since this is the key driver of our results, it bears repeating. We'll do that by pausing to address one more potential concern. There's a common fallacy that you can reduce your risk simply by investing over a longer time horizon. This hokum says that investing $1,000 for each of forty years is less risky than investing $1,000 in each of thirty years. Not so. Both the risk and the reward go up with the increased investment.

We aren't playing that game. Our mean is the same. We take the same total investment dollars that are mostly concentrated over twenty years (under the 75/75 rule) and use leverage to spread them out more evenly over forty-four years (under the 200/50 lifecycle). In effect, the investor has more years for the same total amount of dollars invested—that's the source of our better diversification and reduced risk.

Less Risk or More Return

At this point, you may be thinking that the 20 percent reduction in risk is real but hardly worth the effort. Here is where the diversification gain starts to kick in. Investing is about risk and returns. The 200/50 strategy is structured to channel all the benefits of diversification toward lower risk—holding the expected return constant. But it's possible to move toward the other extreme: channeling the benefits of diversification toward a better return while holding the expected risk constant. By the end of this section, we'll show that with this approach, the impact on returns can be remarkably large.

Under the 75/75 rule, you are exposed to a range of $583,000 up or down. We can provide this same range, but with a higher mean. Instead of using the better diversification to lower volatility, you can gain more exposure to the market with the same volatility.

A 200/61 rule is the lifecycle strategy that generates the same $583,000 range up or down. But the 200/61 rule provides a higher average return, $881,000 compared to $749,000. You end up ahead by $132,000, or 18 percent, and hence are in a better position to take on the risk.

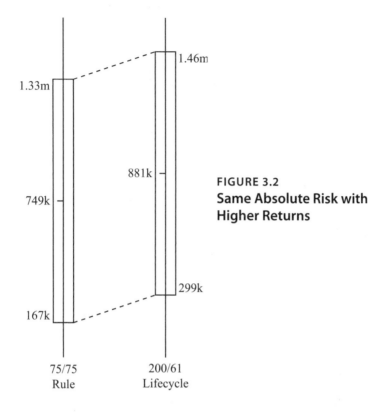

FIGURE 3.2
Same Absolute Risk with Higher Returns

The 200/61 lifecycle strategy doesn't just do better on average or at the bottom. Every outcome is $132,000 better, which is why whatever your preferences toward risk may be, you should prefer the strategy on the right.

Instead of thinking about how much you gain or lose in absolute terms, it makes more sense to measure risk in terms of a percentage of your final accumulation. How would you feel if you were offered the same risk package as 75/75, but now all the payouts are in euros? On average you will end up with €749,000, where the downside is €167,000 and the upside is €1.33 million. This should be an easy call. Since the euro is worth 40 percent more than the dollar (at least when we were writing), whatever happens, you'll be 40 percent ahead of the game.

Moving to a 200/75 lifecycle strategy is just like shifting to euros, only better. You can increase your expected outcome by 45 percent, up to $1.09 million, while maintaining the same percentage swing in outcomes. Under the 75 percent allocation rule, you were living with a potential 78 percent swing in your retirement wealth. The bad outcome ($167,000) was 78 percent below your average accumulation of $749,000, and the good outcome was 78 percent better. Under 200/75, there is the same potential 78 percent swing in outcomes, but the starting point is $1.09 million rather than $749,000. Although your risk is the same in terms of the percentage change, all the outcomes, even the bad ones, are 45 percent better.

If you are willing to accept a small chance of doing worse, there's even more upside potential. Let's say that you wanted to match the worst 1 percent outcome. In the case of the constant 75 percent rule, that number is $167,000. By accepting that same result as the bottom of your range, you can further improve your expected results.

A 200/83 rule is the lifecycle strategy that matches the worst 1 percent result at $167,000. Thus the two bars have the same bottom. Now look at the upside potential. *On average, you will have $1.22 million, a return that is 63 percent higher than a constant 75 percent allocation (and as we'll see almost 90 percent better than the birthday rule).* To put it bluntly, this is the difference between being able to afford your retirement and not.

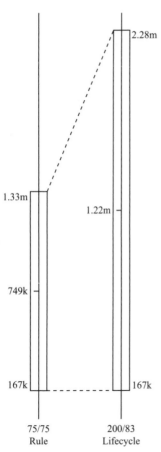

FIGURE 3.3
Same Worst Case with Higher Returns

The 200/83 lifecycle strategy channels the benefits of diversification toward a higher return. While the larger range of outcomes might seem scary at first, it is the upside where the range has expanded. The new average is so much higher that there's a 90 percent chance of beating the $749,000 average result of the 75 percent rule, and the bottom of the 98 percent range is still $167,000, the same as with the 75 percent rule.

Show Me the Money

A limitation of these volatility estimates is that they implicitly assume that stock returns are normally distributed. In reality they aren't. The normality assumption for many purposes isn't a bad approximation. But for something as important as your retirement it's important to dig deeper and see on a case-by-case basis, even year by year, what would have happened to investors who had the temerity to follow these strategies in the past. With that in mind, we've run the numbers on investors born in each of ninety-six different years.

We start with Zachary, an investor born in 1848 (and named after U.S. President Zachary Taylor, who was elected that year). Zachary would have started working in 1871, when he was twenty-three, and retired forty-four years later, at the end of 1914, when he was about to turn sixty-seven. If Zachary had invested his savings following the 90/50 target-date strategy, his $194,573 of savings would have grown to $623,630. Not bad. Still, this number doesn't mean much in and of itself. It's the comparison to the other strategies that's relevant.

Investing a constant 75 percent of current savings does much better, increasing Zachary's accumulation to $667,171. But the 200/83 strategy does even better. By the time Zachary retired in 1914, he would have accumulated $798,481.

Why was our strategy so much more successful? We trace out the performance of all three strategies on a year-by-year basis. You can see in the figure that leverage didn't help him right off the bat. From 1873 to 1879, the 200/83 strategy lagged behind the traditional strategies. But Zachary made out like a bandit using the 200/83 strategy during the late 1870s, when he was still young enough to be leveraged. The stock market earned a whopping 49 percent in 1879 and increased another 27 percent the following year. Because Zachary was leveraged, he would have earned an incredible 101 percent and 49 percent in these years.* This run-up in his

---

*The leveraged returns are not just double the S&P due to margin interest and our rebalancing of the portfolio each month.

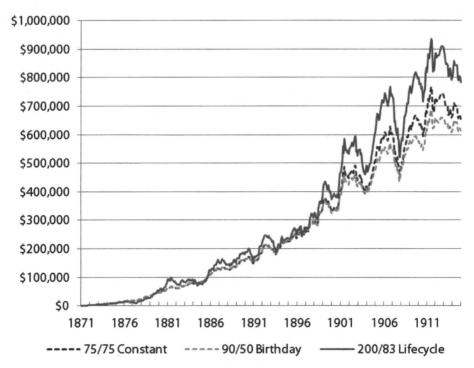

FIGURE 3.4 **Zachary's Savings Under Different Strategies from 1871 to 1914**

leveraged portfolio more than offset the Panic of 1893, when the market fell by 19 percent in a single year. By that time, Zachary was forty-five years old. His portfolio was only slightly leveraged (113 percent in stock), so his portfolio only declined 22 percent during the Panic year. Even after taking into account that he had to pay margin interest early on, when his stock investments were made partially with borrowed money, the 200/83 strategy produced much higher retirement wealth than either of the traditional investment strategies.*

---

*Our advice is to use stock options to gain leverage. Obviously stock options weren't available in the nineteenth century. In our calculations, we assume investors could borrow at the rate that banks offer to brokers. Today, leverage can be obtained for even less through the use of options; see Chapter 7 and the FAQ at the end of this chapter for more on this topic.

Zachary's experience is not an anomaly. What about someone who re-tired at the end of 2009, following the *annus horribilis* returns in 2008? That investor would have been born at the start of 1943—let's call her Eleanor. Holding the basic facts the same, we'll imagine that Eleanor also begins work at age twenty-three in 1966 and makes the same annual sav-ing contributions as Zachary. If Eleanor followed the traditional 90/50 target-date strategy, she would retire with $683,699. The 75/75 strategy produces $634,559. But, once again, the 200/83 strategy produces the biggest nest egg of the three—$766,454.

Eleanor got off to a rough start. Her leveraged portfolio fell 17.4 per-cent when the stock market went down 6.4 percent in 1966. Her portfo-lio took another hit in October 1987, when the stock market declined more than 12 percent in a single month. But by then Eleanor was forty-four and only had 123 percent of her portfolio invested in stock. Although her October return was –15.3 percent, 1987 as a whole wasn't a terrible year and she was only down 5.1 percent. Things turned around in the 1990s, during which time her portfolio quadrupled. Even after absorbing the terrible returns of 2008, when the stock market fell (net of dividends) by 36.6 percent, Eleanor still would have made 21 percent more following our diversified strategy than by investing 75 percent in stock every year and 12 percent more than by following the birthday rule.

So far so good, but the skeptic in you should be concerned that we are somehow cherry-picking our examples. It is possible, of course, to walk you through the investment life of an investor born in every year between Zachary and Eleanor. But we thought a table might be a bit more suc-cinct. Table 3.1 summarizes what we found, and it might well be the most important table in the book. It compares the final retirement accumula-tions under the three investment strategies for investors born in all ninety-six different years (including Zachary and Eleanor). The only difference in these ninety-six investors is the forty-four years of stock returns that they experience. Zachary's portfolio is exposed to stock market returns from 1871 to 1914. We make the same calculation for an investor who works and saves from 1872 to 1915 and so on, all the way up to our ninety-sixth

TABLE 3.1 **Results from 96 Simulated Investors: 1871–2009**

	Birthday Rule	Constant % Stocks	Diversifying Lifecycle Strategy	Improvement over Birthday Rule	Improvement over Constant %
Max. % Inv.	90	75	200		
Min. % Inv.	50	75	83		
Mean Result	$646,575	$748,839	$1,223,105	89.2%	63.3%
Min. Result	$290,310	$308,726	$387,172	33.4%	25.4%
10th pct.	$416,253	$449,266	$701,834	68.6%	56.2%
25th pct.	$539,343	$561,032	$884,138	63.9%	57.6%
Median	$641,555	$691,427	$1,146,812	78.8%	65.9%
75th pct.	$779,044	$922,028	$1,522,653	95.5%	65.1%
90th pct.	$870,921	$1,152,276	$1,929,577	121.6%	67.5%
Max. Result	$1,026,903	$1,252,684	$2,177,424	112.0%	73.8%

investor, Eleanor, whose savings are exposed to the market from 1966 through 2009.

And the winner, by a knockout, is the challenger.

Let's look first at the traditional (90/50) target-date strategy. On average it produced an accumulation of just over $640,000. Of course, each of our ninety-six investors, each born in different years, had different results. The worst year for the strategy turned out to be for people born in 1854 and investing between 1877 and 1920. This investor (named Pierce after Franklin Pierce) had very little to invest during the best parts of the 1870s, partially suffered from the Panic of 1893, and couldn't take full advantage of the recovery because, by that time, he had shifted much of his assets into bonds. Conversely, the best result for the 90/50 strategy occurred for investor Herbert (named after Herbert Hoover), who was born in 1932 and worked between 1955 and 1998. This positive result is largely due to the boom in the 1990s—which, unfortunately, the 90/50 strategy did not allow him to take full advantage of, having then only a relatively small proportion of his portfolio in stock. Had Herbert been following the

200/83 target strategy, he would have done even better—59.6 percent better, to be precise.

This table lets us compare the distributions of all three strategies. As in the specific cases of Zachary and Eleanor, we can immediately see that the 75/75 strategy produces better results than the 90/50 strategy, and that the 200/83 strategy produces by far the best results. The average result for the leveraged 200/83 strategy is nearly double that of the birthday rule, and it's more than 60 percent higher than the 75/75 strategy.

If you've been invested for several years in a traditional target-date fund, this table should give you significant pause. Our preferred strategy so dominates the birthday rule that the *average* of the 200/83 strategy ($1.22 million) is larger than the *maximum* accumulation achieved over ninety-six different periods with the 90/50 strategy ($1.03 million).

Forgoing a higher expected return isn't so troubling in and of itself. After all, the first lesson of financial economics is that risk and reward go hand and hand. We should expect a leveraged strategy to produce a higher average return. But what about the risk of a truly horrible result? How many of the leveraged investors were forced to live on cat food during retirement?

Take a look at the minimum accumulations for each of the three strategies. The worst birthday-rule result was $290,000, whereas, even with leverage, the worst result of the 200/83 strategy was 33 percent higher than that ($387,000) and 25 percent higher than the 75/75 minimum. An even stronger pattern of success emerges from how the bottom 10 percent or 25 percent of investors did under each strategy. The tenth percentile for accumulated savings was nearly 69 percent higher for the 200/83 strategy than for the 90/50 strategy, and 56 percent higher than for the 75/75 strategy. (The bottom quartile result was 64 percent better than for the 90/50 rule and 58 percent better than for the 75/75 strategy.)

To put it simply, the worst-case scenario outcomes are much better under the leveraged strategy than under either of the traditional strategies. The leveraged strategy also produces a substantially higher average. And, of course, it also has a much, much higher upside. The maximum nest egg produced by our diversifying lifecycle was a whopping inflation-adjusted

$2.18 million (for people investing between 1918 and 1961). This is more than double the highest amount produced by the birthday rule and almost 75 percent greater than the 75/75 strategy. What's not to like?

The Crash

You're probably thinking we must have made a mistake in our calculations. What about the poor folks who retired just after the Great Depression? The returns on the S&P 500 in 1929, 1930, and 1931 were −9.5 percent, −22.7 percent, and −44.2 percent. Why didn't leverage kill the portfolios of investors retiring in 1932? The answer is that investors who retired just after the crash were not severely hurt because the leveraged strategy only uses leverage for people in their initial working years. For example, workers retiring in 1932 who followed the 200/83 strategy would have had just 83 percent of their portfolio invested in the market when the market lost more than a third of its value. Because of the success of their investments during the Roaring Twenties, these post-crash retirees would still have a retirement wealth of $729,487—which is above the average of what most people think is the more conservative 90/50 investment strategy. And this accumulation is substantially (32 percent) more than a birthday-rule investor would have made over the same period.

Individuals who began working just before the Depression and adopted the leveraged strategy would have done even better. Those who entered the labor force in 1931 would immediately have experienced a 73 percent loss in their first investment year. Remember, though, that this is a large percentage of a small amount. By the time these investors retired at the end of 1974, they would have accumulated $1,133,421, which is well above the average return for either of the other strategies.*

---

*In case you're concerned that we've only looked at investors who started or ended with the Depression, the results for cohorts in the middle are just as compelling. For example, the cohort investing between 1910 and 1953 (hitting the Depression in their early forties) would have accumulated $1.20 million under the 200/83 strategy, which is more than the $1.13 million for the group who started off during the Depression.

Our leveraged strategy responds to losses in early years by having investors employ leverage for a longer period of time. Remember, the 200/83 strategy aims to invest a constant 83 percent of the present value of your current and future savings in stock. If market losses reduce the value of the current portfolio, then it will take more years of leverage to hit the 83 percent target without the help of a margin loan. The leveraged strategy is more dynamic and dependent on prior returns than either of the traditional strategies. With the target-date or constant-allocation rules, we can write down in advance the exact stock allocation in every year of a person's life. With our strategy, how long you stay leveraged depends on how well the market has performed.

The median investor in our leveraged strategy simulation would have remained fully leveraged—investing 200 percent of her current savings in stock—for the first 12.8 years of her working life and only then began the process of ramping down the amount of leverage. She remained partially leveraged for another 14.2 years—until just after her fiftieth birthday. Only in the last 17 years of work life was the median investor able to implement the overall target without the help of leverage. It's during this final phase when our "leveraged" strategy looks most traditional, with the investor splitting her current savings between stocks and government bonds. But because the leveraged strategy is contingent on past returns, some investors stayed leveraged longer than that. In fact, one of our investor cohorts remained at least partially leveraged until its investors were fifty-six years old.

Take Abraham, for example. He was born in 1863 (and named after Lincoln) and invests in the market between 1886 and 1929. When Abraham is thirty-six, he would be investing 176 percent of his current retirement accumulation in stock. But the run-up to the Philippine-American War in 1899 was not kind to the stock market—that November the S&P fell by 6.5 percent (dividends included). Our target strategy responded by directing Abraham to increase his leverage to 189 percent in December. (This higher leverage is a way to maintain a constant percentage of lifetime savings.) In sharp contrast, when the stock market later crashed in October 1929, the 200/83 rule did not direct Abraham to ramp up just before he retired. By the time of the crash, when Abraham was about to retire, 83 percent of his lifetime savings was equivalent to 83 percent of his cash on hand.

This investment strategy naturally leads investors to take on more risk after a market drop when they still have time to diversify, but it keeps them ramped down when they are close to retirement. Abraham was unlucky to retire immediately after the crash of 1929. However, our leveraged strategy allowed him to navigate these storms in the market. Investing aggressively after downturns when he was younger, he was able to build up a substantial portfolio and ramp down his risk at the end of his working life. Retiring only a few months after the crash, he missed out on the market rebound at the beginning of 1930. Nonetheless, our leveraged strategy worked so well during the middle of his life that Abraham could withstand the loss and retire with a remarkable inflation-adjusted $1,231,861. While his investing life was sandwiched between two major crises, he still pocketed more than any of the investors under the 90/50 strategy in the entire simulation, and beat all but three investors under 75/75.

What we have is a case where theory produces a pragmatic way to adjust how long you remain leveraged. Older investors are protected from a downturn because they will have no leverage in the last ten or fifteen years of their working lives. Younger investors are protected because they have more years to react to a market drop. Leveraging for a few more years is *not* a doubling-down strategy that increases risk; rather it is merely implementing the simple idea that the best way to diversify risk is to invest a constant present-value percentage of current and future saving contributions—spreading some of the risk to your youth so you don't have to bear it later.

The Dominance of Leverage

Table 3.1 showed that the 200/83 strategy produced higher mean, median, minimum, and maximum accumulations than either of the traditional strategies. *There is not a single investor cohort out of the ninety-six in which the 90/50 or the 75/75 strategy beat out the leveraged strategy.* This is the best evidence you could ask for. It is why we are so confident in recommending the leveraged strategy. And now you really know that we didn't pick cherry-pick our examples to support our case.

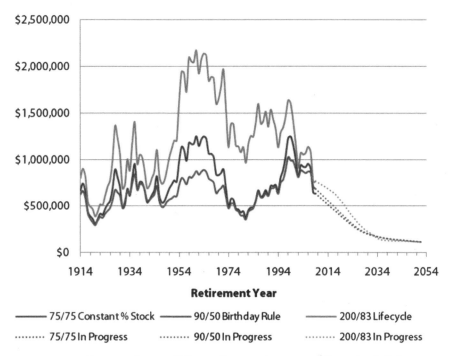

FIGURE 3.5 Comparison of Three Strategies over Historical Cohorts and Cohorts in Progress

Figure 3.5 graphs the accumulations of the three strategies on an investor-by-investor basis indexed by the year in which the investor retired.

Zachary's results live on the far left of the graph because he retired in 1914; we can see that the 200/83 strategy produced a retirement nest egg of $798,481 for him, substantially outpacing the results of the traditional strategies. The figure shows that all three strategies produced their lowest absolute accumulations for workers retiring at the end of 1920 ($290,310–387,172). For these investors, enduring the double-digit market declines in 1893, 1903, 1907, 1917, and 1920 was more limiting than the more severe, but compact, declines of the Depression that other workers experienced.

The dominance of the lifecycle strategy over a constant 75 percent was most challenged for investors retiring in 2002. The relative advantage of the leveraged strategy is smallest in that year because the stock market fell three years in a row (–5.2 percent in 2000; –13.5 percent in 2001; and –20.1 percent in 2002) in the last years before retirement. These declines produced disproportionate losses for the portfolios that were most exposed to the market late in life. Our 200/83 strategy still came out ahead, but the late-inning losses narrowed the size of its victory. In the comparison between the lifecycle and the target-date, 2008 was the closest call: Our strategy came out 6.2 percent ahead. The target-date fund had the advantage of being less exposed to the market in 2008, but that wasn't quite enough to make up for its lower exposure in all the prior years.

Figure 3.5 also includes results of how investors who will retire in the future are currently doing with the various investment plans (and taking into account the present value of their future savings contributions). We don't know for sure how much money someone who retires in 2015 will end up with because we don't know yet how the stock market will do in the homestretch. We can, however, say how his portfolio would be doing so far. For example, consider an investor born in 1954 (named Ike after Eisenhower) who started investing in 1977 and will retire in 2020. At the end of 2009, Ike's portfolio would be worth $400,291 if he was using the 90/50 strategy and slightly less, $373,388, if he had followed the 75/75 strategy. But if he had followed our leveraged strategy, he would have had almost 42 percent more—$529,692. So, even with just thirty-three investment years, we can see that people like Ike can substantially profit from better diversification across time.

The dominance of our preferred rule even extends to people who have a long time to go before retirement. Indeed, in Figure 3.5, you can see that the leveraged strategy dominates the traditional strategies for any investor who has had the chance to invest for at least twenty years. That it doesn't dominate for the under-forty crowd is hardly surprising. Investors who are going to retire in, say, 2043 have only been investing for ten years and simply haven't had enough years over which to spread risk. People who started off leveraged and ran right into the crash of 2008 would have done better—so far—if they had followed the birthday rule. But it is the height of foolishness to choose a long-term strategy based on short-term results. It isn't at all uncommon to start off in the hole. As we saw with both Zachary and Eleanor, the first years were down, and then they more than caught up. Overall, the last 138 years of stock data tell a remarkably consistent story: Our diversifying lifecycle strategy outshines the conventional wisdom, regardless of when the investor happened to be born.

The benefits of leveraged investment under the 200/83 strategy are considerable. While Table 3.1 emphasized the higher expected mean, median, and minimum returns, it is useful to translate what these extra dollars really mean to people's lives. The fact that the expected return for the leveraged strategy is almost double that of the birthday rule means that you could have nearly twice the money to spend during your retirement. Alternatively, it means that you could retire six years earlier and still have the same yearly stipend during retirement. Instead of retiring at sixty-seven, you'd have the freedom to kick back at sixty-one.*

You also have the option of saving less every year of your working life. Instead of saving an ambitious 7.5 percent of your income under the birthday rule, you could save a more realistic 4 percent of your income and still produce the same expected retirement accumulation.

Of course, in an age when people are living longer and longer, you might well decide to fund more years of retirement. Of all the assumptions made in retirement investment plans, the idea that you only need to eat until you're 87 years old is the one that keeps many of us up at night. If you regularly save 4 percent of your income and retire at sixty-seven, under the 200/83 strategy you should have enough to live on till you are 114. That's right. If you take your expected retirement accumulation at age sixty-seven and invest it conservatively from then on (in government bonds), you'll have enough to cover you for forty-seven years of retirement at the same level of real spending that the birthday rule can only support for twenty. Forty-seven years of coverage—that's real security.

Social Security

In spite of its performance, many of you will think that 200/83 is far too aggressive. How could it be prudent to have 83 percent of your money in

---

*Retiring a year earlier is expensive. Not only are you giving up another year of savings contributions, you start spending down the retirement funds a year earlier. Being able to afford to retire six years earlier is a big deal.

the market at retirement age? One reason is that with diversification across time, the lifetime risks are reduced. We've shown that even when you end on a bust, the previous success more than makes up for the final year. This was true for the Great Depression as well as 2008's great recession. It was true for every retirement year in our sample.

And in spite of what we called the 200/83 strategy, you don't really retire with 83 percent of your money in the market. The 83 percent ignores Social Security. We've been emphasizing the point that you should look at all of your assets when deciding upon your allocation between stocks and bonds. In that sense, our allocations are much more conservative because they never put any of your Social Security at risk. Time diversification says that you want to expose some of that future value to the stock market before your retire. But, up to now, we have ignored the value of Social Security. As you approach retirement, your Social Security becomes a very large asset.

In our simulations, we imagined that you retired at age sixty-seven with $100,000 income in your final working year. In that case, Social Security will provide you with a little more than 25 percent replacement income (26.8 percent to be more precise). Even better, the payments are indexed to inflation.* If you wanted to buy an annuity that provided such payments, it would cost roughly $507,000 (see Chapter 7 for details of these calculations).

Thus it is just as if you had, at the time of retirement, a $507,000 bond along with the rest of your portfolio. Under the 200/83 strategy, you ended up with $1.22 million (on average) of which 83 percent or $1 million is invested in equities. Taking Social Security into account, you really have a $1.72 million portfolio. The $1 million invested in equities is only 58 percent of your true portfolio. We've played it conservative by ignoring what is likely to be the biggest bond in your portfolio. At lower incomes levels, the effective allocation is even more conservative.[4]

During the George W. Bush presidency there was a big debate about whether to let people invest their Social Security savings in stocks. The fact is that you can do it now even without a change in law. To show you

*Better still, Social Security payments are given favorable tax treatment. At most, 85 percent of the benefits are subject to taxation.

what we mean, look at a person at age sixty who expects to retire at sixty-seven with a final salary of $100,000. The present value of his Social Security payments is about $420,000. For purpose of illustration, we'll say that this person also had $580,000 in a retirement account, so the total is $1 million. If he wanted to put 60 percent of his Social Security savings in stocks along with 60 percent of his regular retirement savings in stocks, that calls for $600,000 in stocks. He can just about get there by investing all of his $580,000 in stocks and with a little leverage can easily hit the $600,000 target. Money is fungible. You don't need direct access to your Social Security account in order to invest it in stocks.

This all suggests that the right way to do the calculations is to put Social Security into the mix from the start. Even a twenty-three-year-old starting out should take into account the future value of his Social Security bond.

We resimulated a new kind of 200/83 strategy that just like before ramps down from a 200 percent stock allocation to an allocation that on average invests 83 percent of the investor's current savings just before retirement. What's different about the strategy is that it takes account of Social Security by setting the stock allocation target (the Samuelson share) equal to 62 percent, where now the 62 percent applies to the present value of current and future savings *including the present value of Social Security*. We apply a less aggressive Samuelson share (62 percent instead of 83 percent) to a more aggressive assessment of the present value of your future savings. We picked 62 percent because this led to the same effective final allocation in our simulations: Having our investors put 83 percent of their current savings in stock was equivalent to investing 62 percent of their current savings plus the present value of Social Security.

The Social Security–adjusted 200/83 offers the same downside risk as the birthday rule ($760,000, which includes the value of Social Security).* But the upside is much, much better—even better than the previous 200/83 strategy. Although the Social Security–adjusted 200/83 strategy

---

*In the historical simulations, the actual worst case was much better than the predicted 1 percent tail. The 200/62 bottomed at $970,000, which was up roughly 20 percent from the actual worst cases of the birthday rule or the constant 75 percent.

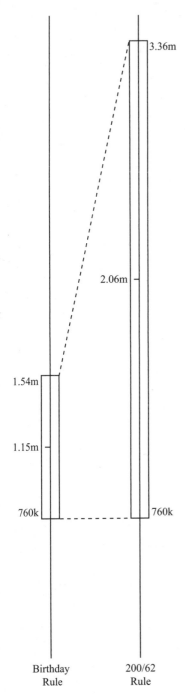

3.36m

2.06m

1.54m

1.15m

760k

760k

Birthday
Rule

200/62
Rule

FIGURE 3.6 Same Worst Case with Higher Returns (Social Security Included)

ends up with the same stock allocation as a percentage of current savings, it doesn't ramp down as quickly as it tries to expose more of Social Security to the market earlier. These additional middle-age leverage years pay substantial dividends. Now, with Social Security factored in, the expected result is $2.06 million, almost double the results from either the birthday rule ($1.15 million) or the constant 75 percent ($1.26 million). Those numbers include the value of the Social Security payoffs. Thus if we just look at your savings on hand at retirement—that is, your non–Social Security wealth—the average results are more than double. The new 200/83 produces an average nest egg of $1.55 million, while the average birthday rule ends up with about $650,000, and the constant 75 percent stock investors end up with about $750,000. That's right: Exposing some of your Social Security to the market before you retire can more than double the size of your personal retirement nest egg—all without increasing your downside risk or asking you to increase your savings contributions.

Figure 3.6 helps illustrate the comparison. It is the same type of chart we showed earlier in the chapter but now includes Social Security as part of the final payoff. We think this makes the choice very clear.

Of course the elephant in the room here is the future of Social Security. For those near retirement, this is something they can reasonably count on. But the long-run future of Social Security is less clear. We come back to these issues in Chapter 7, when we consider how the chance of making your goals depends on your Samuelson share. For now, our next set of simulations in Chapter 4 takes the overly conservative position that there is no Social Security.

Conclusions

At this point, we hope that the data you've seen allows you to believe the results without just taking us on our word. We are talking about a change that will make a substantial difference in your life. This isn't a decision you should make lightly. By the same token, we've shown that there is a huge cost in sticking with the status quo and not doing anything. The stakes are high. This is worth getting right.

In the chapters to come, we provide more empirical evidence that our approach works. Our academic colleagues pushed us to consider a dozen "what if" scenarios. We'll take you through most of them. We show that the results aren't unique to the U.S. stock market. The results still work if stocks don't do as well in the future, or even if the cost of borrowing goes up.

While we believe that leveraged investing makes great sense for most people, it isn't right for everyone. For people whose salaries or job prospects are highly correlated with the market, it turns out that they are, in effect, already highly invested in equities and don't need to increase their exposure. For example, the salary of a stockbroker will likely go up in a bull market and fall in a bear one. Before jumping in, read Chapter 6 to ensure that this advice is right for you. If it is, then Chapters 7 and 8 will help guide you every step of the way.

We know that you still have questions. We try to answer some of them below. You can even kick the tires on the simulation (and customize it to reflect your situation) online at www.lifecycleinvesting.net.

FAQs

Question 1: As they say, past performance is no guarantee of future results. How do I know that the lifecycle strategies will work in the future?

Question 2: If I'm investing with leverage, isn't there the chance of getting a margin call from my broker asking me to come up with more money, which I probably won't have?

Question 3: Don't your results depend on being able to borrow cheaply? I thought margin loans were very expensive.

Question 4: Target-date funds didn't do that well in 2008. Your approach is like a target-date fund, but with a much higher initial stock allocation. Is that a problem for your approach?

Question 5: What about market timing?

QUESTION 1: *As they say, past performance is no guarantee of future results. How do I know that the lifecycle strategies will work in the future?*

This is a point where theory might give you some piece of mind. The reduced risk isn't due to luck or due to the equity premium (i.e., the degree to which stocks outperform bonds), but rather due to an improved ability to spread out your market exposure over time. You can have the same total exposure to the market (measured in total dollar years), but since it is spread out over more years, you have less volatility in your returns and less risk overall.

The fundamental idea is the same as spreading out your investments across more stocks. Instead of investing in just your own company's stock or a handful of stocks, you lower your risk by choosing a broad portfolio, preferably a stock index. Spreading out your investments better over time creates the same free lunch from diversification.

In this chapter, we provided historical data to show you how it worked in the past. But the past is just one data set. To give you additional peace of mind, in Chapter 4 we show that the results aren't limited to the historical returns of the U.S. markets. Similar benefits apply to investors in Japan and the United Kingdom. We also mix things up by doing some Monte Carlo simulations. Instead of taking the actual forty-four years of returns, we pick forty-four years at random based on simulated data where we can adjust the equity premium. As you'll see, the value of leverage does not just depend on the equity premium or the historical pattern of bull and bear markets. We will also show the advantage of our lifecycle strategies for a broad range of stock returns, including those much lower than the historical average. Better diversification lowers risk whatever the equity premium.

QUESTION 2: *If I'm investing with leverage, isn't there the chance of getting a margin call from my broker asking me to come up with more money, which I probably won't have?*

Let's start with how margin calls work. An investor who has $100 in savings and borrows another $100 lets the broker hold $200 in stock as security to guarantee that the loan is repaid. A substantial decline in stock value can trigger a "margin call." This is literally a telephone call from your broker giving you twenty-four hours to come up with some more cash or the broker will sell off some of the underlying stock to make sure that the loan is safe.

The major stock exchanges require that the net value of a leveraged portfolio must not fall below 25 percent of the portfolio's total value (including the margin loan). In the jargon of brokers and exchanges, there is a 25 percent "margin maintenance requirement." So for our example investor with $200 in stock, imagine that the market declines 33 percent. His $200 of stock is now worth just $133. The net value of the portfolio has dropped to $33 ($133 – $100 loan = $33), which is just 25 percent of the total portfolio value ($33/$133 = 25 percent). The 33 percent decline in the market would trigger a margin call and, for most margin investors, would also trigger an involuntary sale of some of their stock.

All the tables and charts reported earlier in this chapter take into account margin calls. We call in the margin loan at the beginning of every month—regardless of the interim returns. The investors pay off their loan and rebalance their portfolios to the desired level of leverage. Of course, it is possible for there to be margin calls due to stock price declines in the middle of the month—but as an empirical matter there has never been an interim daily return that would trigger a margin call. The largest daily stock price drops occurred on Black Monday 1987 (October 19) and Black Monday 1929 (October 26). Given that we are already calling in our loans at the beginning of every month, there were no additional calls as a result of unexpected drops in daily stock returns. In fact, the closest you get to a margin call is not on a particularly dramatic day but on September 30, 1931—the end of a month when repeated losses brought the capital value of stocks down by 31.5 percent. This isn't quite enough to trigger a margin call—and even if it were, it would be just about time to rebalance anyway.

We should emphasize that this "no extra margin calls" result is only true for 2:1 leverage. If you engage in more extreme forms of leverage, you should expect a lot more margin calls, which will limit the benefits of diversification. Margin calls force investors to deleverage their positions by selling stock to pay off some of their loans. They're a natural limit to how much you can use leverage to diversify across time. Investing on a more leveraged basis initially gives you more exposure to the stock market, but it also creates a higher chance of margin calls that will take you out of the market—both immediately and in the subsequent period after your assets are sold off. Another factor is that the cost of borrowing goes up quickly with increased leverage. This shouldn't be too surprising—the loan is much riskier. The cost is so high, in fact, that it quickly exceeds the expected return on stocks.

If the idea of a margin call still makes you nervous, in Chapter 8 we show how to achieve leverage without buying stocks on margin. You can achieve a leveraged portfolio by investing in index futures that are in the money (like Andrew Verstein did in Chapter 1). As it turns out, this is a cheap and safe way to obtain leverage. Thus we have a win-win: Index futures both save you money and eliminate any chance of a margin call.

QUESTION 3: *Don't your results depend on being able to borrow cheaply? I thought margin loans were very expensive.*
The value of using leverage absolutely depends on the cost of borrowing. Unlike traditional investment strategies, time diversification requires you to borrow money to buy stock. The cost of borrowing (the margin rate) is important because you have to pay interest on the money you've borrowed. If this rate becomes too high, it won't be worthwhile to diversify across time. It doesn't make any sense to pay a 10 percent margin rate to buy stock with an expected return of 8 percent.

People think margin loans are expensive because most major brokers charge unreasonably high rates. Perhaps they've decided it's more profitable to take advantage of short-term margin investors who aren't paying attention to the interest rate. When we first started this project, Barry was surprised to discover that he was paying over 10 percent interest on a small margin loan he had with Fidelity. The good news is that online firms have changed the game. InteractiveBrokers.com offers margin loans at 1.65 percent (as of July 2009). That is a great rate and one that properly reflects the low risk to the lender.

This chapter's simulations assumed that the investors were able to borrow at the rate that banks offer to brokers to make margin loans (the "call money" rate). Historically, this rate has been very close to the risk-free rate. Today, even lower cost borrowing alternatives are available from online brokers. You can also implicitly borrow to buy stock through low-cost call options and stock index futures. Chapter 8 provides more detail along with step-by-step instructions on how to create leveraged positions on the cheap.

QUESTION 4: *Target-date funds didn't do that well in 2008. Your approach is like a target-date fund, but with a much higher initial stock allocation. Is that a problem for your approach?*
In 2008, the average performance of thirty-one target funds with a retirement date of 2010 fell by almost 25 percent.[5] That shouldn't be surprising. Target funds are a combination of mutual funds and bonds. Thus if the average 2010 target fund was 60 percent invested in equities and domestic equities fell by 36.6 percent (as they did in 2008, post dividends), then you would expect that the average target fund would fall by 60 percent of that amount or 22 percent.* Target funds did slightly worse than a 22 percent drop because these funds also hold foreign equities, which fell by even more than the U.S. market, and because of the way they rebalance.

---

*There was some question as to whether investors properly understood the extent to which their target-date fund would remain invested in equities. We are big fans of disclosure. Investors should understand what their target-date fund is doing in terms of investing strategy.

As stocks fell, the fraction invested in equities fell below 60 percent, and this led the funds to purchase more equities, which increased the overall loss, since equities continued to fall. In other words, the funds kept buying on the way down. For example, after the market fell by 20 percent, absent rebalancing, the fund would only have been 54 percent in equities. To rebalance, the fund would have bought more stocks, and this led to another 1 percent drop as the market fell another 16.6 percent. The effect of rebalancing means that if the market falls by a steady 36.6 percent, the target 60 percent equity portfolio will fall by 23 percent, not 22 percent.

On top of this poor performance, the funds charge fees, which are all too often above 2 percent. (As we discussed in the previous chapter, Vanguard is the exception, charging one-tenth as much, below 0.2 percent.) These high fees are another drag on performance.

Our lifecycle strategy is a kind of a target-date fund, but one where the stock allocation starts at 200 percent and then ramps down to the desired allocation at the retirement target date. Thus some of the critiques of target-date funds would seem to apply to us, too. While fees are always an issue, you can implement our strategy using LEAPs based on the S&P index and thereby avoid significant management fees.

There are still two critiques that we should address. The first, as leveled by Securities and Exchange Commission chair Mary Schapiro, is that the target-date portfolios for those near retirement are too heavily invested in equities. It is possible that regulation will come in and limit the exposure to equities to, say, 50 percent as the target-date approaches. If that happens, this will only enhance the need to invest more in equities when young.

The problem is that without exposure to equities, it isn't realistic to imagine that people will have a chance to save enough. You can't just plan on ramping down right before a market crash, because you don't know when a crash is going to occur. If you thought that someone should only be 20 percent in equities near retirement, that suggests that they shouldn't be much more than 30 percent in equities at age sixty or 40 percent in equities at age fifty. With exposure that low, most people wouldn't have had much money to lose.

The fair way to make this critique is to ask if people near retirement would have done better to have followed some other rule over their entire investment lifecycle. A glide path that ends up at 83 percent in equities near retirement would have produced a loss of 28 percent in 2008. While that sounds devastating, it turns out that that loss was more than offset by earlier gains that came from having a higher equities exposure. The person may have gotten knocked down more, but he started from a higher perch, and so his final landing place is still higher.

In reading the financial press, a second critique of target-date funds is that they are passive. As *Forbes* columnist Michael Maiello writes, "This is no time to set and forget your 401(k) or IRA. Active markets call for active management."[6] The thought is that somehow investors should have known to avoid financial services firms in 2008. By avoiding those toxic sectors they could have beat the indices. The data says otherwise.

To quote Benjamin Graham, "The investor's chief problem—and even his worst enemy—is likely to be himself." Brad Barber and Terrance Odean show that active traders underperformed the market by 6.5 percent over 1991 to 1996. In a sequel paper, they show that men trade 45 percent more often than women, and this trading ends up lowering their returns by 2.65 percent per year (versus 1.72 percent for women).[7] Worse still, according to Ken French, investors pay out some 0.64 percent annually in fees to get this worse performance.[8]

QUESTION 5: *What about market timing?*
Some investors will want to play a more active role in managing their portfolios. Even if they don't try to pick individual stocks, they might want to try to time the market. Instead of simply investing a fixed percentage of their assets in a mutual or index fund, they will want to invest more aggressively when stocks seem cheap (a low P/E, or price/earnings, ratio) and invest less when stocks seem overpriced. Based on historical data, this approach would have worked well in the past. Our lifecycle approach is compatible with a market-timing strategy. In Chapter 4 we review some approaches to market timing and show you the further improvement that might be possible.

CHAPTER 4

What If . . .

AT THE BEGINNING of the movie *It's a Wonderful Life*, George Bailey (played by Jimmy Stewart) is in a world of trouble. Uncle Billy has lost Bailey Building & Loan's money, and criminal charges for George are looming. Soon we find George standing on a bridge contemplating suicide. George bitterly concludes that it would have been better if he had never been born.

Most of the movie then proves George wrong. Clarence, Angel Second Class, appears and shows George that the world would have been a lot worse without him.

We're suckers for Capra films (and can't keep from crying when George breaks down and kisses Mary), but we've always been troubled by the movie's mode of persuasion. George is shown that he's had a wonderful life so far. But George could react to this information about the counterfactual past by saying, "I was wrong to say that it would have been better if I had never been born. But I still think the future is going to be awful—so I'm still going to commit suicide."

The movie's method of persuasion is indirect. Indeed, the tense of the title itself is a bit of a cheat. At the end of the movie the angel says, "You see, you really *did have* a wonderful life." But George isn't centrally concerned about the past or the present. What he really wants to know about is the future.

Probably the most repeated warning in finance is "Past performance is no guarantee of future results." You might be getting the vague feeling that, like Frank Capra, we've pulled a fast one. The previous chapter showed that a leveraged lifecycle investment strategy would have provided a wonderful return in the past. But what about the future?

It's a Wonderful Stock Market

When we showed our no-nonsense colleague John Langbein the diversification results of the last chapter, he was not impressed. If you remember, John was initially concerned that our fantastic returns were driven by taking more aggressive stock positions. We thought that he'd like our finding that you could generate the same return with 22 percent less risk. We were wrong.

John shot back:

> Your paper, which back-models historical price data, demonstrates that the last few decades have, on balance, been such a fine time to own stocks, and such a poor time to own fixed income assets, that preferring equities and indeed leveraging to buy more would have resulted in outperformance. Accepting that, when I buy a Roth IRA for my kids each tax season, for the domestic allocation I always put them in the Vanguard Balanced Index Fund, which is 60 percent equity, 40 percent debt. Why leave all that free Ayres/Nalebuff gold on the table? Because I think the second half of the twentieth century was uniquely favorable to equity investors, especially 1982 to 2000, and that long term the returns on equities may be much less favorable, especially for pension tax shelters in which fixed income returns compound tax free. Time may prove me wrong, but it may also prove you wrong. If I'm wrong, my kids will have a little less to retire on. If an Ayres/Nalebuff retirement investor is wrong, the downside is much greater, indeed, it can be dog food dinners at the county home.

Yikes. Did we commit the same mistake that Capra made in his movie? We have shown that a leveraged lifecycle strategy worked wonders for U.S. stocks in the past. But the twentieth century was America's century, and U.S. stock returns reflected that success. How do we know that the lifecycle strategy will work in the twenty-first century?

We have a few different ways to answer this question. Our theory tells us that as long as John holds his total dollar years fixed, spreading that exposure over more years will produce the same expected return with less volatility—even if future stock returns are smaller. The benefits of diversifying across time are largely independent of stock returns. But we have a feeling that skeptics want more than a theoretical answer.

Turning to the data, we first show that the historical results aren't peculiar to the United States. That's still backward looking, but it should provide some confidence that the results aren't reliant on the superior performance of the U.S. stock market. We then go and review the theory to see how the optimal investment strategy responds to a more pessimistic future. As you would expect, the overall exposure is reduced, but this is done by reducing the target, not the starting point. Leverage when young still helps diversify risk. To look forward with data, we employ Monte Carlo simulations. We make up thousands of possible futures and then compare our strategies to the traditional alternatives. This also allows us to consider how you'd fare if the equity premium were to fall or stocks were to be more volatile.

The FTSE and the Nikkei

To begin, we look outside the United States. We reran our 200/83 strategy on Japanese and UK stock data and once again found substantial gains over the more traditional 75/75 strategy and the birthday rule. The accumulation for 200/83 was 61.6 percent higher than the 75/75 strategy if you invested in the British FTSE All-Shares Index and 89.5 percent higher if you invested in the Japanese Nikkei Index. This is good news. The lifecycle strategy targeting 83 percent was tailored to the risk and return profile of U.S. stocks, but applying it lock, stock, and barrel to another market still produced superior results. These results, found in Table 4.1, are based on historic returns, but it is clear that the advantages of lifecycle investing aren't simply an artifact of exceptional returns that U.S. stocks experienced in the twentieth century.

The Japanese experiment is revealing on several fronts. As a starting point, it may help to remember that the Japanese market was on a tear

TABLE 4.1 Extension of Lifecycle Results to Foreign Markets

	96 U.S. Cohorts (1871–2009)			30 FTSE All-Shares Cohorts (1937–2009)			17 Nikkei 225 Cohorts (1950–2009)		
	Constant % (75/75) Strategy	Diversifying (200/83%) Strategy	Improvement over Constant %	Constant % (75/75) Strategy	Diversifying (200/83%) Strategy	Improvement over Constant %	Constant % (75/75) Strategy	Diversifying (200/83%) Strategy	Improvement over Constant %
Max. % Inv.	75	200		75	200		75	200	
Min. % Inv.	75	83		75	83		75	83	
Mean Result	$748,839	$1,223,105	63.3%	£538,863	£870,619	61.6%	¥51,120,760	¥96,864,911	89.5%
Min. Result	$308,726	$387,172	25.4%	£258,337	£492,356	90.6%	¥24,626,938	¥32,181,435	30.7%
10th pct.	$449,266	$701,834	56.2%	£328,675	£637,066	93.8%	¥27,480,810	¥37,304,150	35.7%
25th pct.	$561,032	$884,138	57.6%	£457,336	£742,526	62.4%	¥33,088,478	¥47,345,900	43.1%
Median	$691,427	$1,146,812	65.9%	£546,441	£873,400	59.8%	¥42,556,445	¥62,026,139	45.8%
75th pct.	$922,028	$1,522,653	65.1%	£649,572	£1,006,454	54.9%	¥58,724,153	¥107,895,235	83.7%
90th pct.	$1,152,276	$1,929,577	67.5%	£730,990	£1,078,129	47.5%	¥89,853,314	¥207,352,643	130.8%
Max. Result	$1,252,684	$2,177,424	73.8%	£846,333	£1,203,285	42.2%	¥100,875,394	¥290,197,957	187.7%

FIGURE 4.1 Performance of the Nikkei 225 (1950–2009)

from 1950 through 1990. The market index grew by a factor of 100! At the market peak, people feared that the Japanese would take over the world. Instead, Japan has lost two decades, and since that time the Nikkei has lost 75 percent of its value (and a bit more when measured in real terms).

In Figure 4.2, we compare the relative performance of the 200/83 strategy to both the 75/75 and the 90/50. As you can see, not only are the mean and minimum higher, but 200/83 has won for each and every one of the individual cohorts.

The victory for the early cohorts is breathtaking. Investors retired with almost triple the nest egg. The reason is clear: The first cohort retired in 1990 at the very peak of the market, and leverage helped boost their returns during what may have been the biggest bubble the world has ever seen.

More impressive is the fact that the leveraged strategy still won for those retiring in 2009. These investors were only forty-eight and still heavily invested in the market when the Nikkei crashed in 1990. And then it kept falling over the next two decades. While the 200/83 performance has suffered during this period, there was enough of a head start from the pre-1990

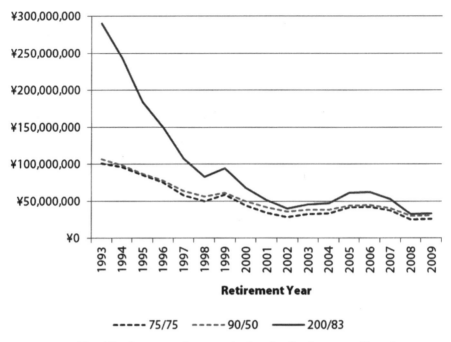

FIGURE 4.2 Final Retirement Accumulation by Retirement Year for Japanese Cohorts

run-up to keep the leveraged strategy ahead of both the constant 75 percent as well as the more conservative 90/50 birthday rule.

It's a Mediocre Life

Still, what if future returns of stocks are generally less rosy than the past? Does lifecycle investing still work? Theory says, "Yes." As long as the expected stock return is greater than the cost of borrowing money, you will want to employ leveraged investing when you are young. You shouldn't borrow money at 6 percent to invest in stock that you think will have an average return of 5 percent. That's a losing proposition. But as long as you expect stocks to earn more than the cost of borrowing (which has averaged just 2.5 percent for the last ten years), you will want to do some lifecycle investing.

How much you'll want to invest in stocks depends on what you think about the prospective risk and return of stocks generally. If, like John Langbein, you think the expected return on stock is going to be lower than it has been in the past, you will want less overall exposure to the market. John intuitively understands this, and that's why he is only exposing 60 percent of his savings to stock market risk.

Nevertheless, deciding to have less exposure to the stock market over the course of your life does *not* mean that you should have less exposure in each and every year. Langbein is right to want to reduce his overall exposure to stock market risk (since he expects the market to have lower returns and/or higher risk). But he is wrong not to try to spread this reduced exposure optimally over multiple years.

One way to think about this is to calculate how many dollar years of stock market exposure you expect to have. Recall that a dollar year of exposure is the risk of exposing one dollar to one year of stock risk. So if you have $100,000 invested in stocks in year 1 and $300,000 invested in stocks in year 2, you have a total of 400,000 dollar years of stock exposure. To diversify across time, you need to spread your dollar years of stock exposure more evenly across the temporal roulette wheel that is the stock market.

In our simulation, the 75/75 strategy exposed investors, on average, to 7.5 million dollar years, but with very little invested in the initial years and the bulk invested later on. You'd do better to spread the dollar years evenly across time—trying to invest $170,000 each year.*

We have no quarrel with Langbein thinking that prudent investors should reduce the dollar years of stock exposure. But whatever number you choose, you would do better to spread the dollar years out more equally across time. Doing this will still require leverage when you are young. For example, imagine that a more-cautious Zachary wanted to cut his dollar years of exposure in half, from $7.5 million down to $3.75 million. As a first cut, he should still want to invest on the order of $85,000 (half of $170,000) each year. Since he doesn't have nearly enough money

---

*$170,000 is the even allocation of $7.5 million over the forty-four years of market exposure.

to do this when he is young, he should prudently invest on a 2:1 basis to come closer to the lifecycle diversification ideal.

Guesstimating your lifetime total dollar years of stock is a great way to see how your exposure is massively unbalanced without the use of leverage. While the strategy of targeting an equal dollar amount in the stock market every year of your life gets you closer to even exposure, it doesn't take into account the compounding of money. Early exposure really matters, as the results get compounded for the next forty years. What we need is a way to adjust the 200/83 strategy to respond to the Langbein prediction of a future with lower stock returns and more risk.

Pessimists Should Still Start Out Leveraged

You might think that the natural adjustment to the 200/83 strategy would be to go to a 100/41.5 strategy. Lowering the beginning and ending percentages reduces the overall exposure to the market. Indeed, one might even think that the truly cautious would embrace the traditional 90/50 target-date strategies that are becoming so prevalent today.

But the logic of diversification suggests something very different.

The simple idea behind our 200/83 strategy was that you should aim to invest a constant percentage of lifetime savings in stock. An investor who has more pessimistic views about the stock market's future returns or risks should reduce her exposure simply by reducing this lifetime percentage. For example, instead of trying to invest 83 percent of lifetime savings in stock you might only try to put 41.5 percent in stock. That still means you should start off fully leveraged.

Here's why. When you're young, the present value of your future savings contributions is still going to be a substantial amount of money. For a college graduate in his early twenties, the present value of lifetime savings is well over $100,000 (even when he has less than $5,000 actually put aside).* Even if he's trying to invest only 20 percent of his lifetime sav-

---

*The representative investor in our historical simulation in Chapter 3 started out with a present value of about $111,000 in future savings contributions.

ings, this investor would need to have more than $20,000 in the stock market. But because he is starting out with only around $5,000 in savings, the closest he can come to this $20,000 target is by investing on a fully leveraged basis—borrowing an amount equal to his current savings and investing 200 percent in stock. And he should stay fully leveraged until his present savings are sufficient to meet his risk-adjusted target.

Pessimism about future stock returns doesn't affect how you start investing in your youth. You still should start out at 200 percent leverage. Pessimism about future returns or greater risk aversion only changes the rate at which you ramp down. Instead of adopting a 200/83 strategy, you might use a 200/50 strategy, in which you start out at 200 percent leverage and ramp down to 50 percent of your savings in stock just before you retire. (Recall that the 200/50 strategy has the same average return as 75/75 and takes all the gain as reduced risk.) This more conservative strategy will affect how long you remain in the three phases of retirement. Under a 200/83 strategy the typical investor remained fully leveraged for nearly thirteen years (phase 1) and partially leveraged for an additional fourteen years (phase 2) before ramping down to an unleveraged portfolio split between stocks and bonds (phase 3). But a more conservative 200/50 strategy would reduce the length of the fully leveraged phase to eight years and the length of the partial leverage to seven years—leaving the remaining twenty-nine years looking much closer to the traditional lifecycle split. The difference between these two strategies can be seen in Table 4.2.

TABLE 4.2 **Years Spent in Each Phase of Investment**

	200/83 Strategy	200/50 Strategy
Phase 1: Fully leveraged	12.8 years	8.3 years
Phase 2: Partially leveraged	14.2 years	7.1 years
Phase 3: Unleveraged	17.0 years	28.6 years

To be clear, if you are sufficiently pessimistic about future stock market returns, you should simply stop investing in stocks altogether. If you think the expected return on the stock market is not high enough, or if you think future returns will be a lot more volatile than in the past, or if you are just really, really risk averse, it is quite reasonable to shift your portfolio toward bonds and treasury bills.

But if, like Langbein and many others, you are investing at all in stock, then you should do so in a way that distributes your risk across time. Even if (indeed *especially* if) you are extremely risk averse and want to ration your exposure to stock, you should try to spread more of your dollar years to your youth.

10,000 Futures

Somehow we don't expect that people like John will be satisfied. We have a powerful theory. We've shown that it would have worked like gangbusters in the past. We've shown theoretically why it should help in the future even if the stock market returns are not as strong as they've been in the past. As long as you hold your total dollar years constant, spreading your stock exposure to more years is bound to produce a more stable result, even if the stock market returns are not as strong. So what's left to do? We could always wait twenty-five years and show that our strategy once again beat the alternatives.[1] But it would then be too late for another generation to take advantage of the core idea—and the next generation would worry about the future once again.

Instead of waiting, we can simulate thousands upon thousands of different scenarios of the future using the Monte Carlo method. Like spinning the roulette wheel in Monte Carlo, a Monte Carlo simulation randomly draws different stock returns from a probability distribution of stock returns. Want to see how lifecycle investing would fare in a world with a lower expected return or more volatility? All you need to do is run the simulation drawing returns from a more pessimistic distribution.

One of the powers of the Monte Carlo approach is that it can be repeated again and again. Instead of limiting ourselves to 96 overlapping cohorts of historic investors, we analyzed how 10,000 different investors would do if they lived in a world where stock returns followed a wide range of possible distributions.

TABLE 4.3 **Constant % Stock Strategy vs. Mean-Preserving Lifecycle 10,000 Monte Carlo Draws from a Lognormal Stock Distribution**

	Constant % Stock	Lifecycle Strategy	Improvement over Constant
Max. % Inv.	50.0	200.0	
Min. % Inv.	50.0	32.1	
Mean Result	$711,746	$711,746	0.0%
St. Dev.	$320,699	$276,903	−13.7%
Min. Result	$130,575	$159,394	22.1%
10th pct.	$384,025	$412,317	7.4%
25th pct.	$490,450	$516,189	5.3%
75th pct.	$856,652	$849,440	−0.8%
90th pct.	$1,112,747	$1,067,025	−4.1%
Max. Result	$3,523,088	$3,084,903	−12.4%
Stock Distribution		Mean	6.1%
		St. Dev.	17.3%

For example, want to know whether a lifecycle strategy could help a more conservative investor like John, who is currently only investing 60 percent of his kids' savings in stock? We compare the results of following a 50/50 strategy versus an equally aggressive lifecycle strategy, which turns out to be 200/32.[2] Which one would a scaredy-cat prefer to invest in? If you were really worried about risk, you'd want a strategy that did well on average but also had a predictable result. The 200/32 has a higher probability of having an accumulation in the middle and a lower probability of being caught in the lower tail. It also has a lower probability of being caught in the upper tail—but that's what less volatile means. It evens out the highs and lows. The numeric results from these 10,000 head-to-head competitions are shown in Table 4.3.

The 200/32 strategy has substantially less risk. Its standard deviation is 13.7 percent lower than the 50/50 strategy. In Chapter 3, we compared a 75/75 strategy to an equally aggressive 200/50 strategy and showed that the standard deviation dropped 21 percent. The smaller diversification benefit in Table 4.3 is just what our theory would predict. You see, if you played a 0/0 strategy—investing all of your money in government bonds—your exposure to stock would be perfectly diversified (because you'd have no exposure in any period). Investing a constant 1 percent of current savings in every period would make you only slightly undiversified with little room for better diversification over time. (With a 1 percent goal, you'd hit your target very soon and so wouldn't be far out of balance.) Table 4.3 shows, however, that there still is substantial room for diversification benefits against a long-term 50 percent stock investment. This is relevant because few financial advisors would suggest that young people put less than 50 percent of their retirement savings in stock—even if they are very risk averse.

It's also striking that the minimum accumulation is a healthy 22 percent higher for the 200/32 strategy. We saw similar results in the last chapter. But it's more surprising here because the Monte Carlo method allows an investor to encounter much worse luck than has ever been seen in the real world. In American history, an actual investor would only have to live through at most one Great Depression. But in a Monte Carlo simulation, it is possible for an unlucky investor to draw a year like 1929 over and over and over again. Indeed, when you are simulating 10,000 different future scenarios, it becomes inevitable that some unlucky investor will draw repeated market crashes.* One of our investors had six years when his stocks lost more than 20 percent of their value.** But such gruesome luck not withstanding, the leveraged strategy still prevailed. Exposing the investor to more risk when young (200 percent versus 50 percent) and less

---

*If you had 10,000 people each flip a coin forty-four times, there would be a 60 percent chance at least one would have more than thirty-five tails. That unlucky person is like an investor who draws thirty-five years' worth of below average stock returns.

**One point to remember is that we used the same simulated returns to compare the 50/50 rule to the 200/31.5 rule. Thus both the 50/50 investor and the 200/32 investor experienced the same six years with −20 percent returns. This is how you'd want us to do it. The approach is like duplicate bridge. The comparison shouldn't depend on one strategy getting a better history than the other.

risk when old (32 percent versus 50 percent) turns out to be a better way to weather even the worst-case perfect storm.

A Meaner Mean

So far we have run our simulation under the assumption that stock returns will have the same mean and standard deviation as in the past. What if the mean expected returns from stock are meaner? This is a real possibility—especially with regard to U.S. stock. In the twentieth century, returns on U.S. stocks were substantially higher than their foreign counterparts.[3] From 1871 to 2009, U.S. stock returns outpaced bond returns by almost 4 percent compounded.[4] However, a 2004 *Wall Street Journal* survey of economists predicted a much more modest risk premium for stocks—only 1.7 percent—over the next forty-four years. Our theory suggests that there should still be diversification benefits as long the expected return on stock is higher than the expected cost of borrowing. But seeing is believing.

So we reran the simulations, generating 10,000 more possible futures—but drew our stock returns from a more pessimistic distribution, in which the expected average return was about 30 percent less (4.26 percent versus 6.13 percent) than in the last table. And the results, seen in Table 4.4, are quite reassuring.

As expected, all the returns are worse. But what we care about is the relative performance of 200/32 to 50/50. As promised, the benefits of diversification are largely unchanged from the earlier simulation. This is just what you should expect. The benefits of diversification come from better handling of volatility in stock returns across years. Merely shifting down the average return shouldn't affect the size of the benefits.

Second, you can start to see that the optimal lifecycle strategy depends on your expectations about future stock returns. If you believe that investing in the stock market is riskier, you will want to expose yourself to less stock. As we saw earlier, this doesn't mean reducing your exposure in every period. Instead, risk-averse investors should still start out fully leveraged but ramp down faster and to a lower terminal stock allocation.

TABLE 4.4 **Constant % Stock Strategy vs. Mean-Preserving Lifecycle
10,000 Monte Carlo Draws from a Lognormal Stock Distribution with a
Lower Mean**

	Constant % Stock	Lifecycle Strategy	Improvement over Constant
Max. % Inv.	50.0	200.0	
Min. % Inv.	50.0	31.6	
Mean Result	$544,785	$544,785	0.0%
St. Dev.	$234,763	$204,868	−12.7%
Min. Result	$109,267	$126,532	15.8%
10th pct.	$302,382	$322,261	6.6%
25th pct.	$382,266	$399,713	4.6%
75th pct.	$652,709	$648,084	−0.7%
90th pct.	$838,548	$810,276	−3.4%
Max. Result	$2,521,100	$2,258,514	−10.4%
Stock Distribution		Mean	4.3%
		St. Dev.	17.3%

Fat Tail Fears

Nassim Taleb, the author of *Fooled by Randomness* and *The Black Swan*, has made a pile of money by exploiting the tendency of the distribution of stock returns to have slightly fatter tails than suggested by a normal bell curve.[5] In the 1990s, Taleb's company bought thousands of options on the cheap. These far out-of-the-money options would be worthless unless the stock price moved substantially. Most of the options did end up being worthless, but Taleb figured out that those "rare" stock jumps, which the market thought would only happen once every 10,000 times were likely to occur once every 1,000 times. He was right. One-in-a-thousand is still pretty rare, but if you're only paying the price for a one-in-ten-thousand long shot, it's a bet you'd want to play over and over again.

We love Taleb's books. We agree with him that it is foolhardy to predict the future price of individual stocks or even the market in aggregate. But when he goes further and suggests that numbers can't guide you in your investing decisions, that's hogwash.[6] Indeed, Taleb's own success as a quant shows the power of exploiting better information about likely future stock returns. We think it is possible to make noisy unbiased predictions about future stock prices. We can predict that the S&P 500 will increase 7 percent next year. The problem is that we also estimate that the standard error of our prediction is 20 percent. Like Taleb, we agree that a prediction that is right on average isn't helpful if there's a large range of how it could go wrong. This uncertainty is a big reason why we think it's so important to diversify. But that doesn't mean that predictions of future risk and return of stock are useless. They can and should be used to craft superior investment strategies.

Nowadays, savvy hedge funds have pushed the market to do a much better job at pricing the fat tails. It's become much harder for casual investors to beat the market by betting on fat tails. That said, your optimal diversification across time still depends on what you think future volatility will be.

If, like Taleb, you think that stock market returns have fatter tails than they've displayed in the past, then diversifying your risk over time makes all the more sense. Risk-averse investors will want to expose themselves less to a riskier market. Of course, lowering your portfolio exposure to stock risk does not mean an end to leverage. Just like those who are pessimistic about the future average return, you can reduce your exposure to a riskier market by lowering your terminal allocation and ramping down more quickly.

Table 4.5 shows just this result. In this final Monte Carlo simulation, we looked at 10,000 stock iterations that come from a distribution where the variability of stock returns (measured by standard deviation) is almost 50 percent higher.

Far from extinguishing the benefits of diversification, fatter tails reinforce the dominance of the leveraged strategy. Comparing Tables 4.3 and 4.5, we can see that the leveraged strategy reduces the volatility in retirement savings accumulations more when stock returns are more volatile. The standard deviation of outcomes falls by almost 16 percent. Of course, what we really care about are the bad outcomes. The worst 1 in 10,000 (the minimum) case is up by over 15 percent. Normally we next present the 1 in 10 case. To be extra cautious, here we also provide the results for

TABLE 4.5 **Constant % Stock Strategy vs. Mean-Preserving Ramp Down 10,000 Monte Carlo Draws from a Lognormal Stock Distribution with Increased Volatility**

	Constant % Stock	Lifecycle Strategy	Improvement over Constant
Max. % Inv.	50.0	200.0	
Min. % Inv.	50.0	33.0	
Mean	$911,087	$911,087	0.0%
St. Dev.	$668,540	$564,139	−15.6%
Min.	$80,625	$92,893	15.2%
0.1 pct.	$153,436	$169,983	10.8%
1st pct.	$209,694	$236,705	12.9%
10th pct.	$348,005	$385,503	10.8%
25th pct.	$491,757	$535,653	8.9%
75th pct.	$1,116,997	$1,122,598	0.5%
90th pct.	$1,647,642	$1,589,371	−3.5%
Max.	$9,865,224	$7,921,964	−19.7%
Stock Distribution		Mean	6.1%
		St. Dev.	25.0%

the worst 1 in 1,000 and 1 in 100 cases along with the 1 in 10. As you can see above, all three show at least a 10 percent improvement. Your downside risk is substantially reduced. At the end of the day, the greater volatility still leads to a worse risk-reward tradeoff, and so you may decide to forgo investing in stocks altogether. But if you invest, even at a reduced level, the take-home lesson of Table 4.5 is that it's safer to use leverage early on and spread your risk out over time.[7]

But Is Now the Right Time?

As we write this in the summer of 2009, people are still nervous about the stock market, and the economy in general. The subprime mortgage crisis and an anemic economy led to a market low of 676.5 for the S&P 500 in March. Even after an impressive recovery, the Nasdaq Index is still only back to where it was eleven years ago. And to many, the future does not look much brighter.

Fat tails aren't a reason to reject a lifecycle investment strategy, but how do we respond to readers who think the market is currently overpriced? They might ask, "Surely you can't be asking me to take a leveraged position when the market is about to tank?"

Our first response is to be skeptical. We don't think that we can predict when the market is going to tank or rally. And to be honest, we don't think other people can either. People bet real money when they bought, sold, or held stock yesterday at the market price. If there was a true consensus that stock prices would fall tomorrow, then everyone would sell today, and so prices would fall today instead.

We're leery about the ability of market timers to time their investments. People are prone to overrate their ability to time when it is propitious to hold stock and when it is better to transfer their savings to a less risky asset, such as government bonds. This book is not about making money by buying low and selling high. It's about making money by diversifying.

You can't time the market. But you can time yourself. You know how many years you have left till retirement and how much of your income you are likely to put aside during that time. You can use this self-knowledge to diversify your exposure to the market.

And because our diversification strategy doesn't depend on any assumption that stocks are mispriced, people playing our strategy aren't in competition with other investors. In sharp contrast, market timers should be worried that someone will beat them to the punch. If today's price is too high, some other guy has every incentive to start selling it short. Arbitrageurs and hedge funds are constantly trying to put market timers out of business. Because of their corrective power, we tend to throw our lot with the random-walkers.

Nevertheless, the research of our colleague Robert Shiller gives us pause. In 1996, Shiller testified before the Federal Reserve that stock prices were overvalued. He presented the graph in Figure 4.3 (which we've updated through 1999 showing a negative correlation in historical stock data between the current price/earnings (P/E) ratio and stock returns over the following ten years.

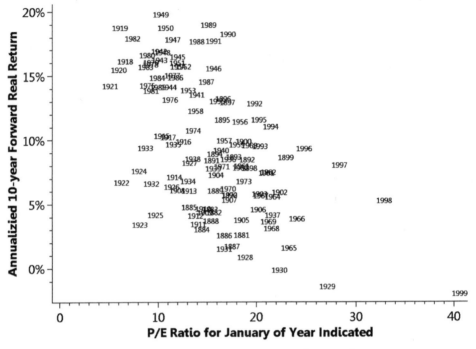

FIGURE 4.3 Ten-Year Forward Return Compared to Market

The overall market's price/earnings ratio is simply a comparison of the total value of stocks to their combined earnings. A P/E ratio of 20 means that for every $20 of stock price companies had $1 in earnings. When stock prices are low relative to earnings, say 5 to 1, then stock market returns for the next ten years are much higher than when the same P/E ratio is 20 or higher. Shiller's preferred measure of the market P/E ratio (which we adopt) compares current stock values to their average earnings over the previous ten years. At the time of his testimony, this P/E was hovering at 25.9. Shiller was testifying before the Fed because he was concerned that the markets were headed for a fall. As it turned out, the next ten-year return averaged a more than respectable 9 percent. By 1999, the market P/E had risen to 40.6, a number that is almost off the right edge of the chart. At that point, his Chicken Little scenario was around the corner, and the next ten years brought the crash of the dot-coms in 2001 and the meltdown in 2008, for a negative 1.99 percent annual return over that decade. Shiller's claim of "irrational exuberance" was largely vindicated.

Historically, high P/E ratios don't assure you that the stock market is about to decline. When we crunched the numbers, we found that when the market P/E ratio is 25, you'd still expected a positive but anemic annual return of about 3 percent. In contrast, investing in the market when stocks are cheap relative to earnings, with a P/E ratio of 8, will produce expected annual stock returns of about 13 percent.

People who have embraced Shiller's P/E analysis have proposed a variety of simple market timing strategies. Buy and hold stocks when the P/E ratio is below the historic average of 15, and sell your stocks and hold government bonds when the P/E ratio goes above 15.* Shiller's empiricism has made even skeptics like us more open to the potential of timing strategies.

Before we dive in, a problem with these timing strategies is that they sacrifice the value of diversifying across time.[8] If you believe Shiller, is there a way to have your cake and eat it too? Indeed there is.

Up until now, we've been advocating multiplying the present value of your current and future savings by a single percentage target, your Samuelson share—in most of our examples, 83 percent. The Samuelson share that is right for you is based on your personal risk preferences and your expectations about future stock returns. In Chapter 7, we'll help you quantify your attitudes toward risk. For now, we'll stick with 83 percent, since it is an appropriate target for a typically risk-averse investor who thinks the market is going to have generally the same risk and return in the future as in the past. This target is constant because we've been assuming that investors' risk preferences don't vary and that their expectations about market returns don't vary.

If we accept Shiller, however, we should have varying expectations about the market and, therefore, a varying percentage target. It's fairly simple to create a P/E–adjusted target by just making the percentage a function

---

*Actor, comedian, and economist Ben Stein argues for a modified version of this strategy in *Yes, You Can Time the Market.* He and his coauthor, Phil Demuth, suggest that you hold on to all additional savings in cash during periods when the P/E is high and only convert the cash to stock when the P/E is low again.

TABLE 4.6 **Market P/E 10 and the Associated Samuelson Share**

P/E 10	Samuelson Share
6	163%
10	118%
14	83%
18	57%
22	33%
26	12%

of the P/E ratio. When we did this for a range of P/Es (and the associated range of expected returns), we found that our fairly conservative 83 percent investor would invest higher percentages in stock when the P/E ratio was low and lower percentages in stock when the P/E ratio was high. These findings are shown in Table 4.6.

When the P/E ratio is 22, our Shiller-inspired strategy more than halves the target Samuelson share from 83 percent to 33 percent; when it is 26, the recommended percentage drops to just 12 percent. But as before, pessimism doesn't stop the young from being fully leveraged. After all, 13 percent of (the present value of) your lifetime savings is still a lot more money than most twenty-five-year-olds have in cash.

Instead of the all-or-nothing timing strategies advanced by others, our P/E–adjusted strategy naturally combines evolving expectations about the stock market together with the benefits of a lifecycle strategy. It's only when the P/E ratio goes above 27.7 that our number crunching suggests that people should completely stop investing in stock. When the market is this overpriced, the expected future stock returns don't justify the risk. The market has entered this danger zone only twice—in 1929 just before the crash and again in the late 1990s just before the tech bubble burst.

To P/E or Not to P/E

This market-timing strategy isn't perfect. Shiller's approach doesn't provide us with a crystal ball for knowing exactly when a bull or bear market will descend. Remember, he was warning about a crash five years before it actually happened. That said, looking at the onslaught of the Great Depression gives you a pretty good idea of how a market-timing strategy sacrifices some of the upside but protects you from the downside. Following the P/E–adjusted strategy in 1929 would have caused you to hold no stocks in July and August when the S&P had huge run-ups of 6 percent and 4 percent. But the strategy would have also kept you out of the market in September, when the S&P fell 10 percent, and though you would have reentered the market in October, when it fell a staggering 26 percent, you would have had 50 percent as much in stock as you would have had otherwise.

Of course, you should be wary of any strategy that is sold to you by anecdote. How does the P/E–adjusted 83 percent strategy fare compared to the other contenders? Table 4.7 provides parallel analysis for 86 investor cohorts.[9]

The table shows that the P/E–adjusted strategy (which targets 83 percent when the market has a P/E ratio of 14, the historical average) produces substantially higher expected accumulations than any of the traditional strategies, and higher even than our previously touted unadjusted 200/83 strategy. This is the kind of striking improvement—coming on top of our already improved results—that should give even the most ardent skeptic pause. Adopting a lifecycle strategy that takes you out of the market completely when the market seems overpriced produces expected returns that are more than twice that generated by either of the traditional strategies.

The mean accumulation of the P/E–adjusted strategy is 26 percent higher than that of the unadjusted 200/83 strategy. And this higher mean does not come at the expense of additional risk—the minimum stays the same while the tenth percentile and above all increase with the P/E adjustments. Yet, if we display the two accumulations over time, as in Figure 4.4, we see that only about 70 percent (fifty-nine out of eighty-six) of the cohorts experience higher accumulations using the P/E–adjusted 83 percent strategy rather than the unadjusted 200/83 strategy.

TABLE 4.7 Results from 86 Simulated Investors: 1881–2009

	Birthday Rule	Constant % Stock	Unadjusted Lifecycle Strategy	Adjusted Lifecycle Strategy	Improvement over Birthday	Improvement over Constant	Improvement over Unadjusted
Max. % Inv.	90	75	200	200	—	—	—
Min. % Inv.	50	75	83	0	—	—	—
Mean Result	$671,239	$771,214	$1,296,998	$1,639,374	144.2%	112.6%	26.4%
Min. Result	$351,550	$390,988	$611,774	$611,515	73.9%	56.4%	0.0%
10th pct.	$465,921	$476,942	$768,404	$903,884	94.0%	89.5%	17.6%
25th pct.	$564,012	$587,319	$1,010,702	$1,086,915	92.7%	85.1%	7.5%
Median	$670,886	$711,777	$1,204,712	$1,365,441	103.5%	91.8%	13.3%
75th pct.	$793,996	$944,026	$1,587,704	$1,963,838	147.3%	108.0%	23.7%
90th pct.	$872,311	$1,154,342	$1,939,646	$3,205,714	267.5%	177.7%	65.3%
Max. Result	$1,026,903	$1,286,285	$2,177,424	$3,522,336	243.0%	173.8%	61.8%

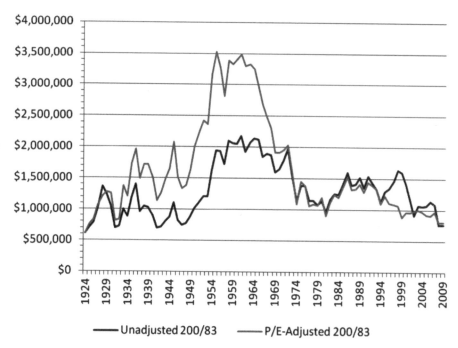

FIGURE 4.4 **Final Retirement Accumulation by Year for P/E–Adjusted vs. Unadjusted Strategies**

From a quick look at the chart, you'll see that when the unadjusted strategy beats the P/E–adjusted strategy, it does so by a smaller amount than when the adjusted strategy wins. While you can't know which strategy will win in the end for your particular cohort, the potential upside of investing with the P/E–adjusted strategy is sufficiently large that it deserves serious consideration. On the other hand, for recent history, 1972 to 1996, the two approaches were essentially tied, and from 1996 to 2008 the nonadjusted P/E strategy was nearly always out on top.*

Despite the improvement in the average return, we can't bring ourselves to wholly abandon the notion that the market follows a random walk. Market timers' theories tend to put themselves out of business. If

---

*Of course these results are for people retiring in those years. For folks starting out, they would have done better to start out with less exposure in 2008, and so the P/E–adjusted strategy would have given them a head start.

everyone believed Shiller's results, then the market would never display aberrational P/E ratios. If the expected future returns are abnormally high, smart investors would rush in and bid up the current price of stock until it reached the point at which the future expected return was no longer abnormal.

Including a P/E adjustment also adds another degree of complexity to an investment strategy, which will make it harder for many investors to execute it in a disciplined manner. It might require more psychological restraint, in that when the market is increasing by leaps and bounds month after month, it will be difficult for some investors to take their foot off the gas.

Then again, our theory suggests that your Samuelson share should decline if you have more pessimistic views about the future risk or return of the stock market. Our P/E adjustment reduces the Samuelson share when a high P/E suggests that future returns are expected to be low. In the end, we suggest that you follow the temperate advice of Samuelson:

> Whenever you discern a tempting 'edge,' yield to it, but yield only a little. 'Sin'—but only a little. . . . Among the asset allocators there are *confident* ones; they move from ninety-ten in stocks-bonds to five-ninety-five in stocks-bonds. That implies a degree of self-confidence bordering on *hubris* and self-deception. Over the decades, when both groups of asset allocators have an equal *limited* (!) ability to 'time,' the *cautious* chaps who alternate between sixty-five-thirty-five in stocks bonds and sixty-forty are likely to end up with a superior risk-corrected total return score.[10]

A small amount of timing may help with the return and won't cost you much in terms of extra risk. By small, we mean that you might want to adjust your target share up or down by 10 percent depending on the P/E ratio. When done at this scale, market timing is a bit like Pascal's wager, there's not much to lose, and there's the chance of some upside.

You should also reduce your Samuelson share when the expected future risk or volatility of stocks is high. Even with Shiller's P/E, it is difficult to predict the future return of the stock market. But if you use future prices, it is possible to derive measures of the market's current expectation of stock volatility. When volatility measures like the VIX rose fourfold in 2008, the market was sending a loud and clear message that the risk had gone up, and our theory then says that you should reduce your share. So even if you don't adjust your share based on difficult-to-measure changes in expected returns, we are attracted to making adjustments based on easier-to-measure changes in expected volatility (and in Chapter 7, we'll show you how).

CHAPTER 5

Starting and Stopping

DERIVING AND PROVING the benefits of a lifecycle investment strategy has been one of the most exciting things we have ever done. There is something truly satisfying about waiting for the computer to kick out the results of a simulation and seeing that the theory holds up to another data set or to a different Monte Carlo simulation. But in another sense, it's also been slightly depressing.

You see, as we write this, we've just turned fifty, and it is hard to confront over and over again the mistakes of our youth. We would be in a much better position if we had bought stock on leverage when we were young. Merlin may be able to live life in reverse, but we mortals come this way only once. The lost opportunities to diversify in our twenties and thirties and forties are just that—lost.

But all is not doom and gloom. Diversification across time can still help you if you're in your fifties and sixties—and even if you're already retired. We'll show you how to give your kids the gift of diversification. We'll even show that a lifecycle investment strategy has concrete things to say to organizations that don't plan on ever dying.

Starting Late

While we are late to the game, we have taken some steps to drink our own diversification Kool-Aid. Let's look at Ian, a real-life fifty-something. Financially, Ian and his beloved spouse (and coauthor) Jennifer have been faithful savers—both for retirement and for looming college expenses (their kids are now twelve and fifteen). For most of his working years, Ian has invested virtually all of his savings in stocks—low-cost index funds and ETFs of U.S. and non-U.S. equities. He doesn't try to beat the market, and he hasn't engaged in market timing. He also doesn't spend much time thinking about it. Once a year, just before tax time, he updates a spreadsheet summing up what has happened to his savings in the past year. And really, just once a year, he and his spouse talk about what kind of investments they plan to make in the coming year. Since they invest all their savings in stock, it's a pretty quick conversation—usually limited to simple questions like whether they should put a higher proportion of their savings in foreign or small-cap index funds.

Ian's all-stock strategy is more aggressive than the financial strategies of many of his law school colleagues. Friends of his who put 60 percent of their money in stocks (and 40 percent in bonds) missed out on the huge run-up in the market that occurred in the eighties and nineties. The problem is that so did Ian. Even though he was 100 percent in stock, as an absolute matter, he still didn't have very many dollars invested and so he, too, largely missed out on the run-up. For the moment, his friends can gloat a bit. After the market drop of 2008, their 60/40 portfolios would (as of June 2009) be worth about 8 percent more than Ian's 100 percent stock portfolio. What Ian is really kicking himself for, though, is not taking on a leveraged position when he was young. If he had anticipated this book's advice and followed the 200/83 strategy, then (as of June 2009) his portfolio would have been 23 percent higher than it currently stands and 14 percent ahead of his colleagues.

Ian's problem is that, like most investors, he hasn't kept anything like an equal amount of money invested in the market. His exposure to the market has grown tenfold from the time he was thirty to now when he is fifty. His experience is the poster child for this book. The fact that he was so poorly diversified across time meant that the 2008 market hit him especially hard. The solution isn't to invest less in his fifties, but to have invested more earlier on. He thought that 100 percent equities was aggressive, but measured as a percent of his lifetime savings, he was under 20 percent in equities during his thirties and even his early forties. He can't go back and correct that mistake, but he can get it right going forward.

When Ian now takes account of his expected future retirement savings, he figures that his discounted future savings add another 50 percent to his current total. (Those savings are after putting money aside for his children's college educations and taking care of his dad.) So even a 100 percent stock portfolio is really like a 67 percent lifecycle allocation.

Remedying this underexposure doesn't mean that Ian as a fifty-year-old should be investing 200 percent of his current savings in stock. But it does mean that he should be more exposed to the market today since he expects to have significant savings in the future. Ian and Jennifer love their jobs and figure that they have at least twenty, maybe twenty-three, years until retirement. Teaching smart students is a truly great gig, and Ian can see himself, like many of his colleagues, waiting until he is seventy-three to retire. In our simulations, the average person following our 200/83 strategy who has twenty-three years until retirement is forty-four years old and would be investing 126 percent of his or her present savings in stock. Ian calculates that he should be investing nearly the same—125 percent of his current worth in stocks.[1] And he's

> We could analyze Barry's portfolio, but it's much more complicated because of his involvement with Honest Tea. In 1998, Barry and one of his former students, Seth Goldman, cofounded a company to make bottled iced tea that actually tastes like tea (rather than liquid candy). It's organic, true brewed, and not too sweet.* The business has grown from zero to fifty million in annual sales and in 2008 Coca-Cola bought a 40 percent stake at a valuation above $100 million. For the time being, Barry has the vast majority of his net worth tied up in the business. While he would like to be more diversified, that's the fate of an entrepreneur.

*Learn more at honesttea.com. When you are a startup, you take product placement wherever you can, including books on investment.

taken action to make it so. In 2009, he and his wife invested over $100,000 in call options on the S&P index—which effectively increases his exposure to stocks.

Having missed out on almost three decades of opportunities, will Ian's move to lifecycle investing be too little, too late? Thankfully, the appropriate adage here is "better late than never." Even if your youth has passed you by and you find yourself in your thirties, forties, or even your fifties, diversification across time can still help you. That's the good news. The bad news is that you can't turn back the clock (even if fifty is the new thirty). Missed opportunities for temporal diversifications are forever lost, but there are still substantial gains from switching to a lifecycle strategy even if you start late.

Table 5.1 shows just how large these gains can be. This is the same scenario as in the last two chapters. We ask what would happen if representative investors—like Zachary and Eleanor—saving the same amounts over their lives had used alternative strategies. But in this version, we ask what the impact is on your final retirement nest egg of switching from the traditional birthday rule (90/50) strategy to a lifecycle strategy at different stages of your life. For comparison, the first two columns report the results that we saw earlier in Table 3.1 for the 90/50 rule and our 200/83 lifecycle. The remaining columns estimate the impact of starting late.

You can see that starting late still produces better results. For example, if you are twenty years from retirement, switching from a traditional strategy to our lifecycle strategy raises your expected accumulation by almost 40 percent. And you can quickly see that this increase in return is not accompanied by an increase in risk—as the worst-case accumulation increases by nearly 16 percent. Indeed, even doing a better job of diversifying across the last ten years of work life helps. Across the ninety-six historical investors, switching for the last decade of one's working life increases the average retirement nest egg by 17 percent.* To be clear, much of this gain

---

*For those with only five years to go, we can improve the mean but not the minimum (although the downside is less than 1 percent worse). This shouldn't be surprising—five years doesn't offer much time to get the benefits of diversification.

is coming from being more exposed to equities. But the simulation still shows that historically the additional exposure is sufficiently spread across years so that even the worst-case scenario sees a slight improvement. Now these increases are not as impressive as the 89 percent increase we found for someone who takes full advantage of diversification throughout their entire working life. A forty-year-old (stock) virgin will not be able to double his money by diversifying time. But Ian, at age 50, is still happy to take a 40 percent increase in his retirement funds.

The "Undercover Economist," Tim Harford, described the results of our first academic analysis of temporal diversification in an article in *Slate* with the memorable title "Only the Good Buy Young." But the results in Table 5.1 show that while the best buy young, it can also be good to buy when you're starting to gray.

In the Introduction, we wrote about how we should have invested part of our book advance before we actually received it. The same thought process leads us to think that many middle-age investors should start exposing some of their expected bequests to the stock market even *before* their parents or grandparents die. Ian has a friend from high school who begged his wealthy octogenarian grandmother for nearly a decade to shift some of her retirement portfolio from bonds to stocks. His family was close and all the grandkids were assured of receiving a hefty inheritance. But grandma's money was left languishing largely in fixed-income securities. We now think Ian's friend should have stopped cajoling his grandmother and just reallocated the money himself. He could have replaced some of the bonds in his portfolio with stock (and even used leverage if need be) to start exposing his expected inheritance to the stock market *before* his grandmother passed away.

Inheritance in America is increasingly the phenomena of the very old (the surviving spouse in her 80s or 90s) giving to the old (the children in their 60s or 70s). Even grandchildren now are often in their 40s by the time they receive a check from the dearly departed's estate. If you're lucky enough to have an inheritance in your future that is currently invested in bonds, you don't have to convince your grandmother to buy stock, you can do it yourself.

TABLE 5.1 Switching from Birthday Rule to Lifecycle Strategy Later in Work Life

	Birthday Rule	200/83 Lifecycle Strategy	Improvement over Birthday	Switch to Lifecycle for Last 40 Years	Improvement over Birthday	Switch to Lifecycle for Last 35 Years	Improvement over Birthday
Mean Result	$646,575	$1,223,105	89.2%	$1,200,075	85.6%	$1,128,916	74.6%
Min. Result	$290,310	$387,172	33.4%	$355,710	22.5%	$368,754	27.0%
10th pct.	$416,253	$701,834	68.6%	$696,726	67.4%	$719,691	72.9%
25th pct.	$539,343	$884,138	63.9%	$869,564	61.2%	$825,371	53.0%
Median	$641,555	$1,146,812	78.8%	$1,139,359	77.6%	$1,064,119	65.9%
75th pct.	$779,044	$1,522,653	95.5%	$1,443,402	85.3%	$1,381,705	77.4%
90th pct.	$870,921	$1,929,577	121.6%	$1,887,323	116.7%	$1,771,132	103.4%
Max. Result	$1,026,903	$2,177,424	112.0%	$2,237,399	117.9%	$2,378,396	131.6%
Avg. % Inv. at Switch		200		200		200	

	Switch to Lifecycle for Last 30 Years	Improvement over Birthday	Switch to Lifecycle for Last 25 Years	Improvement over Birthday	Switch to Lifecycle for Last 20 Years	Improvement over Birthday
Mean Result	$1,044,939	61.6%	$972,221	50.4%	$898,173	38.9%
Min. Result	$388,864	34.0%	$399,330	37.6%	$336,199	15.8%
10th pct.	$635,924	52.8%	$563,407	35.4%	$497,530	19.5%
25th pct.	$778,659	44.4%	$676,065	25.4%	$591,064	9.6%

	Switch to Lifecycle for Last 15 Years	Improvement over Birthday	Switch to Lifecycle for Last 10 Years	Improvement over Birthday	Switch to Lifecycle for Last 5 Years	Improvement over Birthday
Median	$909,276	41.7%	$797,963	24.4%	$811,275	26.5%
75th pct.	$1,180,967	51.6%	$1,175,825	50.9%	$1,086,152	39.4%
90th pct.	$1,676,114	92.5%	$1,691,259	94.2%	$1,541,586	77.0%
Max. Result	$2,338,557	127.7%	$2,129,773	107.4%	$1,943,502	89.3%
Avg. % Inv. at Switch	191		152		121	

	Switch to Lifecycle for Last 15 Years	Improvement over Birthday	Switch to Lifecycle for Last 10 Years	Improvement over Birthday	Switch to Lifecycle for Last 5 Years	Improvement over Birthday
Mean Result	$825,553	27.7%	$755,535	16.9%	$698,956	8.1%
Min. Result	$299,142	3.0%	$296,963	2.3%	$287,949	−0.8%
10th pct.	$454,665	9.2%	$431,217	3.6%	$418,161	0.5%
25th pct.	$571,529	6.0%	$564,212	4.6%	$525,010	−2.7%
Median	$751,761	17.2%	$712,307	11.0%	$679,321	5.9%
75th pct.	$989,416	27.0%	$917,150	17.7%	$848,698	8.9%
90th pct.	$1,406,078	61.5%	$1,200,602	37.9%	$996,685	14.4%
Max. Result	$1,592,337	55.1%	$1,359,755	32.4%	$1,291,251	25.7%
Avg. % Inv. at Switch	103		92		86	

Starting Early

You can also use the logic of temporal diversification to help your progeny. Even without being cajoled, you can make it possible for your kids and grandkids to start diversifying well before they start working. Up to now, we've been emphasizing the advantages of diversifying risk for forty-four years. If you could diversify over fifty or sixty years, that would be even better. Of course, that would mean starting to buy stock at birth. Leverage alone is not going to make this possible. You have to have some savings in order to borrow to buy stock. If you have $4,000, it is possible to borrow another $4,000 through your broker and invest $8,000 in stock.

The problem is that you can't borrow if you don't have savings to begin with—which is generally true for kids, teens, students, and recent college grads. The broker lending $4,000 wants the security cushion of having $8,000 in stock backing up the loan, so that it knows the loan will ultimately be repaid. Without the coinvestment by the borrower, the broker would charge an excessively high interest rate. That means that this is a context in which it takes money to borrow money. We are advising young people to invest on a 2:1 basis. But that's not going to help you if you don't have a 1 to leverage.

This coinvestment constraint limits temporal diversification in two important ways. First, it keeps young workers from fully diversifying risk throughout their working lives. A 2:1 leverage gets them closer to full leverage. But most are constrained by the 2:1 cap for the first ten years of their working lives. This leverage limitation has been a central part of all of our analysis up to now.

But the coinvestment constraint has a second and even more profound limitation on the ability of people to diversify. Most people really can't start diversifying until they're in their twenties and start working. Ian didn't invest in the stock market until he was twenty-seven, when he finally finished school and got his first job. (For a while it looked as if Ian would be a perpetual student—after college he went for both a Ph.D. in economics at MIT and a J.D. at Yale.) These were twenty-seven years of potential added diversification that he threw away by being completely out of the market.

Again, we reject the notion that nothing can be done. Parents and grandparents can give their kids the gift of diversification. There is already a tradition of investing for your kids. Ian's grandmother gave him a U.S. savings bond when he was born. But sadly, that did nothing to help diversify Ian's exposure to stock risk. By investing on a leveraged basis on behalf of your children, you can substantially increase the number of years they are exposed to the market. And by exposing them more when they are young, they can then reduce their exposure as they age.

Of course, this advice is only true for parents or grandparents who intend to leave something behind to succeeding generations. Many of us have enough trouble making sure that we have enough for our own retirement. Others don't feel the need to give. (Perhaps that's a reason why the book *Die Broke* was such a big seller.)

Even if you don't have the means to help your kids start out, you can give your kids the gift of diversification by educating them about the benefits of better spreading their exposure to stock market risk across time. You can tell your teens and young adults why it is important to invest at least 100 percent in equities until their thirties—and even convince them that 2:1 leverage during their youth is the way to be truly cautious with their retirement savings. We've pitched most of the book on how to invest *your* retirement investments, but in some ways our more important audience is parents and grandparents who can help prevent their children and grandchildren from repeating the mistakes of their past. Call this the educational gift of diversification.

We recognize that this won't be easy. Parents are often extra conservative when it comes to the investment advice they give their kids. As much as it hurts to lose money in your portfolio, it can hurt even more when the loss hits your kids—they trusted you and you let them down. Therefore you say nothing and don't take the risk. Even if the wisdom of your advice is clear by the time the kids retire, you may not be around to be thanked.

This fear of regret is why many parents don't give investment advice to their children. But how are your twenty-somethings supposed to learn how to allocate their investments? Getting it right is especially hard when the standard advice they'll be given is wrong. Though you may not be a certified financial planner, the fact that you are reading this book and made it to Chapter 5 says something good about your level of sophistication.

Consider the following approach. You can tell them about this book and how you wished you had this advice when you were their age. You can talk about how your portfolio was overexposed to 2008 and underexposed to the 1980s and 1990s. You can't promise that starting out with 100 percent stocks (or more) will leave them ahead all along the way, but it can lower their risk and improve the odds.

Better than giving advice is doing the investment for them. If your kids are young, the issue of regret won't be such a factor as the kids don't have to see the ups and downs along the way. What we're proposing is not some cataclysmic change in behavior. If you have a custodial account, everything should be in equities. If you want to use leverage, that investment will have to be in one of your own accounts, though you can earmark it for the kid. Investing as little as $1,000 on a leveraged basis when a child is born can pay big dividends with regard to the child's ability to diversify across time.

To test this hypothesis, we reran our historical simulations, this time looking at the diversification difference among different ways of investing a small pot of money given to your child at birth. The seventy-three cohorts we considered had their inheritance invested for them until age twenty-three and then followed the 200/83 lifecycle strategy during their working years.[2] We compared three different ways to invest the money during those initial twenty-three years of life. In the first simulation, we invested the gift all in bonds. In the second simulation, we invested it all in stocks. And in the third simulation, we invested it on a leveraged basis 200 percent in stock.

Table 5.2 runs these simulations for investments (at birth) of $500, $1,000, and $5,000. (For our average Joe, this represents in present-value terms 0.46 percent, 0.92 percent, and 4.6 percent, respectively, of expected future savings contributions.)

TABLE 5.2 **Impact of $500, $1,000, and $5,000 Inheritance Invested at 200% Stock, 100% Stock, and 100% Bonds from Birth to Age 22 and Following a Diversifying 200/83 Strategy Thereafter**

	$500 Inheritance at 100% Bonds	$500 Inheritance at 100% Stock	Improvement over 100% Bonds	$500 Inheritance at 200% Stock	Improvement over 100% Bonds
Mean Result	$1,378,031	$1,410,573	2.4%	$1,490,899	8.2%
Min. Result	$727,570	$736,572	1.2%	$733,416	0.8%
10th pct.	$844,958	$859,045	1.7%	$939,261	11.2%
25th pct.	$1,087,263	$1,106,721	1.8%	$1,161,063	6.8%
Median	$1,327,069	$1,352,427	1.9%	$1,457,633	9.8%
75th pct.	$1,655,024	$1,729,245	4.5%	$1,803,963	9.0%
90th pct.	$1,968,761	$1,981,700	0.7%	$2,167,269	10.1%
Max. Result	$2,220,573	$2,265,918	2.0%	$2,991,801	34.7%
	$1,000 Inheritance at 100% Bonds	$1,000 Inheritance at 100% Stock	Improvement over 100% Bonds	$1,000 Inheritance at 200% Stock	Improvement over 100% Bonds
Mean Result	$1,400,825	$1,464,596	4.6%	$1,620,486	15.7%
Min. Result	$760,323	$773,853	1.8%	$769,655	1.2%
10th pct.	$859,708	$904,163	5.2%	$994,446	15.7%
25th pct.	$1,089,626	$1,152,625	5.8%	$1,183,069	8.6%
Median	$1,360,025	$1,424,139	4.7%	$1,552,222	14.1%
75th pct.	$1,659,814	$1,802,864	8.6%	$1,949,127	17.4%
90th pct.	$1,976,648	$2,039,670	3.2%	$2,297,024	16.2%
Max. Result	$2,256,302	$2,345,004	3.9%	$3,902,278	73.0%
	$5,000 Inheritance at 100% Bonds	$5,000 Inheritance at 100% Stock	Improvement over 100% Bonds	$5,000 Inheritance at 200% Stock	Improvement over 100% Bonds
Mean Result	$1,568,369	$1,852,215	18.1%	$2,445,979	56.0%
Min. Result	$776,811	$913,078	17.5%	$889,470	14.5%
10th pct.	$974,506	$1,133,555	16.3%	$1,240,896	27.3%
25th pct.	$1,177,094	$1,419,360	20.6%	$1,473,687	25.2%
Median	$1,570,632	$1,705,009	8.6%	$2,086,440	32.8%
75th pct.	$1,911,256	$2,284,061	19.5%	$2,768,188	44.8%
90th pct.	$2,220,743	$2,597,872	17.0%	$4,688,804	111.1%
Max. Result	$2,514,668	$3,237,877	28.8%	$9,945,576	295.5%

An extra $1,000 invested in all stock leads to a $64,000 gain (in real dollars) over buying the kid a savings bond. The gain comes from both the higher returns during the first twenty-three years and then the ability to invest more with leverage starting at age twenty-three.

Investing on a leveraged basis right from the start pays even bigger dividends. The extra kick of just $500 invested on a leveraged basis increases the average retirement nest egg by more than 8 percent relative to the impact of investing the same early money in bonds. And early leverage of $5,000 beats early bonds by a staggering 56 percent increase in the final retirement nest egg.

The larger $5,000 gift is particularly helpful at diversifying because it loosens the coinvestment constraint. Adolescent accounts that have more cash on hand can come closer to hitting the Samuelson target. The average person playing a traditional investment strategy only takes advantage of fifteen or twenty years of time diversification. Sure, people have a little money in stocks when they're young, but it is so small that the number of "effective" years of exposure is also relatively small. But by investing on a leveraged basis on behalf of your children you can double the number of effective years of diversification.

The benefits from the gift of enhanced time diversification are so great that some parents who otherwise were planning to invest most of their money in relatively safe, nonstock assets might be moved toward more of a "buy young" strategy on the part of their children. Indeed, the intergenerational bang-for-the-buck is so great that some parents who had not been planning on making a bequest might be moved to do so, and those planning to leave an inheritance may increase the amount. The gift of diversification is a new technology that rational people should move toward. Just as you might give more if the government matched your gift, you might also give more knowing that giving early pays these additional benefits. Whatever you decide, Table 5.2 makes it clear that giving a child or grandchild a stock index fund is a far, far better present than the more traditional savings bond.

By the way, the government may one day help you invest in stock on behalf of your kids. In 2007, Hillary Clinton proposed that the government give parents $5,000 to invest on behalf of their kids.[3] Under her (admittedly provisional) plan, every child would receive a "baby bond" at birth, which would grow over time, creating a nest egg for the child's future educational expenses or home purchase.

The cynical might view Clinton's proposal as just another feel-good campaign promise that had little chance of passage. (Indeed, Clinton abandoned this proposal shortly after putting it forth.) But "baby bonds" are already a reality in England, with the Child Trust Fund. In 2003, Tony Blair's Labour government started giving parents £250 (approximately $370)—low-income families receive up to twice that amount—to invest on behalf of newborns. An additional £250 to £500 (approximately $370 to $740) is given to children when they are seven.[4] The funds must be put into a savings or investment account in a financial institution. If parents do not choose an account to put the money into, the government will automatically put a child's funds into a stakeholder account. When the child turns eighteen, he or she can either withdraw the funds in the account or roll them over into a new savings or investment account.

The baby bond idea is derived from a more ambitious proposal from Bruce Ackerman and Anne Alstott for the government to give each eighteen-year-old $80,000.[5] Blair's $1,480 for seven-year-olds seems rather paltry by comparison. But Table 5.2 shows that even $1,000 invested correctly can yield substantial returns. An advantage of the Blair bond is that it is given eighteen years earlier than the Ackerman and Alstott bond. That's eighteen extra years of potential stock market exposure. Ackerman and Alstott want to give each citizen a literal economic stake in society. But a palpable additional reason to endorse government baby bonds is that they relax the coinvestment constraint. With baby bonds, every child, regardless of economic status, can start to diversify across time.

Ramping Up for Retirement

In 2008, three experts in retirement investments—Francisco Gomes at London Business School, Laurence Kotlikoff at Boston University, and Luis Viceira at the Harvard Business School—published a painstaking simulation to derive their own estimates of "optimal lifecycle investing."

Like us, they wanted to know on a year-by-year basis what proportion of savings should be invested in the stock market (and what proportion should be invested in government bonds).

But instead of deriving an optimal strategy, they let a computer churn away, evaluating literally millions of different investment strategies to figure out the strategy that produced the best trade-off of risk and return within their lifecycle model. Their analysis also differed from ours because they wanted to know how much retirees should invest in the stock market. We shut down our analysis on the day of retirement, but they assumed that some proportion of people would live to one hundred and kept the computer running to see what strategy worked best over the entire lifespan. After crunching a gazillion numbers, the computer spit out a strategy that is summarized in a single figure.[6]

Figure 5.1 sets out for a typical working family a vision of the optimal lifecycle. In some ways, it is reminiscent of the birthday rule—which starts investors at 90 percent in stock and ramps them down to 45 percent in stock when they reach age sixty-five. But look again at the figure. Think of it as a kind of *Highlights* magazine picture test. What part of the allocation line looks incorrect given what we know about the lifecycle strategy? Can it really represent an optimal lifecycle and, if so, can both it and our theory of diversification across time be right? When we look at the figure, we see three conundrums: two with regard to how people invest before retiring and one big conundrum regarding how they invest after retiring. Let's take a look at them one at a time.

1. Why isn't the stock allocation higher at the beginning of the investor's work life? If our lifecycle strategy approach is right, why didn't it pop out as a natural by-product of Gomes, Kotlikoff, and Viceira's search for the optimal investment strategy?

The answer to this conundrum is pretty easy. Our strategy didn't pop out because they didn't allow it to. They capped the maximum allocation in stock at 100 percent of current savings, so 200/83 never had a chance. But look at what did happen: The optimal strategy was trying to invest as much as possible in stock for about the first decade of the worker's life.

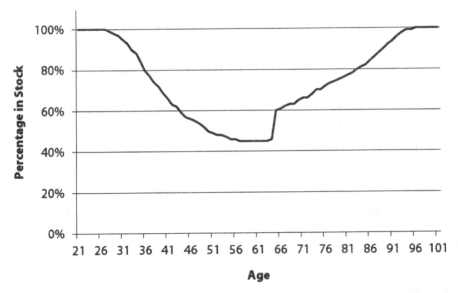

FIGURE 5.1 **Optimal Stock Allocation by Age from Gomes, Kotlikoff, and Viceira**

The simulation is telling us that it would like to invest more, and it is only the cap that is keeping it from doing so.

Actually, the period at 100 percent in stocks would have been much longer had they not artificially knocked down the expected stock premium to 4 percent. As they write: "This equity premium is lower than the historical equity premium based on a comparison of average stock and T-bill returns, but accords with the forward-looking estimates reported in Fama and French (2002). Higher premiums generate unrealistically high equity portfolio shares." We don't think high equity shares are unrealistic. They are unconventional, but it is the conventional advice that's wrong.

And there's one more reason why the interval at 100 percent only lasts ten years: Their investors are highly averse to risk. This explains the next conundrum.

2. *Why isn't the stock allocation higher at the end of the investor's work life?*

Our investors aimed for a preretirement stock allocation of 83 percent, while the Gomes et al. simulation has the investor end his working life with a stock allocation of about 45 percent. When Social Security wealth is taken into account, the Gomes simulation has investors allocating only some 20 percent of their portfolio to stocks.

Why the difference? The Gomes simulation assumes a high level of risk aversion that leads to a very conservative investment strategy.[7] Combine this with a reduced equity premium, and it should not be surprising that they end up investing less in stock along the way. A more realistic level of risk aversion would shift up the stock allocation not only at the end of the investor's working life but throughout his working life. Indeed, if they used a more realistic level of risk aversion, the historical equity premium, and allowed for leverage, their strategy would come very close to the 200/83 strategy that starts at a 200 percent allocation for ten years and ramps down to 83 percent. As emphasized in Chapter 4, even true scaredy cats will want to go beyond 100 percent investments in stock when they are young.

The main reason we've included the Gomes figure isn't because of the ramp-down during the investor's working life, it's because Gomes and his coauthors derived that the allocation in stock should ramp *up*—that's right, the huge conundrum lurking in the figure is:

3. Why do the stock allocations increase during retirement?
You can look long and hard, but you'll be hard pressed to find an investment advisor who would suggest that a ninety-nine-year-old should invest 100 percent of his or her savings in stock. But the Gomes simulation suggests a new kind of birthday rule for retirement—basically telling you that by age eighty you should invest your age in stock. If you didn't see this when we asked you what looked wrong with the figure, you should probably take a break and come back to this when you're feeling better rested.

The big clue is that Gomes makes a very reasonable assumption for anyone retiring since the New Deal. The Gomes simulation assumes that people in retirement receive Social Security. Now, to be honest, we're not completely assured that Social Security will be there for us when we retire. It may be so means-tested and taxed that it becomes only a shell of its current self for people with high income. But as we emphasized in Chapter 3, the prospect of receiving Social Security adds a substantial amount to the total value of retirement savings—especially as you get close to retirement.

It's the presence of this bond-like Social Security payment that leads to the ramp-up result. Remember that our simple idea is that people should try to invest a constant percentage of the present value of their current and future savings. Social Security represents a substantial chunk of risk-free future savings contributions. We argued in Chapter 2 that people should try to expose some of that expected future money to the stock market even before they retire, but in an abundance of caution we excluded Social Security from our simulations in the last two chapters. It is the consideration of Social Security payments that explains why the allocation increases over time in Figure 5.1.

And as retirees age, they disproportionately deplete their current savings relative to the present value of future Social Security payments. When Social Security (or a defined benefit plan) becomes an increasing proportion of your present wealth, then it becomes time to rebalance your portfolio. Without doing anything, you end up almost all in bond-like investments. Ramping up your stock allocation does *not* mean that you are taking inordinate risks. Gomes has a ninety-year-old investor investing nearly all of his current cash in stock, but by that point in his life the current cash represented a very small proportion of his overall retirement wealth. For a ninety-year-old who has $10,000 left in savings and a $25,000 annual check from Social Security, private savings are less than 10 percent of total wealth, and so even a 90 percent allocation of the $10,000 to stock is still limited exposure.

Retirees who have large private savings relative to Social Security should not find themselves increasing their stock allocation as they age (at least, not a lot) because their private retirement portfolio will not become a disappearing proportion of their total present wealth. Another rough-and-ready rule is that if you don't need your Social Security payments, you don't need to ramp up.

While we may disagree over some modeling assumptions, we shouldn't lose sight of where we fundamentally agree: *You should continue to invest in stocks during retirement.*

Whether the optimal percentage goes up or down over time is much less important than the realization that retirement doesn't imply an end to market exposure. Indeed, fifteen to thirty years of retirement is a significant number of years which you could use to gain better diversification over time.[8]

Our simulations don't look beyond retirement age. But you should. Social Security is like a big bond in your portfolio. As a result, even if you continue to invest 50 percent or even 83 percent of your retirement savings in stocks, you will still be below 60 percent in stocks when you take Social Security into account.[9]

As to how to invest, at the end of the day, we will suggest the use of life annuities as a powerful and simple way to manage retirement risk. In a world where few know their death date, we are attracted to a vehicle that guarantees payments for just as long as we need it. One of the greatest risks we all face is that of living too long. It is hard, perhaps impossible, to save for a thirty-year or longer retirement. Think of annuities as a private version of a defined benefit plan or of Social Security. But unlike defined benefit plans or Social Security, you can buy an immediate annuity in which the payments are linked to stock market performance. These are called variable annuities. Putting some of your money into immediate variable annuities provides financial protection against living too long and maintains exposure to the market.

A Road That Never Ends?

You'd think that by now we have spanned the space of potential applications—literally—from cradle to grave. But, as a final bonus, let's see if you can apply our theory to institutions that plan to be around forever. We're talking about corporations, trusts, and especially endowments and pension funds. You can also think of this section as a final test of whether you grok lifecycle investing.

So here's the question: *Should the Ford Foundation and Yale University invest their endowments differently?*

Roll this question around in your mind before proceeding: In the case of individual investors, what is it that gives lifecycle investing the advantage over traditional strategies? To keep the question simpler, imagine that the institutions are equally risk averse, each wanting to ensure that they will be around to fulfill their respective missions in perpetuity. And let's also assume—consistent with the rest of this book—that the central investing goal of the endowment managers is to figure out what proportion of the current endowment to invest in stock. Is there any reason for the two endowments to invest different proportions in stock?

Okay, here's a hint. For endowment management purposes there's a key difference between Yale and Ford, and that difference is alumni giving. Yale has current and future graduates who are going to keep on giving like clockwork to their alma mater (as beneficiaries of this largesse, we thank you). On the other hand, while Edsel Ford has many illustrious offspring, they have not been giving, and will not give, to the foundation. This is no knock on the Ford scions—the Ford Foundation is formally closed to further contributions.[10]

With this key difference in mind, should their investment strategies be the same? We think not. The reason is that, just like individuals saving for retirement, institutions need to take future income into account. Yale is like a forty-year-old who expects to still make significant contributions to her nest egg, while Ford is like a retiree whose earning days are over.

The first two columns of Table 5.3 lay out the basic facts about endowment size and annual contributions not just for Ford and Yale but also for the Rockefeller Foundation and MIT. (There's no particular reason to focus on MIT and Yale, other than the fact that we're alumni.)

TABLE 5.3 Endowments (in Billions)

	2008 Endowment Value	2008 Contributions and Pledges	Present Value of Future Contributions and Pledges*	2008 Present & Future Endowment	% Increase	Stock Allocation (50% Target)	Stock Allocation (83% Target)
Ford	$10.87	$0.00	$0.00	$10.87	0.0	50.0%	83.0%
Rockefeller**	$4.10	$0.00	$0.00	$4.10	0.0	50.0%	83.0%
MIT	$10.07	$0.39	$15.08	$25.15	149.7	124.9%	219.8%
Yale	$22.87	$0.37	$14.45	$37.32	63.2	81.6%	143.6%

*Assumed annual risk-free interest rate of 2.56%.
**2008 endowment value was unavailable for Rockefeller; $4.1 billion is the 2007 value.

The Ford and Rockefeller Foundations are both "closed-end" endowments with, respectively, $11 billion and $4 billion endowments—but with no annual contributions. MIT and Yale, in contrast, also have substantial endowments ($10 and $23 billion, respectively, in 2008) and substantial alumni giving.* MIT received $386 million in gifts in 2008, and Yale's gifts totaled $370 million.[11]

Of course, past giving doesn't ensure that alumni will continue to give in the future. But both schools have a seasoned track record of success. A central—indeed maybe *the* central—point of this book is that investors should take account of expected future savings contributions today. In the same way, MIT and Yale should discount their alumni contributions before they hatch. We do just this in the third column of the table, assuming that alumni giving stays constant indefinitely into the future, but discounting these future contributions just as we do future salary at a 2.56 percent real risk-free interest rate. We think the real interest rate is the right one to use, as donations are likely to keep pace with inflation. Indeed, as the institutions grow in size the donor pool will be ever larger, and so donations will likely grow faster than inflation.

The present value of future endowment contributions for Ford and Rockefeller is of course zero, because they expect none. However, the present value of future endowment contributions for MIT is $15.08 billion and for Yale, close to $14.45 billion. These are not only substantial amounts in and of themselves—in MIT's case, they are bigger than its current endowment. In that sense, MIT is more like a thirty-year-old who is still very early in the game; most of its endowment is yet to come in the future.** As shown in the fifth column of the table, Yale's endowment grows by more than 60 percent if one considers the present value of future contributions, and MIT's endowment swells by 150 percent.

---

*After the market fall in 2008, MIT's endowment shrunk to $8 billion, Yale's to $16.3 billion, and annual donations fell substantially, too. We discuss below how the correlation between donations and stock prices influences our investment strategy recommendations.

**While MIT has been around since 1861, few of its early alums were of old money. The technology boom has done wonders for creating wealthy alumni able to make significant contributions.

So even if MIT and Yale are equally cautious, it would seem that MIT's endowment managers should invest a higher proportion of its current endowment in stock than Yale. How much more? Well, to expose 50 percent of the *total* endowment present value, Yale would need to invest 82 percent of its current endowment in stock, and MIT would need to invest about 125 percent of its current endowment. Yes, MIT should be leveraged since investing all of its current endowment is still less than half of the total value.

That's not really our recommendation, and the reason why is important since it applies to some individual investors as well. The problem isn't with the theory, but with the nature of those future contributions. Alumni give more in bull markets than in bear markets.[12] What that means is that some portion of the future donations are already like stocks. In 2008–2009, donations to Yale fell by 28 percent while the market fell by 38 percent. This suggests that alumni contributions are like 74 percent stock. Over at MIT, individual donations fell by 32 percent in 2008–2009.[13] Thus Yale and MIT are already investing most of their future donations in the market indirectly through their donors' portfolios.*

Were MIT trying to be 50 percent in stocks, that 50 percent should apply to both the current $10 billion and the future $15 billion—which comes to $12.6 billion total in equities. But of the future $15 billion, it is as if 84 percent of that amount is already in stocks (as the 32 percent fall was 84 percent of the market fall). Now 84 percent of $15 billion is $12.6 billion, and that's the full exposure MIT would be looking for. So if MIT only wants to be 50 percent in equities, it should invest none of its current $10 billion in equities. More realistically, MIT might like to be 84 percent exposed to equities. The future portfolio is already at that level, and so investing 84 percent of the current $10 billion in equities will get to the desired allocation. In this case, MIT can, in effect, ignore the future gifts since the alums are already allocating their gifts just as MIT would if it had the money in hand.

---

*This is a one-year fall and there is some thinking that donations will recover, even if markets do not, as alumni will adjust to the new reality. Even if long-run donations do recover, they will still end up lower compared to where they would have been with a market rise.

For Yale, a 50 percent target implies $18.7 billion exposure. Of the future $14.45 billion in donations, it is as if $10.7 billion are in equities, which leaves $8 billion out of the $22.9 billion, or only 35 percent exposure to equities from the current endowment. More realistically, the investment committee would target an allocation closer to 83 percent. (This may seem like a high number, but it takes into account international, private equities, commodities, and other unconventional investments.) That suggests a $31 billion overall equity allocation, of which $10.7 billion comes from future gifts. That leaves $20.3 billion to be invested from the current portfolio, or 89 percent exposure.

To get your allocation right, you have to do this same exercise for yourself. Are the future contributions to your retirement account more like a bond or a stock? The answer depends on what you do: Civil servants and professors are more like bonds, while investment bankers are more like stocks. In Chapter 6 we look at this issue in more detail.

The real purpose of this example is to make sure that you understand the larger application of diversification. Universities should take into account the discounted value of their future contributions when thinking about how to invest. They should take into account not only the amount but its composition. To the extent that future gifts are more heavily weighted toward stocks than the desired allocation, the university should be more conservative with its current investments. Or if future giving is more like a bond, then the university should be more aggressive with its current investments.

Sure, the devil is in the details. Our estimate that future contributions are highly correlated with the market is based on one data point, though a prominent one, and the view that 50 percent or 83 percent is the goal may not be what the trustees have in mind. So don't hold us to the final figures.

But the big picture is that investors should be discounting future contributions. This is true not only for the family saving for retirement and the university investing its endowment, but for any financial planner. In fact, by now it should be easy to see how dynamic diversification could be used by pension funds too. Pension fund managers have long taken into account their future expected payouts, but we think they should also start diversifying future expected pay*ins*.[14]

So ends our affirmative case. We've now led you through both the theoretical and the empirical evidence for the benefits of temporal diversification. If you're not convinced that the basic idea makes sense and has the potential to produce substantial real-world benefits, it is time to put this book down and tend to other pursuits. Many people have lived happy lives while missing out on these benefits, and you can too. In fact, the next chapter identifies circumstances when young people *shouldn't* lever their retirement portfolio. But for the intrepid, those who are willing to dare to diversify, Chapters 7 and 8 try to show you when and how to turn this theory into action.

CHAPTER 6

Contraindications

BEFORE RUSHING TO embrace our advice, consider the cautionary tale of "MT" (short for "Market Timer"), who lost everything following his home-brewed version of a leveraged investment strategy.[1] MT is an economics graduate student. All on his own, he came up with the idea of investing more when young so as to spread out his market exposure across time. Unfortunately, he decided to put this idea into practice in the fall of 2007, just at the market peak. By November 2008, he was forced to liquidate his portfolio. At that point, MT owed some $210,000.

MT didn't just leverage at 2:1. He went all in. He increased his leverage by selling puts, bets that created almost unbounded losses as the market fell. And he didn't just put the money into a simple index fund. Instead, he made concentrated side bets on what he thought was a significantly undervalued financial services sector. He had the misfortune of betting on individual bank stocks, specifically Citibank. As Citibank fell precipitously from $57 to $45, MT "felt compelled to sell more puts." In the end, Citibank shares dipped below $1 per share, but MT was wiped out long before that.

As a graduate student, MT didn't have $210,000 to lose. The source of his loans was those credit card solicitations that most of us throw away. While many entrepreneurs have been known to finance their start-ups using credit cards, MT used them as a way to borrow and more than double his bets.

The rational decision would have been to pare down exposure to the banks and invest it in the broader market. This is where my life takes an unfortunate turn. As part of my new interest in finance, I'd stumbled across the App-O-Rama concept on FatWallet, where you apply for a bunch of credit card promotional offers and invest the balance transfer money into higher yielding savings accounts. Instead of reducing exposure to the banks where I was losing money, I could simply double or triple the size of my portfolio by leveraging balance transfer money using LEAPs and by selling naked puts on the S&P 500. As I paced around the pool, I was trying to convince my superego that risking several hundred thousand dollars was prudent.

We hope you appreciate that MT broke pretty much every rule we have. We want you to limit leverage to 200 percent; MT started out at 400 percent and then increased his leverage as stocks fell. As stocks fall, our rebalancing strategy has you reduce your exposure; MT bought more. That meant his leverage became unbounded as his assets fell to zero. We want you to diversify across time; MT ended up placing big bets on a single stock. He financed the purchases with credit card debt, which soon cost him 15 percent in interest.

In reality, my stepdad knew that I was exactly the type of immature, booksmart doofus who could be lured by a false sense of superiority into blowing up his personal account. . . . I've read the accounts of LTCM and Neiderhoffer's memoirs, but it took night after night of insomnia in October 2008 to drive home the message that leverage is unforgiving, it's unfeeling, and it will force you to come to terms with whatever delusions you hold about fair value. I can only hope my memories won't fade with time.

For reasons that should be obvious, MT prefers to stay anonymous. His online picture is an image of Don Quixote tilting at windmills. And the story has a surprise ending. In a recent post, MT tells of making back a good chunk of his losses and paying off debts. After a reflective period in Asia, MT discovered a new arbitrage strategy for making money. One day you may be able to read about his adventure in the book he's writing.

Most investors end up with relatively too much market exposure near retirement age. MT went to the other extreme: "Retirement investing is a four-decade poker game, and I should never have felt the urgency to go all-in as I did." The better strategy is to avoid either extreme and spread your exposure across time.

MT's experience provides a cautionary tale of what not to do. Later we return to his experience to consider psychological factors that can get you in trouble. But first we start with some of the more mundane issues, such as the use of credit cards. Some credit cards offer a "no interest rate" teaser deal. Those deals look great on paper, but there's a host of fine print. And then the rates go up. And up. And up again. Not only do we advise against borrowing on credit cards to get leverage, you shouldn't be buying *any* stocks until you've first paid off all your credit card debt.

Not Having Credit Card Debt: Priceless

There is no point investing in stocks that might return 8 percent when you have an option of getting a 100 percent safe tax-free return that's far higher. As we write this, the average interest rate on consumer credit cards is 14.67 percent.[2] Paying off your credit card debt is the best financial investment you can make, period.

Let's say that you are lucky enough to pay just 8 percent interest on your credit card balance. By paying down that debt you are effectively paying yourself a return of 8 percent. Even better, you won't have to pay any tax on that return. You won't have to pay tax because it is interest you don't have to pay, as opposed to interest you end up earning.

Here's an example that illustrates the point. You owe $10,000 on a credit card with an 8 percent APR.

Year 0 (now): You owe $10,000.
Year 1: You will owe $10,800.
Year 2: You will owe $11,664.
Year 3: you will owe $12,597.
Year 4: You will owe $13,604.

Year 5: You will owe $14,693.
Year 6: You will owe $15,869.

Let's say that you somehow had the full $10,000 to pay off the debt. By paying off your credit card debt today (versus waiting six years), you will be $5,869 ahead.

If, instead, you put that same $10,000 in the stock market and the market returned a steady 8 percent each year, then at the end of year 6 you'd have $15,869. That would be just enough to pay off the debt.

Except it wouldn't be. You wouldn't have the full $15,869, as you would have to pay taxes on the $5,869 capital gains. Furthermore, you would have been exposed to substantial risk. It's unlikely that the market will go up 8 percent each and every year.

The reason to invest in stocks is that on average they outperform bonds. That's true enough. But stocks don't on average outperform the interest you have to pay on credit card debt. Stocks don't return 14.67 percent tax-free.

To put this in as stark terms as possible, even Bernie Madoff didn't return 14.67 percent tax-free. And he was a scam artist. Yet by paying off your credit card debt, you save yourself from falling 14.67 percent in the hole. You would have to earn 14.67 percent after tax on other investments to keep even. By paying down the debt now, you don't have to pay an extra 14.67 percent later, and that is every bit as valuable as earning 14.67 percent on your investments—risk-free and tax-free.[3]

All too often, credit cards end up charging interest rates well above 14.67 percent. Remember, that 14.67 percent is the *average* rate. Interest rates around 20 percent are not uncommon. The higher the rate, the better the return you'll make in paying down those debts.

Credit card debt doesn't create a problem with the 200/83 allocation rule. The problem isn't the allocation rule, but rather how much money you put aside to invest. You shouldn't put any money into stocks or bonds while you have credit card debts that remain outstanding—200 percent of $0 is still $0.[4]

Along with credit card debt, there are five other situations that militate against investing with leverage.

1. You have less than $4,000 to invest.
2. Your employer matches contributions to a 401(k) plan.
3. You need the money to pay for your kids' college education.
4. Your salary is correlated with the market.
5. You would worry too much about losing money.

Minimum Investments

A cost-effective way to gain leverage is to buy a deep-in-the-money call option. The problem is that options are sold in packages, or "contracts," of 100, and the cheapest ones you can buy (that provide 2:1 leverage) cost about $4,500.

To get 2:1 leverage, you will want a call option with an exercise price of roughly half the market price. Recall that the options are on the SPDR index, which is designed to mimic the performance of the S&P 500 index at one-tenth the price. As of the summer of 2009, the SPDR contracts were trading at around $90. That suggests a strike price of around $45 and a corresponding option price just above $45 per share. Each option contract on the SPDR is for 100 shares. Thus the smallest amount of leverage you can buy is one contract with a price tag of around $4,500.

You could reduce the price just a bit by buying an option contract with a strike price of $50, rather than $45. But, however you slice it, the minimum purchase is one contract and that will expose you to around $9,000 of S&P returns. Therefore if you have much less than $4,000 to invest you will end up with too much leverage.

Another option is to use a margin loan to gain leverage. Traditional brokers, including Fidelity and Vanguard, charge way too much for margin loans to make them worthwhile. There are some great online options such as Interactive Brokers, but they require a minimum account size of $10,000. Once again, it won't work.

If you have less than $4,000 to invest, all is not lost. You can still invest in stocks directly. Stick with 100 percent in equities. That's a step in the right direction until your account grows to the point where this is no longer an issue.

Even if you do have more than $4,000 to invest, you may get started on the right path but then have trouble rebalancing your portfolio. To see the problem, let's go back to Andrew Verstein. He had roughly $5,000 invested in LEAPs that gave him exposure to $10,000 of stock. If the market were to rise by 10 percent, the value of his investment would rise by 20 percent, from $5,000 to $6,000. Meanwhile, his stock portfolio would be worth $11,000. At this point, he isn't quite at 2:1 leverage. To get to that level, he would need to buy another $1,000 of stock.

Index contracts aren't sold in $1,000 increments, so he can't use LEAPs to get there. The easiest way is to buy stock on margin, but Andrew doesn't have another spare $500 that he could use to buy $1,000 of stock on margin. In theory, Andrew could sell his current LEAP for $6,000 and then use that $6,000 to buy another LEAP or stock on margin. But that would lead to short-term capital gains tax and excess transaction costs (including bid-ask spreads).

For those starting out, short-term rebalancing isn't practical. We've rerun the historical simulations using annual data and rebalancing only once a year. The results are almost identical, and so being a little slow to rebalance doesn't create a big problem. But you do need to make incremental investments and do some rebalancing when the market makes a big move. This becomes a bigger challenge if you don't have the resources to have an account at Interactive Brokers and don't have the scale to employ LEAPs to gain leverage.

Another take-away message here is that if you just want to set and forget your retirement portfolio, the leveraged lifecycle strategies probably aren't for you. Using leverage requires paying some attention. We hope that there will soon be target-date funds that employ leverage and do all the work for you—rebalancing and ramping down as you age. In fact, we've filed a patent application based on the leveraged lifecycle and are working to bring this product to market. But in the meantime, if you are the set-it-and-forget-it type, you can still start with 100 percent equities and then follow a 100/S strategy (where S is your Samuelson share).

Matching 401(k) Plans

Those of you lucky enough to have an employer who matches contributions to your 401(k) plan should take full advantage of that option. When you put in $100, you get $200 in your account. That's like making an immediate 100 percent return on your investment.

Ideally, you would employ leverage on that $200 (at least while you're young). In that case, you would get exposure to $400 of stock. The only problem is that—at least for now—regulations won't let you employ leverage inside a 401(k) plan.

Thus your choice is either to put the money in an IRA (or another after-tax account) where you can employ leverage or to put it in a 401(k) plan and give up leverage. The combination of the tax advantages of a 401(k) plan and the employer matching make the 401(k) plan the clear winner. It's always better to have $200 invested outright than to have only $100 invested at 2:1 leverage.

Both options give you the same exposure to the market, but look what happens if the market goes up 25 percent. In the case where you started with $200, you end up with $250. In the case where you had the $100 invested with leverage, you still make $50 (actually a bit less due to interest), but that leaves you with $150.

The comparison is easy when the employer matches dollar for dollar. Even if your employer only matches at 1:2, so a $200 contribution from you brings a $100 match, you are better off taking the match and forgoing the leverage. You've got an unbeatable head start: a 50 percent risk-free return on your investment.

Just because you have the good fortune to have a matching 401(k) plan doesn't mean that our book can't help you. Even inside a 401(k) plan you can take a step in the right direction. Instead of following a 200/S plan, you can follow a 100/S plan. Whenever you were supposed to be more than 100 percent in the market, you can go up to 100 percent. Your ultimate target is still the Samuelson share, but now you are capped at 100 percent exposure.

While the results aren't as dramatic, following a 100/S allocation is well worthwhile. Compared to the constant 75 percent rule, a 100/58 strategy yields the same average return but lowers the standard deviation by 24 percent. A 100/80 strategy leads to the same risk profile but improves the mean by (coincidentally) the same 24 percent. You can beat the birthday rule, too. A 100/71 target beats the birthday rule mean return by 33 percent and lifts the historical worst case by 20 percent, all while preserving the theoretical 1 percent worst outcome.

Of course, if you have enough money to both fund the 401(k) plan and have other money to invest in the market or in an IRA account, then you can apply the leverage approach with your other assets. Most employers offer matching up to some maximum employee contribution. A typical plan might match employee contributions up to 5 percent of salary. Contributions above this amount do not benefit from employer matching. If you are able to contribute more, you could put that money on a leveraged basis in a Roth IRA (assuming you qualify).[5]

Our point here is that before you put any money into an IRA account with the idea of leverage, you should first take full advantage of any employer matching within a 401(k) plan. You won't be able to apply leverage, but matching is better. And you can still go for a 100/S allocation.

Saving for College (and a Rainy Day)

Most of us have lots of different cookie jars for savings. One jar is for retirement, another for the kids' college, another for an emergency. Even if the jars aren't real, we keep mental accounts of how our savings is to be allocated across different pots. This begs the question of whether it's okay to commingle the different funds and, if so, how you should do it.

To answer that question, let's say that you are forty with $90,000 already saved for retirement and $50,000 saved for your kids' college tuition, and the value of your future savings contributions adds another $310,000. Thus your total savings are $450,000. How much of that $450,000 should you invest in equities?

The first part of the answer depends on your strategy. Say, you choose to follow a 200/50 path, so you'd like to put half of your total retirement savings into equities. But your total retirement savings isn't $450,000 because $50,000 of that amount is earmarked for tuition. Therefore, you should apply the 50 percent Samuelson share to $400,000, for a goal of $200,000. Of course, you don't have $200,000 available today, so you'll need to use some leverage.

Now the question is whether you should leverage the $90,000 earmarked for retirement at 200 percent leverage or take the full $140,000 and leverage that amount at just 143 percent to hit your $200,000 goal. Here, commingling is a good idea. It lets you get to your $200,000 goal that you otherwise wouldn't quite make investing only the $90,000. What that means in practice is that you might borrow $60,000 on margin or invest $60,000 at 2:1 leverage and invest the other $80,000 without leverage.[6]

What you've really done is "borrow" the $50,000 earmarked for college and put it to use temporarily in equities. The fact that you have this cash available today allows you to take a bit more market exposure: You can get all the way to $200,000 rather than limiting yourself to $180,000. And using the $50,000 in savings reduces your need for outside borrowing. You are borrowing from yourself before going elsewhere.

But what if a $20,000 tuition bill arrives, and you have all your liquid assets invested in stocks? At this point you have to come up with the money. One option is to take out a loan. The Federal PLUS loan program (for parents with good credit) offers loans at 8.5 percent, minus 0.25 percent if you enroll in automatic debit.[7] While that is better than most credit cards, it is still too high to justify borrowing in order to buy stocks with leverage. Not taking the loan is like getting an 8.25 percent risk-free, tax-free return on your money. That's a better deal than investing in stocks. So don't take out the loan if you have any other assets available.

In our example, you had $140,000 available that was invested at 143 percent leverage. The solution to your liquidity needs is to take $20,000 out of the equity, leaving $120,000. That remaining amount can then be invested at 167 percent leverage to reach the target of $200,000 exposure to equities. After paying the bill, you still have the same exposure to equities, but it requires more leverage.

The general principle here is that you should pay for tuition first out of your liquid assets. This might lead you to temporarily increase your leverage. So be it. If you don't have enough liquid assets to pay for the parental contribution, then you'll have little choice but to take out a loan. If that's the case, paying off the loan should be your first priority.

There's one more caveat to take into account. If the value of your account ever drops to your earmarked savings number, then it's time to cash out. For example, if you had $140,000 invested with 143 percent leverage and the market were to fall by 45 percent then the value of your account would drop to $50,000. That $50,000 is your college savings, and so it is time to walk away.

College tuition in this example is really a placeholder for the larger class of nonretirement savings. People also save to take care of their parents, pay for their children's weddings, and as a rainy day precaution. The general principle is that in order to figure out the present value of retirement savings, you need to do the hard work of deducting the present value of your retirement savings. You only apply the Samuelson share to the net amount—which in the previous example was $400,000 ($450,000 minus the $50,000 tuition expenditure). If you also expected to have to pay $80,000 to care for your parents, the net present value would decline to $320,000 (and the net investment target would decline to $160,000). Here's a case where mental accounting is a good thing, because it helps us separate what parts of our savings should be exposed to the diversifying strategy. And as our example shows, the other forms of savings can help ease your liquidity constraint and help you hit your target even sooner.

Wall Street Is Close to Home

This is the most serious contraindication for you to consider. For most readers, we venture that the value of your future income is relatively uncorrelated with the market. If you work in government or are a teacher, car mechanic, or lawyer, your salary won't go up and down with the market, or at least not very much. Although if you are a lawyer who works on mergers and acquisitions, then you might well find your income to be highly correlated with the market.

Recent history will have provided a good test for you. What happened to your income in 2008 and 2009? If your income didn't fall that much, then your correlation to the market probably isn't too large.

Faculty salaries, for example, are mostly protected from the vicissitudes of the market. In 2009, endowments fell sharply and many universities imposed salary freezes so that salaries remained flat instead of going up with inflation and seniority. This suggests that for most professors, the correlation is small, perhaps 5 or 10 percent. What that means is that when academics look at the value of their future savings that is currently tied up in their human capital, most of that money, over 90 percent, is like a bond, not a stock.

For finance professors, the correlation is higher. From 2000 through 2007, universities were losing finance professors to Wall Street. As a result, salaries rose rapidly. Now that Wall Street looks less attractive and few investment banks are trying to hire away professors, there is no pressure to raise salaries. Indeed, it may be some time before their salaries increase at all.

Focusing on salary leaves out two important features. Instead of getting a raise or a freeze, you could be laid off. In that case, your salary ends up taking a large fall. To the extent that both your job and the stock market are tied to the overall health of the economy, then your future income has some characteristics of a stock.

For homeowners, a second hidden source of correlation is the value of your home. During the current crisis, if you live in Michigan, then not only is your job at risk, but the value of your home is likely to have dropped as well.

John Heaton and Deborah Lucas have looked at this issue for a broad selection of workers.[8] Based on a 1979–1990 panel of individual tax returns, they find that for the average person there is a small negative correlation between salary increases and stock market performance. And there is a large negative correlation (–20 percent) between house price appreciation and stocks. Both these factors suggest that future salary and home values may actually reduce your effective exposure to the market.

While the raises of the average wage earner are negatively correlated to the market, there is substantial heterogeneity across the population: 32 percent of the population have a correlation between –15 percent and +15 percent, another 33 percent have a correlation below –15 percent, and 35 percent have a correlation above 15 percent. That tells us that for 65 percent of the population (without significant business income), there shouldn't be a large concern about the relationship between future earnings and the market.

Even if you are in the 35 percent of the population with a positive correlation, you will still want to employ leverage, just less leverage. Let's look at a case where the correlation is positive and reasonably high at 20 percent. Take a forty-year-old who has $150,000 already saved for retirement and for whom the present value of his future savings contributions is $250,000, making his total savings $400,000. Say that his goal is to be 60 percent in equities, which amounts to $240,000. Because his future income is correlated with the market, it's as if 20 percent of his future savings or $50,000 is invested in stock.

Here's why. If the market were to go up 10 percent, then we expect his future earnings and thus savings to go up by 20 percent of that rise, or 2 percent. Of the $250,000 that he expects to add to his savings pool, it is like 80 percent of that amount or $200,000 is in bonds and 20 percent or $50,000 is in stocks. If the market goes up 10 percent, we expect the $250,000 to rise by 2 percent, to $255,000, which is just like holding the $200,000 bond portfolio constant and having his $50,000 in stocks rise by 10 percent along with the market.

To get to his $240,000 goal, this investor will need to put another $190,000 in stock. If he invests his current $150,000 with 126 percent leverage, he'll get there. This situation is illustrated in Figure 6.1.

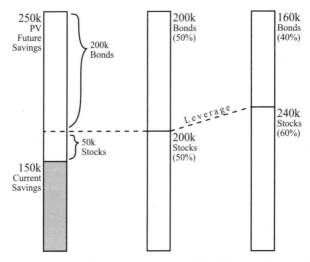

FIGURE 6.1 **Adjusting Leverage for Human Capital**

Recent work by Vladyslav Kyrychenko looks at the correlation between human capital and the stock market for people in different industries.[9] For those working in finance, insurance, and real estate, the correlation is 21 percent. For those in manufacturing, the correlation is 17 percent. For those in public administration the correlation falls to 4 percent and to –7 percent for those in wholesale and retail trade.[10]

Whether your future income is more like a stock or a bond is the subject of a terrific book by Moshe Milevsky.[11] (As it turns out, Milevsky is Kyrychenko's Ph.D. thesis advisor.) For a typical forty-five-year-old tenured professor, Milevsky suggests a 280 percent allocation to equities. This falls to 170 percent for a bankruptcy lawyer, 125 percent for a mechanical engineer, and 60 percent for an investment banker.[12]

The situation is different for people who have significant business income (for example, entrepreneurs and small business owners). Because of their business income, their market exposure is greater than that of regular wage earners. The correlation of business income to the market is 14 percent. Moreover, this group tends to hold a large fraction of their equities in their company stock, so they are not well diversified. If you are in this group, you will have less need to employ leverage to get to the desired level of overall market exposure.

Once Burned, Twice Shy

How would you react if you lost most of your retirement savings at age thirty? We expect your answer would be *NOT WELL*. That's okay. While the chance of losing most of your money is low, it is something to consider. Had you been leveraged at 2:1 in 2008, you would have lost 64 percent of your savings.

That seems like a lot, and it is. But the key point is that while the percentage is high, the absolute dollar amount will still be low. Consider two investors, one age thirty with $10,000 invested at 2:1 leverage and one age sixty with $250,000 in retirement savings, only 50 percent invested in equities.

In 2008, the thirty-year-old would have lost 64 percent of $10,000, or $6,400. The sixty-year-old would have lost $36,500 (15 percent), or almost six times as much in absolute dollars. Our view is that the sixty-year-old is in a much worse position than the thirty-year-old. What ultimately matters is the size of your loss in relation to your lifetime savings.

Young investors have so little in the market that even a large percentage loss at the time won't have a crippling impact on their ultimate retirement amount. By investing more when young, you can have less exposure when near retirement age. While losses are never pleasant, they are easier to handle when young, both because they tend to be smaller in magnitude and because you have more time to adjust.

With that advice, here is our caveat. You might be able to understand this exercise on an intellectual level, but if you were to lose, say, 64 percent of your retirement account at age thirty, would that scar you to the point that you wouldn't be able to stick with the plan? Our plan requires you to go back and continue to invest at 2:1 leverage. If you think you would give up at that point, then you shouldn't put yourself in that position to start with. You would do better to settle for being 100 percent in equities.

There's another psychological factor to consider: the urge to double your bets. If you are down 64 percent, you might feel, think, believe—even know in your bones—that the market is wrong and now is the time to invest more. Stocks are on sale, and so this is the time to buy. That's what Market Timer did, and that is what sealed his fate.

When the market falls and you're leveraged, then your equity goes down even faster, and so your leverage creeps up. Once the market moves by more than 10 percent, it is time to sell and *reduce* your exposure. This rebalancing made a big difference in 2008. Although the market fell by 36.6 percent, our 2:1 leveraged portfolio only dropped by 64 percent, not 73.2 percent. The reason is that rebalancing required selling along the way down and that reduced losses as the market continued to drop.[13]

Selling is how you limit your leverage to 2:1. This is what our disciplined plan calls for. If you are the type who has trouble cutting your losses, then leverage might not be for you.

Some of the diary entries from Market Timer will give you a sense of how a smart, financially literate young man let his emotions take control:

Rationally, I should reduce leverage, realize some losses, and come back with more capital as soon as it is feasible. At this time, I almost feel like Ahab, having lost a leg and seeking revenge against my white whale.

Sept 15, 2008, S&P 1193, net worth –$105K

I never expected to go this far into a hole.

Oct 10, 2008, S&P 899, net worth –$165K

I'm about to risk what is probably my last investment for a while, and the plan is to start at 4–5x leverage, and if I'm wiped out, then I'm simply wiped out. In effect, it is a bet that the S&P will not trade much below 800.

Oct 15, 2008 S&P 908, net worth –$180K

The margin violation warning emails have started again. S&P futures around 855. I'm not sure what happens now. These scenarios weren't in my original playbook. . . . These losses are incomprehensible for me. I'd be pissed if I lost $100 on a World Series bet. Losing $210K? I don't even know what to feel. . . . If I thought there was any chance a year ago that I'd find myself in this situation now, I would not have implemented the strategy the same way.

Oct 24, 2008 S&P 855, net worth −$205K

My taxable account is next in line for liquidation and I wonder, if these losses had been spread over the next 5 years, would I feel any differently? It's easier to lose conventionally. Then it's just bad luck, right?

Oct 27, 2008 S&P 836 net worth −$210K

As MT's case so clearly reveals, it is hard to predict the emotional reaction one will have to losing money. Of course his case was extreme. Not only was his timing exquisitely bad, but his excessive leverage and undiversified bets led to losses that were truly beyond his ability to pay. (Following our strategy, MT might have lost $50,000—a bad outcome but one that would have left him with $30,000 in the bank and a chance to participate in the 2009 recovery.) Before taking on leverage, even 2:1, ask yourself if you are prepared to stick to the plan and move on.

It is easier said than done. A few of Market Timer's friends were convinced by his analysis, and they followed his lead, though more cautiously. They had significant money at stake and started out with 2:1 leverage. Although they didn't double down, their leverage naturally increased as the markets fell. The disastrous results of 2008 led to more than just financial losses. One thirty-five-year-old colleague had accumulated an impressive $450,000 in savings and lost almost $350,000 when the market hit bottom. These losses created a strain in his marriage and as a result, he no longer invests in the stock market (and therefore missed the recovery in 2009). The colleague had also leveraged his sister's portfolio, and she, too, lost 75 percent of her account and no longer trusts him to manage her money.

We are under no illusions that losing 75 percent of your retirement savings won't lead you and your loved ones to rethink the wisdom of the lifecycle investment strategy. The only way to keep going is to put the losses in perspective. You wouldn't have lost that much with rebalancing. And even without rebalancing, you wouldn't have lost 75 percent of your true lifetime retirement portfolio—you would have lost 75 percent of your *current* retirement savings. Say that your goal was to be 83 percent invested in the market. Even with leverage, you would never be above that level. When the market fell 36.6 percent in 2008, you would have lost less than 30 percent of your lifetime retirement savings, and less still when taking Social Security into account. That is a big hit, but not one that should prevent you from staying the course.

Conflicting Advice

We don't think our diversifying lifecycle is appropriate for everyone. These six contraindications will help you decide if the advice is right for you. But at the other end of the spectrum, our strongest critics will claim our approach is bad advice for everyone. For them, any strategy with leverage is contraindicated for the entire population. What do we say to the growing number of "keep it all in cash" investment advisors? For example, Zvi Bodie and Michael Clowes have a book called *Worry-Free Investing* that provides advice that is just about diametrically opposite to ours. They suggest that people should put essentially all of their savings into inflation-protected bonds. Since we are proposing that people invest significantly in stocks, even borrowing to do so when young, we can't both be right.

We agree that inflation-protected securities are the safest investment out there. When it comes time to hold bonds, we, too, are big fans of TIPS, the inflation-indexed Treasury securities. The problem is that bonds, TIPS or otherwise, charge a high price for safety. The low returns that go along with that safety mean that most people will never be able to save enough for their retirement.

Bodie and Clowes propose buying the government's I-series bonds. When their book came out in 2003, those bonds were paying 3 percent interest (above the inflation rate). As we write, the return on those bonds has fallen to just 0.10 percent interest, and the government has put a cap of $5,000 per Social Security number in terms of how much you are allowed to buy. At that rate, you'll need to save over 15 percent of your income to reach your retirement goal, and that's simply out of the question for most people.[14]

Instead of investing in I-series bonds, you could try TIPS (Treasury Inflation Protected Securities), since both are inflation-protected securities. A ten-year TIPS bond offers to pay 1.589 percent interest (as of April 2009). That makes things better, but still practically impossible. Now you'd only have to save 10.8 percent of your income.[15]

If you are able to save 10.8 percent of your income, starting at age twenty-three and continuing on straight for forty-four years, then you can indeed have a risk-free way to achieve your retirement goals. But as we'll show in the next chapter, our approach offers a way that gives you a better than 90 percent chance you can hit the same goals while saving a more realistic 4 percent.[16]

Risk, or chance, isn't all bad. Would you prefer a sure $1,000 to a gamble in which you will make either $2,000 or $4,000? The latter choice might sound scary in that it has a $2,000 spread, which is a big number compared to the sure thing of a $1,000 payoff. But this risk shouldn't scare you at all in that the risk is all upside. Even in the bad scenario, you will end up with twice as much money under the gamble.

Here's one more way of putting things in perspective. Say that you can only save 4 percent of your income for retirement. What's the chance that you will succeed by putting everything in TIPS? The chance is zero! There's no risk at all. You can know now that you won't make it to amassing an amount that will adequately fund your retirement. You can confidently predict that, when it comes time for retirement, you will have saved an amount equal to three times your final salary and that's not enough, not even close.[17] For most people, that certainty of failure would keep them up at night.

Yes, there is risk in everything you do—from crossing the street to investing for retirement. Our objective is to help minimize your investment risk by spreading it out better across time. That should allow you to have enough market exposure so that you can afford to live while working and retire thereafter. If you have run the gauntlet of these six contraindications and are ready to start diversifying across time, the next two chapters get down to the brass tacks of showing you how to choose a strategy and implement it.

CHAPTER 7

What's Your Share?

SUPPOSE THAT YOU are the only income earner in your family and you have a good job guaranteed to give you your current income for life. You are given an opportunity to take a new and equally good job, with a 50 percent chance that it will double your family income and a 50 percent chance that it will cut your family income by a third. Would you take the new job?

This new job question is hypothetical. But it represents one of the more sophisticated ways of trying to put an actual number on your tolerance for risk.[1] For economists, the granddaddy of all risk-tolerance measures is something called "relative risk aversion" or RRA for short. If you said you were willing to take this new job, you implicitly indicated that your RRA is below 2; if not, then your RRA is above 2.

The lower your RRA, the higher your tolerance for risk. Someone who is indifferent to risk has an RRA of 0. Such a person is willing to take any gamble, just so long as on average he'll come out ahead.

By answering a laddered series of questions you can pin down your own RRA. For example, for those who said yes to the move, would you be willing to move your family if the downside put half your family's income at risk—that is, if there were a 50 percent chance that the move would cut your family income by half? If the answer is still yes, than you have even more tolerance for risk, and we can infer that your implicit risk parameter is below 1. (If you are willing to risk a third but not a half, then your risk parameter is somewhere between 1 and 2.)

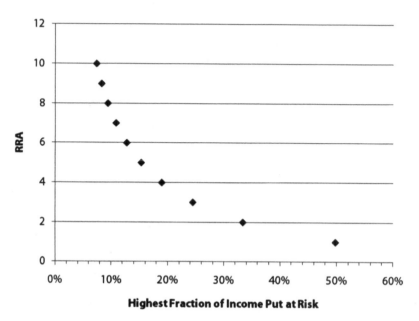

FIGURE 7.1 RRA as a Function of Willingness to Put Income at Risk

More generally, by determining the highest proportion of your family income you would be willing to put at risk to get a 50 percent chance of doubling it, you can calculate your RRA by reading it off Figure 7.1.

For example, if the most you are willing to put at risk in the bad scenario is 20 percent of your income, then you have less risk tolerance, and your implicit RRA is 3.76.

Thousands of people have been asked questions like these, and their answers reveal substantial differences in tolerance for risk.[2]

Relative Risk Aversion	*Proportion of Respondents*
3.76 < RRA	64.6%
2 < RRA < 3.76	11.4%
1 < RRA < 2	10.9%
RRA < 1	12.8%

Of the respondents, 64.6 percent were not even willing to risk 20 percent of their income to get an equal chance of doubling it and hence revealed strong risk aversion, exceeding 3.76. Close to a quarter were willing to risk at least a third of their safe current income for a chance to double. If you ask us, that's about our threshold. Wake us up in the middle of the night, and our first guess is that our RRA is about 2. But you shouldn't choose your risk tolerance to match ours; you should choose it to match your own comfort with taking on risk.

Ultimately, we are not big fans of the new job question. But if (and it's a big if) you actually trusted your answer to this move/not move question, it would be incredibly easy to tailor the diversifying lifecycle strategy to your preferences. Your new job answer gives you your RRA, and, at least as a first cut, you can then plug your RRA into a formula to find out the holy grail of lifecycle investing, your Samuelson share:

$$\text{Samuelson share} = \frac{1.58}{\text{RRA}}$$

This simple equation says that if your relative risk aversion is 2, you would want to be 79 percent in stocks. If you have less tolerance for risk, your RRA will increase, and, as you would expect, your Samuelson share will fall. So, for example, if your relative risk aversion is 3, you would want be at about 53 percent invested in stocks.

You still have to do the hard work of figuring out the present value of your future savings contributions (and you still need to keep in mind the caveats and contraindications from the previous chapter). But as a first cut, you take your Samuelson share and multiply it by the present value of your current and future savings, and voilà: You know how much you should want to invest in stocks. As we've emphasized above, even risk-averse investors will start out leveraged. Someone who was willing put at most 20 percent of her income at risk in the new job question would still have a Samuelson share of 42 percent (1.58/3.76 = 0.42) and would still need to take a leverage position while she was young to come closer to her target.

But before you take this formula to the bank (or your brokerage house), you should be asking yourself, Where did the 1.58 come from? Our answer will help you further tailor your Samuelson share.

How much you want to invest in the stock market turns not just on your risk tolerance but also on your expectation about the future risk and return of investing in the stock market.

A more general statement of the Samuelson share equation is this:

$$\text{Samuelson share} = \text{RETURN}/(\text{RISK}^2 \times \text{RRA})$$

where "RETURN" is measured by the expected equity premium—the amount by which stock returns are expected to exceed the return on government bonds—and "RISK" is measured by volatility, the expected standard deviation, of stock returns.[3]

Historically, the average annual real return on stocks (including dividends) has been about 7.9 percent, and the volatility has been 17.86 percent.[4] What we really want to know is how much more stocks return than government bonds. You get paid for two things when investing in stocks. One is taking on some risk, and the second is getting your money in the future. The bond rates provide a return for patience. It is the equity premium or the amount by which stocks outperform bonds that determines how much you are being compensated for taking risk. Even after the market fall in 2008, the historical equity premium is 7.87 percent on stocks – 2.83 percent on boards = 5.04 percent.

Our magical 1.58 constant was derived by assuming that the risk and the return on the stock market going forward is likely to be what it has been in the past:

$$\text{Samuelson share} = 5.04\% / (17.86\%^2 \times \text{RRA}) = 1.58 / \text{RRA}$$

If you have different expectations about the market's prospective risk and return, 1.58 might not be the right number for you. In making our calculations, we have used the historical equity premium going back to 1871. We took the average of real stock and bond returns over 138 years, including the crash of 2008.

If we had instead limited ourselves to more recent data, from 1926 onwards, we'd have produced a more conservative estimate.[5] From 1926 through 2008, the real equity return has been 6.00 percent, while the average one-year real bond rate has been 1.58 percent, leading to an equity premium that was only 4.42 percent. To make matters worse, volatility has also been higher over this period, 19.59 percent rather than 17.86 percent. Putting these two factors together leads to the following investment rule:

(Post-1926) Samuelson share = 1.15 / RRA

This revised formula leads to about a 25 percent smaller allocation to stocks. Thus with RRA = 2, it follows that 57.5 percent should be in stocks, down from 79 percent. For simplicity, we'll round down to 57 percent.

As we sit here in 2009, it is hard to dispute those who have even more pessimistic views about risk and return than the above.[6] The implicit stock risk found in stock futures suggests that volatility is still high, and our colleague Robert Shiller has argued that we should expect even lower equity premiums for U.S. stocks in the future. If you expect only a 4 percent equity premium with 20 percent risk, the revised 1.15 factor falls further to 1.0, so that if you also had a relative risk aversion of 2, you would only want to invest half of your savings (future and current) in the market.

Conceptually, you could wake up at the beginning of every month and think about adjusting your Samuelson share based on how risk tolerant you were feeling that day and how optimistic you were feeling about risk and return. Indeed, in Chapter 4, the Shiller adjustment simulations did just this. When the P/E ratio was high, Shiller told us to expect lower stock returns, and we accordingly reduced the Samuelson share. When the P/E ratio was low, we increased the Samuelson share because we expected higher prospective returns. Similarly, you can adjust the RISK term by plugging in the current value of the VIX or some other broad-based volatility index.

One Cheer for RRAs

Oh, if it were only that simple. Answer a relatively simple new-job question and before you know it you have your own personalized Samuelson share. Unfortunately, we don't really trust your answer, and neither should you.

The good news is that the new-job question is a massive improvement over the alternatives. If you go to websites like www.myrisktolerance.com, you will be asked a series of questions like the following:

When you think of the word *risk* in a financial context, which of the following words comes to mind first?

A. Danger
B. Uncertainty
C. Opportunity
D. Thrill

This kind of question drives us nuts, because it seems like folly to go from it to any kind of a number on tolerance for risk, much less a percentage stock allocation. It is hard to believe, but multiple-choice questions like this are the dominant way that financial advisors try to assess their clients' tolerance for risk in order to give advice on how to allocate a portfolio between stocks and bonds. The new-job question at least is soliciting information about your willingness to trade off a particular type of risk and return.

The bad news is that the answers that people give to new-job questions are notoriously fragile. For example, imagine that we instead gave you the following scenario:

The Acme Company will be making its earnings announcement tomorrow before the markets have opened. If sales hit or exceed the target, the stock will open at $110. If sales are below target, the stock will open at $90. In your view, there is a 50 percent chance that the sales will hit or exceed the target. What is the highest price the stock could be today for you to be willing to invest 10 percent of your wealth in this single stock?

In trying to answer, we want you to ignore taxes and any interaction between this decision and your other investments. Also ignore the fact that today's price might give some market indication of the likelihood that the news will be good or bad. We simply ask you to play along and accept that there is a 50 percent chance that the stock will open at \$110 and a 50 percent chance that it will open at \$90.

As you think about your answer, note that picking 90 (or anything below that) isn't a legitimate response. Everyone should be willing to take a bet with no downside and a 50 percent chance of a significant upside.

Conversely, if your answer is above 110, then you are sure to lose money, and so there would be no point in making this investment. Even if the price is only 100, you shouldn't make this investment. On average, you'll lose as much money as you make and thus won't be compensated for taking risk.

In short, we expect your answer to be somewhere in between 90 and 100. How much of a discount from an average opening price of \$100 do you need to make this an acceptable gamble? If you are more risk averse, you need to buy at more of a discount to make it worth your while. Go ahead and pick a number between 90 and 100.

What scares us about the Acme and new-job questions is that there is a very good chance that your answers are inconsistent. Our guess is that most of you picked an Acme number between 96 and 99. That seems like a reasonable answer. But it turns out to be far too conservative and inconsistent with what we think we know about risk.

If you thought 97 was a reasonable price, then you would need a relative risk aversion of 63 to justify requiring that large of a return. That level of risk aversion would also suggest that you shouldn't get out of bed in the morning, you should never drive a car, and you should be just about 98 percent invested in bonds.

It doesn't make sense to have a RRA less than 4 when answering the new-job question, and an RRA greater than 50 when answering the Acme question. This makes us suspicious of both answers. Your tolerance for risk shouldn't depend on how the question is framed.

One reason for the inconsistency is that the Acme bet was on only a small fraction of your wealth. People have a hard time distinguishing between a risk to 10 percent of their portfolio and a risk to 100 percent of their portfolio. If your entire portfolio is at stake and you are quite risk averse (RRA = 4), then a stock price of 98 is required to make this an attractive bet. A stock price of 98 implies a return of 2 percent. The volatility (or standard deviation) of this bet is 10 percent. To put this in perspective, recall that the overall stock market has had an annual volatility of roughly 18 percent, and the average return is a 5 percent premium over bonds. That might help you appreciate that 2 percent is a reasonable return for taking a risk that your portfolio could go up or down by 10 percent. This gamble is much like six months' exposure to the market.

Economic theory says that when you invest 10 percent of your wealth in something, as opposed to all your money, the risk goes down by a factor of ten. Correspondingly, so should the required return. Thus if you need 2 percent to invest everything, you would only require 0.2 percent to invest 10 percent. You should buy the stock at a price of 99.8.

We know that is hard to accept. A return of 0.2 percent seems so very small. But the risk to your overall wealth is only 1 percent up or down. If we look at some numbers from the stock market, they may help put the 0.2 percent return in context. Consider the return you expect for investing in the market over a two-week period. The equity premium is 5 percent per year, which translates to a 0.2 percent return over a two-week period. During a two-week period, you can expect that stocks will move up or down by about 3 percent.[7] Being required to hold all your money in stocks for two weeks is worse than investing 10 percent of your money in Acme with the 0.2 percent return. They both offer the same expected return, but Acme has less risk.

Most people aren't very good at evaluating risk. It is scary to follow the daily ups and downs of the market. People have a hard time figuring out just how much they need to be compensated for risk. Indeed, an excessive fear of small risks leads many folks to make some very poor financial decisions. Inside wire insurance for phone lines is an example that illustrates the point.

Inside (Wire) Job

The typical telephone customer pays $0.45 per month to protect against repair charges in the event that the phone lines inside his house are damaged. This is a very unlikely scenario. According to economists Charles Cicchetti and Jeffrey Dubin, the chance of this problem is only 0.477 percent per month, and when a problem does arise, the cost of having it fixed is only $55 (on average).[8] Thus the consumer pays $0.45 to avoid something that has an expected cost of $55 × 0.477 percent = $0.26. The phone company charges a fee that is almost double what the repair costs, and many people seem willing to pay this high premium in order to avoid the risk.

Let's turn the problem on its head. We want you to think of *not* buying the insurance as if you're making an investment in the stock market. Say that you had an opportunity to buy a stock that costs $100. Most of the time, 94 percent of the time to be precise, that stock went up in value by $5.40 annually. But 6 percent of the time, the value fell to $50.40. (So that we don't have to take into account the issue of forgone interest on the $100, we will assume that you are able to take this risk without having to put up the $100 today.)

This is a great investment opportunity. On average, you expect to end up $2.10 ahead.[9] While losing $49.60 is painful, it isn't so bad that it should prevent you from taking this gamble.

What we've done here is take the phone repair risk and turn it into a stock. By not buying the insurance, you are in effect paying yourself $0.45 a month, or $5.40 per year. The chance of a problem is 0.477 percent per month or 5.7 percent annually, which we'll round up to 6 percent. That means 94 percent of the time, you won't have any repair needs and will end up $5.40 ahead. The other 6 percent of the time, you will have to pay $55, but you can still use the saved premiums to offset this loss, so you'll be $49.60 behind.

If you still aren't convinced, consider the following perspective. Take the $0.45 that you would have sent to the phone company each month for inside line insurance and put it in a jar. You will be able to sock away $5.40 a year. In a little over 10 years, you will have enough to pay for one repair. But given the low frequency of problems, you only expect to have an issue every 17.5 years. Thus over a 17.5-year cycle, you expect to come out $39.50 ahead.

Not only should you not buy inside-line insurance, you should offer to sell the product to all your neighbors. Okay, maybe that isn't practical, and your neighbors would probably look at you funny if you offered. That said, if you are currently buying inside-line insurance, cancel it, and we've saved you well more than the cost of this book. Along similar lines, your water company might be trying to convince you that $5 a month is a good price to pay for protection against a break in the water line to your house. Don't bet on that, either.[10] And while we're at it, you probably have too small a deductible for your homeowners policy and your auto insurance.

There are many reasons why people might buy inside-line or water-line insurance. As economist Edi Grgeta explains, you could be systematically overestimating the risk of a problem.[11] If you thought the chance of needing repair is 1 percent per month, not 0.5 percent, then the insurance contract is a fair deal. A related explanation is that many people tend to overweight small probabilities. In their minds, they treat a 0.5 percent chance as if it were a 1 percent chance.

Even if you understand that this is a bad bet, you could worry about regret. If there is a problem and you haven't bought the insurance, then you will feel stupid, or your spouse will make you feel that way. Better to buy the insurance and not think about the issue.

Of course, for the small amount of money involved, it probably isn't worth doing the calculation. But here's an easy shortcut. If someone is selling you the insurance, they expect to make money. Few insurance products operate with less than 30 percent overhead and profit margin. Thus you can expect to make at least 30 percent if you don't buy the insurance.

If you are able to get your head into the mode of thinking about insurance contracts as an investment, then you will want to self-insure, at least for small risks. Using the investment frame, look at the decision from the perspective of the phone company. They take in $5.40 a year for something that only costs them less than $3.30. Their profit on this $5.40 premium is $2.10, or 40 percent. That is a stunningly high rate of return.

When seen from this lens, there is no credible way we can explain why people are so scared of losing $55 that they would let the phone company make a 40 percent return on this investment, year after year.

Ditto for water-line insurance. Ditto for low deductibles on auto and home insurance.

Our point in all this is that people have lots of inconsistencies in how they approach risky situations. While we are happy to take people as they are, we think that we can help you see the world from a different vantage point and thereby help you be happier and wealthier. When it comes to assessing your own tolerance for risk, asking how much risk you're willing to take with regard to a big, long-term question, like the new-job question, is more likely to give you a reasonable answer than asking the Acme question, which concerned a short-term, small-percentage investment.

Even here, we worry that your answers will depend too much on how we frame the question. Behavioral economists have had a field day showing how fragile these kind of self-assessments can be (you can see some examples on our website). As a complement to these personal surveys that work forward from self-assessments of risk tolerance, we also want to work backward from your required nest egg to find the Samuelson share that will likely provide you with enough to retire happily.

How Much Is Enough?

An elderly Floridian gentleman is hit by a car while crossing the street. A bystander runs up and asks, "Sir, are you all right?!" The man responds, "I'm not rich, but I'm comfortable."

In order to work backwards, you need to know how much money is enough to retire comfortably. The answer, of course, depends on your goal. The standard advice is that you will need roughly 70 percent of your preretirement income each year to maintain your standard of living. We don't really know if that is right or not. One justification for the 70 percent rule is that it leads to roughly the same after-tax consumption level.[12] Larry Kotlikoff has argued that this is more than most people will need.[13] On the other hand, a 2007 survey from the Employee Benefit Research Institute suggests that over half of retirees spend at least as much annually in their first five years postretirement as during their working years.[14] Given that

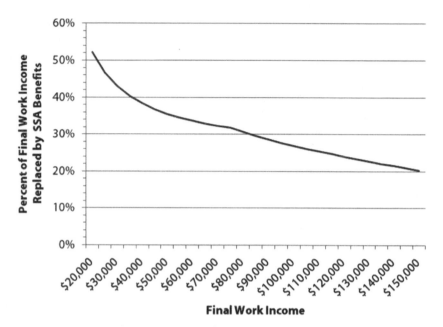

FIGURE 7.2 **Social Security Benefits as a Percentage of Final Income**

this is something that depends on your health, your enjoyment of travel, grandchildren, and more, there's no single answer for all readers. We'll stick with the 70 percent rule of thumb, and you can adjust everything up or down based on your anticipated needs.

Social Security has you partially covered—assuming that it is still in business when you retire.[15] If your ending salary is $150,000, Social Security covers about 20 percent, so your personal savings need to cover 50 percent of your preretirement income if you want to reach our rule of thumb replacement rate. If your ending salary is $75,000, Social Security replaces 32 percent of your salary, meaning that you only need to cover 38 percent to make up the gap. Figure 7.2 provides replacement rates based on the Social Security Administration's online calculator.[16]

The big question is: How much of a nest egg will you need at the beginning of your retirement in order to finance the gap between Social Security and 70 percent?

This seems like an impossible question to answer, because when you retire you don't know how many years left you have to live. If you get "lucky" and live longer than actuarially expected, you may end up poor.

But even without foreknowledge of your death date, it's actually not so hard to figure out how much of a nest egg you'll need.

We are fans of life annuities as a way of financing your retirement. With a life annuity, you don't have to worry that you might live too long. While that is a good thing, few have the resources to pay for a forty-year retirement. Living to 105 isn't so unusual anymore and might well become commonplace by the time many of this book's readers retire. Annuities solve that problem by giving you an income for as long as you live.

What's more, life annuities can protect you against the risk that inflation might eat away at the purchasing power of your income. Social Security has inflation protection built in, so the problem is only with the gap amount. Annuities come in many varieties, and we suggest paying the extra amount to get one where the payments are indexed to inflation.

Since inflation-adjusted life annuities can solve your problem, the relevant question is how much it will cost to get an annuity that provides the income you'll need. That will tell us how much you need to save to hit that target. To do that right, we would have to forecast what annuity prices will be at the time of your retirement, and that depends on both longevity and interest rates at the time, neither of which is easy to predict.

To give you some idea of this pricing, we can tell you what the annuity payments would be like if you were to retire in 2009. For a sixty-seven year old man, the price of an annuity is roughly fourteen times the annual benefit.[17] What that means is that for every $1,000 of annual benefit, the upfront price will be $14,000. (In this case, we've saved a bit of money by not having any minimum guaranteed payout. We've also assumed that the man was married and wanted to protect his sixty-five year old wife; when one partner passes on, the annuity payouts are then reduced to 66.67 percent of the original level.)[18]

Unfortunately, the cost is more if you want to get inflation protection. And you should. When we talk about replacing 70 percent of your income, you need to do that in real terms. Vanguard provides an annuity that has inflation protection built in.[19] The payments go up each year with the consumer price index. As you will guess, this increases the cost substantially, to about nineteen times the annual payout.[20] Basically, for every

$19 you give Vanguard, they'll provide a life annuity that pays an inflation-adjusted $1 a year.

The standard advice is that you can spend 4 percent of your assets and maintain your real standard of living. That would imply you need to save an amount equal to twenty-five times your annual payout. Inflation-adjusted annuities offer a much better deal. In effect, they allow you to spend 5.3 percent of your assets for as many years as you need. They guarantee the real payout and take away the risk of outliving your assets. They also eliminate any risk that your portfolio won't keep up with inflation. The downsides are that there's no money at the end left for inheritance, and you can't dip into the principal for an emergency.[21]

If you follow the annuity path, you'll need the nineteen multiple on the gap in your salary. This suggests that most of our readers will need to have savings equal to seven to nine times their final salary. If your final salary is $100,000, then Social Security will replace 27 percent of that income. Your savings at retirement will need to be large enough to fill a 43 percent gap (70% – 27%). Buying a life annuity on the first day of retirement that replaces 43 percent of income would cost 19 × 43% = 8.2 × final salary. If you retire with eight or more times your final salary, you can rest assured that, together with Social Security, you'll have enough to live on during retirement. As your final salary rises, the Social Security gap rises, too, and so the required multiple is also bigger. At lifecycleinvesting.net, we provide a widget that will make this calculation for any projected final income.

Will I Have Enough?

Now that we have an estimate of how much is required, let's return to our simulations to give you a sense of whether you have a chance of making it or not. For someone with an ending salary of $100,000 who saves 4 percent of her income throughout her life, we've projected the probability of making the requisite 8.2 savings multiple.

Over the ninety-six different cohorts of investors—from Zachary, who started investing in 1871, to Eleanor who started investing in 1966 and retired in 2009—we found the following median accumulations:

The 90/50 rule ends up with $642,000, which is 6.4 × final income

The 200/57 rule ends up with $834,000, which is 8.3 × final income

The 200/83 rule ends up with $1.15 million, which is 11.5 × final income

Half the investors did better than the median amount, and half did worse. For the lucky half, saving 4 percent of income was more than enough to cover their retirement needs under either the 200/57 or the 200/83 lifecycle strategies, but not under the birthday rule. The 90/50 rule is low-risk, but it's also a very low return. It produces a very low chance of actually meeting the multiple of 8.2 × final income.

Focusing on the median result isn't really enough reassurance. You should want more than a 50 percent chance of financing your retirement. By looking at the tenth percentile of outcomes, we can see what number you'll beat 90 percent of the time.

The 90/50 rule ends up with $416,000, which is 4.2 × final income

The 200/57 rule ends up with $552,000, which is 5.5 × final income

The 200/83 rule ends up with $702,000, which is 7.0 × final income

Here we see that the 90/50 rule won't get most people where they need to be. It will only provide enough income to fill in 22 percent of replacement income. For a couple retiring with $100,000 income, the annuity plus Social Security will only replace 49 percent of their income, a figure that suggests a significant decline in standard of living.

Ensuring that you will hit your goal in the worst 10 percent case is a tough test, and even the 200/83 doesn't quite pass for the $100,000 earner. The $702,000 result leads to 37 percent replacement income, which along with the 27 percent from Social Security is a 64 percent replacement level.* Like horseshoes and hand grenades, here is a case where close counts. People who are unlucky enough to be in the worst 10 percent for

---

*For a $75,000 earner, Social Security comes up with 32 percent, and so the combined replacement income will be 69 percent, just about there.

stock returns will only have to make a small cutback in their standard of living. Overall, under the 200/83 strategy there is about a 79 percent chance of making the full 70 percent goal if you have a $100,000 income. These calculations are conservative, as they don't consider the possibility of tapping into any home equity to make up the difference.

If you have a lower tolerance for risk (RRA = 2.7), you might embrace a 200/57 lifecycle, instead of 200/83. A 57 percent Samuelson share channels most of the benefits of temporal diversification to risk reduction. However, if your goal is a 70 percent income replacement this might lead you to the more aggressive 200/83 lifecycle. While our initial analysis suggests that an 83 percent Samuelson share is for people with a fair amount of risk tolerance (those with an RRA of 1.9), our nest-egg simulations suggest that channeling all the benefits of diversification toward higher return can increase the chance of having enough to retire—by shifting the bulk of the distribution above the line of comfort.

What Is My Income Stream?

At this point, you are in the home stretch in terms of figuring out how to allocate your retirement savings. Let's say that you've decided to save 4 percent and adopt the 200/57 rule. Now all you have to figure out is how to actually implement this decision. What do you have to do to follow the 200/57 path?

At first, you have an easy strategy: Take whatever you have, and invest it at 2:1 leverage. That's the 200 part. Over time, your assets will grow, and you will come closer to hitting your goal of 57 percent. Here we provide calculations that show how to determine when you are hitting the 57 percent goal. This will tell you when you should start to delever and when you should be investing without any leverage at all.

The key challenge is figuring out the number that gets multiplied by 57 percent. To put the target allocation into practice, you need to come up with a total savings wealth number. How much you have today is easy. The hard part is figuring out how much more there is to come in future savings. To do that, you have to estimate the path of your lifetime income.

As a starting point, it is useful to look at how wages tend to vary over a lifetime. For most people, wages follow a hump-shaped pattern over time: Real wages go up with your age until you're in your early fifties, and then they tend to decline slowly until you retire. The exact height of the hump depends on what kind of training you have: College graduates tend to have a higher hump than high school graduates, and professionals have a higher hump still. But what's remarkable is that the basic shape of the hump doesn't vary that much across different kinds of workers.

The Social Security Administration estimates that for an average person, real wages at age twenty-three start at about $20,000 and rise to a maximum of almost $59,000 at age fifty-one. Real wages then tend to fall to around $42,500 by the time the worker retires at age sixty-five or so. Note that we are putting everything in terms of real wages, as we expect that salaries will keep pace with inflation. It is easier to forecast how much your real salary will increase when you can look around and see what today's wages are like for people in more senior positions.

To calculate the present value of your future savings contributions you should start out by estimating the present value of your future income. It turns out that for young workers under age twenty-five, the present value of future income tends to be about forty-five times current income. Our average worker at thirty has future income that is thirty-two times her current annual income. If you've been working for a year or two, take your average annual income and multiply it by thirty, and you'll have a conservative estimate of your future income. Of course, we can't guarantee future success: Some people lose their jobs and fall on hard times. Others start slow and race ahead of their peers. But the income profile is surprisingly consistent. We don't hold by the Jesuit maxim: "Show me the boy at seven, and I will show you the man." But show us the income at twenty-seven, and we can come a lot closer to showing you the lifetime value.

If you consistently save 4 percent, the present value of your savings contributions will just be 4 percent of the present value of future income. Be sure to include employer matching as well. If you're in the kind of job in which employers match on a 1:2 basis, then your 4 percent contribution becomes 6 percent.[22]

So if you're twenty-seven and earning $50,000 a year, as a first cut we'd conservatively predict that the present value of your future income is at least $1,500,000 (30 × $50,000). If you're a 4 percent saver, the present value of your future saving contributions is $60,000. The logic of time diversification tells us that you should start exposing some of this present value to the market now. It is as if you have a $60,000 bond. Thus if your Samuelson share is 57 percent, then you should have $34,200 in equities. Most twenty-seven-year-olds earning $50,000 won't have anything close to that amount available, so they should simply max out at 200 percent in equities.

Over time, the present value of future income as a multiple of current income declines. By age thirty-five, the multiple is down to twenty-six. At forty, it's twenty-one, and sixteen at age forty-five. By the time you're our age (fifty), it's just about twelve. (At lifecycleinvesting.net, we'll help you calculate the multiple for your age.) So if you are fifty and earning about $90,000 a year, you should, as a first cut, expect that the present value of your future income will be $1,080,000. And if you're a 4 percent saver, the present value of your future saving contributions is $43,200. Say that you have $65,000 saved up so far. Then your total amount of savings is the two combined or $108,200. You goal is to be at 57 percent, which is $61,674. Since you have $65,000 available, you can get there without any leverage, investing the extra $3,326 in bonds.

We go back to Andrew as one last example to help illustrate how to put all these numbers together. At age twenty-five, his starting salary is $160,000. Law firms typically don't offer matching 401(k) plans, and Andrew has decided to put aside 5 percent a year. That implies the present value of his future contributions is by our estimation equal to 225 percent of his salary ($360,000 = $160,000 × 45 × 0.05). To that amount, we should add what he currently has saved up, namely $4,800, bringing the total to $364,800. Let's say that his glide path would ideally take him to 57 percent equities. That suggests he would want to have about $208,000 in equities today. But he only has $4,800 today. Even investing at 200 percent leverage only brings him to 5 percent of his goal.

If Andrew were more risk averse, so that he only wanted to be 40 percent in equities, that would lead him to a desired portfolio of $145,920.

Investing $4,800 at 2:1 leverage brings him a step in the right direction, but still only 7 percent of the way to his goal.

What this says in bold letters is that if you are starting out, you don't need to do these calculations. Whatever you have in your IRA, you should invest with maximum (2:1) leverage. Whatever you have in your 401(k) plan, you should invest at 100 percent equities.

While these numbers are an extremely rough estimate for someone starting out, that turns out not to be a problem. The asset allocation is going to be the same pretty much whatever number you put in: 200 percent. You should take advantage of any opportunity to leverage up to 2:1.

By the time you are thirty, you will have a more meaningful ability to forecast your future income. That's about the time you will have to start re-balancing your portfolio. As we saw in Chapter 4, under a 200/83 strategy the typical investor remained fully leveraged for 12.8 years. An investor following a 200/57 strategy would be fully leveraged for nine years. Assuming that you start at twenty-three, it will be around age thirty-two that you will start moving down from 200 percent. Late starters will take longer to delever.

At this point, we hope to have explained how you should allocate your portfolio between stocks and bonds. In the next chapter we turn to the real nitty-gritty—what you should buy to get leverage at a reasonable price.

CHAPTER 8

The Mechanics

AT SOME POINT in the future, we hope that following our strategy will be as simple as investing in a target-date fund, one that employs leverage in the early years. But as we discuss in Chapter 9, it may take some time for regulations to catch up with our advice. In the meantime, you will have to follow a DIY strategy.

This chapter provides the nuts and bolts of how to invest with leverage. Here we explain where to buy options, what strike price to employ, how much they will cost, and what leverage they will provide. Our starting point is the different types of retirement accounts and the constraints they impose.

401(k), 403(b), and 457 Plans

Practically speaking, the money you have in a 401(k) plan can't be leveraged. The same thing goes for the nonprofit and government 403(b) and 457 retirement plans. That's because you are limited to the investment choices designated by your employer. At this time, none of these choices will be a mutual fund with leverage, and you aren't allowed to just go out and buy options.

What is to be done? Go to the limit. To the extent that you are in Phase I or II, and thus you want to be more than 100 percent invested in equities, you can get as close as possible to your desired allocation by allocating all your funds to equities. If you want to be 200 percent in equities, then 100 percent is better than 80/20. And if you want to be 150 percent in equities, 100 percent is again better than 80/20.

155

There is another approach, but it isn't something we recommend. In some cases, you could borrow against your 401(k) account, generally up to 50 percent of the vested amount, or $50,000, whichever is less. The interest rate is set by the plan, but as you are paying yourself interest, the rate isn't that important.

Employers may restrict your borrowing to specific purposes, such as education, unreimbursed medical bills, avoiding eviction, or buying a first home. Even if the loan were allowed, you only have five years to pay it back. The loan also comes due immediately if you change jobs.

If you don't pay the loan back, the amount borrowed will be treated as if it were a premature withdrawal, which leads to immediate tax liability along with a 10 percent tax penalty. You will be hit with a large tax bill at a time when you can least afford it.

For money in a 401(k) plan, going to 100 percent is a good step in the right direction, but trying to go beyond that isn't worth the risk.

IRA

An IRA, be it a traditional or a Roth IRA, gives you more flexibility with your investment options. Most important, for our purposes, you have the ability to self-direct how it is invested.

To the extent that you are looking to be leveraged, there are three approaches: (1) You can buy options on a stock index. (2) You can buy a stock index on margin. (3) You can invest in a mutual fund that does the leverage for you. We discuss each of these options in turn.

For now, we favor the option alternative as the best way to proceed. More specifically, we like two-year, deep-in-the-money LEAP call options on the S&P. But the margin alternative is very competitive, and there is a general trend toward ease of use (e.g., the proliferation of smartphone apps makes it possible to execute trades just about anywhere). This is a horse race that is likely to only get tighter.

You can also follow a leveraged strategy in a regular (non-IRA) account. The disadvantage is that you will be taxed on gains along the way. This is a more serious issue with options than with buying the S&P index itself, because every two years the LEAP options expire, which leads to recognized gains or losses. Moreover, our strategy requires you to rebalance your portfolio along the way. You can't just buy and hold.

How to Find an Option with 2:1 Leverage

Call options—option to buy stock indexes—allow you to get a leveraged exposure to the stock market. Let's say that you are seeking exposure to $10,000 of stock. You'd like to find something that costs much less than $10,000 but goes up or down dollar for dollar with $10,000 of stock.

What you are looking for is a call option that is deep in the money. What that means is the option has a low enough exercise price that you can be highly confident that it will be exercised. For example, if the stock index is trading at $100 and the option gives you the right to buy the index at $50, then you will exercise the option so long as the index ends up above $50 prior to expiration. As you can guess, the odds of that are quite high.

Let's say that you were required to exercise the option at the end. Then all you have done is delay a payment of $50 (the exercise price) from the time you bought the option to when it expires. In effect, the person selling you the option has lent you $50. Even if you aren't forced to exercise, since the odds are so high that you will want to, the economics of the transaction are almost identical.[1]

An option to buy an index at 50 that is trading at 100 will cost just a little over $50. That means you can obtain 2:1 leverage by buying an option that has an exercise price roughly half of the current index value. If we go back to Andrew Verstein's case in Chapter 1, the SPDR was at 92.00, and the call was at 45, a near perfect match. You don't have to get the match perfect. If the call had been at 50, he would have had a bit more than 2:1 leverage, and if the call had been at 40, then a bit less than 2:1 leverage.

If you want less leverage, there are two ways to go. You can use 2:1 leverage on only part of your portfolio, or you can buy an option that gives less leverage. For example, say that you have $10,000 and would like exposure to $15,000 of equities. You want 150 percent or 3:2 leverage. You can buy 2:1 leverage on $5,000 (giving you $10,000 of exposure) and invest the other $5,000 entirely in stocks (giving you the remaining $5,000 of exposure). Or, you can buy an option that is even deeper in the money, namely, one that is around one-third of the current price. If the index is at $100 and your call price is at $33, then you are only borrowing $33, or one-third of the total purchase. The cost of such an option will be close to $67. Buying 1.5 of these options will end up costing $10,000 and provide exposure to $15,000 of stock. In practice you can't buy a fraction of an option—they come in 100 share lots—and so you will do better to invest $5,000 at 2:1 leverage and the other $5,000 without leverage. Another problem with the second approach is that not all strike prices are available in the market, and as one gets to options with such low strike prices, they may be illiquid or not even exist.

In terms of where to go buy the options, you have choices here too. Options can be bought in pretty much any brokerage account, although you have to demonstrate that you have some degree of financial sophistication.[2] There are also online brokerage houses, such as OptionsXpress.com, that are designed to trade options with low commissions.

As far as which index to purchase options on, since you should be looking for a well-diversified portfolio we suggest the S&P 500. You can buy an option that is directly connected to the index or one that follows the index via an exchange-traded fund (EFT) such as the SPDR. The SPDR is designed to track the S&P 500 at one-tenth the price.

We like options on the SPDR (ticker symbol: SPY) because it is affordable and one of the more actively traded ETFs in the market. Without enough liquidity, you will end up paying a large bid-ask spread in order to first buy and then sell the contract.

For Andrew, his long-term call option traded under the ticker symbol .CYULS. That ticker will continue to work so long as the December 2010 contract remains active. You will want to go out and find the long-term contract that is best for you. Thus in January 2010, you would look for the December 2011 contract.

It is also possible to buy a call option directly on the S&P 500 (ticker symbol: SPX). For example, the December 2011 contract with an exercise price of $450 trades under the ticker .SZJLI. These contracts are also fairly liquid. In May 2009 there were 5,000 contracts outstanding with a December 2010 exercise price of $500. This represents roughly $20 million worth of options. The problem, as you may have already inferred, is that each option contract is for 100 shares of the index. Thus a single contract with an exercise price of $500 will go for roughly $40,000 (when the index is around 900). That is a lot more money than most investors have starting out. That's why option contracts on the SPDR are a good alternative. Since the SPDR trades at one-tenth the price of the S&P, its options contracts will cost closer to $4,000 each.

What Is the Cost of Borrowing?

An option serves two roles. It allows you to borrow money, and it limits your downside to the price of the option. In the case of an option priced at half the index, the downside protection is worth very little. The primary cost of the option is that you end up paying more in total than if you had simply bought the index at the start, rather than the option. The extra amount you pay is the implied interest rate.

Let's go back and review Andrew's LEAP transaction to figure out his implicit cost of borrowing. Recall that he paid $47.70 a share for the right to buy the SPDR at a price of $45 a share in December 2011. At the time he bought the contract, the SPDR was trading at 92.00. Thus, compared to buying the SPDR at that moment, Andrew saved himself $44.30.

In effect, Andrew borrowed $44.30. He is getting all the upside and downside associated with the SPDR contract, except that he paid $47.70 rather than the full $92.00. When December 2011 comes along, Andrew will have to pay another $45 a share. That is more than he would have paid if he had simply bought the shares in January 2009 for $92.00. All told, Andrew will pay $47.70 + $45.00 = $92.70. Thus Andrew is paying an extra $0.70 for the right to wait until December 2011 to pay for the rest of the contract.[3]

That $0.70 is part of the implied interest cost for borrowing $44.30 for twenty-three months. It comes out to slightly less than 0.8 percent annually, which is almost nothing. The larger cost is that Andrew will miss out on dividends.

A SPDR holder gets a quarterly dividend payment reflecting all dividends paid out by companies in the S&P 500. As an option holder, Andrew doesn't get those payments. So when we compare the cost of buying the option versus owning 100 shares in the SPDR, we have to take into account the forgone dividend yield on the S&P stocks.

Under more normal times, one might simply look at the historical dividend payout on the S&P index. In 2008, the total dividend payments across all the S&P 500 firms added up to $28.05, which means $2.805 per share in the SPDR contract. The problem is that with the 2008 drop in stock prices, the dividend yield increased from about 1.8 percent in 2006 and 2007 to 3.7 percent in early 2009. That rate is too good to be true, or at least sustainable. Investors don't expect firms to continue paying the same level of dividends, especially those whose earnings have taken a large hit. We don't know what the eventual dividend payouts will be over 2009 and 2010. For our calculation, we will assume that firms will cut their dividend back to the level of five years earlier, 2004, when they were $1.94 per SPDR share. (With the S&P index at 900, this implies a dividend yield of 2.2 percent.) Because Andrew's option contract expires in December 2011, he will miss out on two full years of dividend payments.

Finally, we have to add the cost of commission. To buy and sell the option contract costs $15 each way, or $0.30 per share for the round trip. That is a high estimate of the cost because the commission is the same price for one through ten contracts. Thus the cost would be reduced to $0.03 per share for someone buying options on $90,000 of SPDR rather than $9,000. Since Andrew bought just one contract, we apply the full $30 to his costs.

Adding up the $0.70, the forgone dividends ($3.88), and the trading costs ($0.30) comes to $4.88. That extra cost would have been avoided if Andrew had spent an extra $44.30 and bought the SPDR rather than the

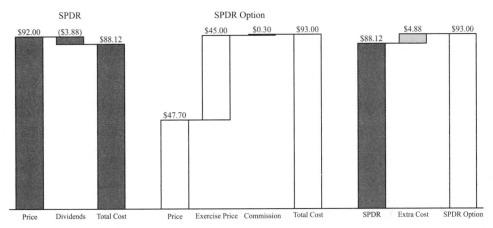

FIGURE 8.1 Andrew's Implied Cost of Borrowing

option. Thus the implied annual interest rate (over twenty-three months) was 5.75 percent.

As it turns out, this was a relatively high cost for buying an options contract when compared to the data in our sample. The reason is that in January 2009, the market volatility index (VIX) was over 40, more than twice the historical average. That suggests that the possibility of not exercising the option might well have been worth something. Someone who bought the SPDR could lose all $9,200, while Andrew's losses are limited to $4,770.

We've done calculations of implicit costs for hundreds of different LEAP options between 1996 and 2008. Over this period, we find that the average implied interest rate was 4 percent. For example, on May 26, 2009 (2:00 PM), the S&P 500 Index was trading at 911.23. At that time, the asking price for a December 2010 option on the index directly with a strike price of $500 was $404.50. Thus it was $6.73 cheaper to buy the index via the option than outright.[4] On the other hand, the option holder lost out on dividends. If the annual dividend payout on the S&P were to fall back to its 2004 level of $19.40, then the forgone dividends over the 569 days until the contract expires in December 2011 is (569/365) × 19.40 = $30.24. That makes the total cost ($30.24 – $6.73) = $23.51, which translates to an implied interest cost of 2.98 percent.

Even if dividends were to stay at their 2008 level of $28.05, the total cost would be ($43.73 – $6.73) = $37.00 or 4.68 percent. Depending on what dividends turn out to be, the interest cost will be between 2.98 percent and 4.68 percent.

If you want to figure out the potential cost for your own transaction, you can go to www.lifecycleinvesting.net, where we have a spreadsheet all set up that takes you through the calculations on a step-by-step basis.

Another Approach

A cheap way to get 2:1 exposure on the S&P 500 index is to buy an E-mini S&P futures contract. Each of these contracts is designed to give you the exposure to 50 "shares" of the S&P 500. If the index goes up 1 point, you make $50. With the S&P 500 trading around 950, each contract gives you exposure to around $47,500 of stock.

The way E-mini futures work is that you don't pay any money up front, except for collateral. When the contract expires, you owe (or collect) the difference between the original purchase price and the price of the S&P 500.[5] Until that point, the price of the E-mini is based on supply and demand. For example, on July 27, 2009, the price for the December E-mini was $975.50, while the S&P index was at 979.26.[6]

Because the E-mini was trading for less than the index, this was like buying the S&P at a slight discount. If the index were to hold steady through December, the buyer of the E-mini would make roughly 3.76 × $50 = $188. (The contract would be bought at $975.50 and sold at $979.26, for a gain of $3.76.) Another way of putting this is that whatever happens to the S&P, it is $188 cheaper to buy the E-mini than the S&P.

However, the buyer of the futures contract again forgoes dividends. Over this time, the buyer is giving up roughly $385 in dividends (assuming a 1.94 percent dividend yield). Thus the net cost is really $385 – $188 = $195. This is a trivial borrowing cost: $195 to get access to $49,000 of stock for four months leads to an implied interest rate of 1.2 percent.

Of course you are required to put up collateral. Since you are buying a futures contract rather than the stock itself, you have to put up money as collateral against losses. The folks at Interactive Brokers require an initial collateral amount of $5,625 (and that at least $4,500 be maintained in your account at all times). Thus, for about $5,000 you get exposure to close to $50,000 of stock market risk. That's a whopping 10:1 leverage for the small time investor.

Don't get carried away and think that you can prudently use index futures to get even closer to your lifecycle target. If the price of the futures contract were to fall, you will quickly need to come up with that collateral. You need to keep at least $4,500. Say that the index fell from 950 down to 500. Over this period, you would need to come up with $450 × 50 = $21,500 of additional collateral. That's why you should have at least this much equity behind each one of the contracts so as to keep the leverage at around 2:1.

The advantage of these contracts is that they provide a cheap form of leverage. A disadvantage is that you may be required to keep putting up money. And you have to pay attention. These contracts only go out a few months, so you will have to regularly roll them over. Unlike the option contracts, if the market were to fall 50 percent and then recover, you wouldn't get the chance to ride the stocks back up, since your position would be closed. Another disadvantage, perhaps more of a nuisance, is that many of the major brokers (such as Fidelity) don't permit futures trading, period. Thus if you want to pursue this approach, you will have to open an account with a company like Lind-Waldock or Interactive Brokers. We've tried them, but at the end of the day, they are too much of a hassle relative to the call option alternative.

Investing with ProFunds UltraBull

Instead of dealing with options or futures to get leverage, there are several mutual funds that are designed to do all the work for you. They apply leverage so as to give you a return equal to twice that of the S&P index.

In practice, the situation is a bit more complicated. First, the funds charge high fees. The ProFunds UltraBull has an expense ratio of 1.50 percent (which is eight times what Vanguard charges on a similar unleveraged index funds). A second issue is that these funds are constantly adjusting their portfolio so that you will maintain 2:1 leverage on a daily basis. This leads to returns quite different than 2:1 leverage that is rebalanced on a monthly or annual basis. In particular, when the market oscillates up and down, that volatility leads to a significant reduction in the performance of their mutual fund.

To explain the issue, let's look at an example. Say that the S&P index starts at 1,000, so the SPDR would be at 100. We follow two investors who each have $1,000 to invest. One, "Margie," uses margin to buy 20 shares of the SPDR, and the other, "PF," gets 2:1 leverage via a $1,000 investment in ProFund's UltraBull fund (which like the SPDR mimics the S&P 500, but with 2:1 leverage). Let's imagine that the S&P index falls from 1,000 to 750 and then rebounds to 1,000.

In Margie's case, she first loses half her investment when the index falls 25 percent, but then gets it all back as the index recovers. She ends up net zero.

In PF's case, when the index falls to 750, the fund rebalances. At this point, he has lost twice the 250 decline in the index, so the value of PF's account is only $500. For his $500 to be leveraged 2:1, he needs to be getting the returns on $1,000 of stock.[7] Unfortunately for PF, when the index recovers to 1,000, his portfolio only gains back $333 (33 percent on a $1,000 portfolio), leaving him down by a net $167.

To maintain 2:1 leverage, ProFunds sells shares when prices fall and buys shares when prices rise. This hurts performance whenever prices bounce around, since ProFunds will be buying high and selling low. On the other hand, if prices move in one direction, then ProFunds' rebalancing will help performance. For example, if the SPDR had fallen from 75 down to 50, then Margie would have lost her entire remaining $500, while PF would only have lost $333 of his remaining $500.

As you can see from this example, ProFund's rebalancing isn't necessarily good or bad; it is just different. Its impact is largely dependent on the path of stock prices, not just the endpoints. Volatility lowers returns for a portfolio that is rebalanced on a daily basis, since this strategy sells when the market is down and buys when it is up.[8] In contrast, rebalancing is helpful to returns when the market moves consistently in one direction. It boosts returns in the good times and acts as a safeguard in the bad.[9]

Rebalancing

The issue of rebalancing isn't limited to ProFunds. Even Andrew Verstein should be rebalancing his portfolio.[10] When Andrew bought the SPY contract in January 2009, the index was at 927. Three months later, the index was at 835, and with that decline the value of his equity stake fell from $4,770 to something like $3,850. Since he was then exposed to $8,350 of S&P, his leverage grew to 2.17.

In theory, Andrew should have sold some stock. They problem is that he can't just go and sell a small amount to bring him back to 2.0. Contracts are sold in units of 100. He could go and close out his trade, recognize the loss, and then rebuy a new LEAP with a strike price closer to 41 or 42. But the transaction costs of doing this type of trade would be prohibitive. Each time he would have to pay the bid-ask spread.

An additional cost of having a small amount to invest is that it makes rebalancing impractical. In the case where prices go up, Andrew would be called on to invest more money. The problem is that he doesn't have more money to invest. He could close out his position and rebalance. The capital gains would provide the additional funds to do so. Provided the account is inside an IRA, taxes wouldn't be an issue. (Outside an IRA, this would be a real problem.) The remaining question is whether the time hassle along with the transaction costs make this worthwhile. Our view is that it isn't worth the cost of small changes in leverage. The goal is to be at 2:1. If you end up at 2.2:1 or 1.8:1, that's close enough. The market needs to move 10 percent before you should worry about rebalancing.

You might have noticed that the nature of the rebalancing above is exactly above the opposite from the traditional rebalancing. If you want to have 60 percent of your current savings in equities and equities fall by 20 percent, then you end up only being 48/88, or 55 percent in equities. Falling prices mean you need to sell some bonds and *buy* more stock.[11]

The traditional target-date funds were buying stock all the way down as the market fell in 2008, and this only added to their poor performance.

In contrast, to obtain constant 200 percent leverage (in Phase I), you should be *selling* shares on the way down (and buying on the way up). As stocks fall, you are indeed getting even further away from your desired Samuelson share, and that would lead you to buy more stocks. But the problem is that with your reduced equity, your leverage rises past 200 percent. The 2:1 leverage constraint says that you need to reduce your holdings.

To sum up, when you are not constrained by leverage, rebalancing requires you to buy additional stock when prices fall and sell when prices rise. However, when you are starting out and thus constrained by the maximum 2:1 leverage, then rebalancing your portfolio leads you to sell shares when prices fall and buy when they rise. When markets make large movements, rebalancing makes a difference. A monthly rebalancing of our 2:1 leveraged portfolio reduced the market losses in 2008 from 76 percent to 64 percent.

Don't get too caught up with rebalancing, either. There are transaction costs and too much rebalancing also means that you end up paying a big price for volatility. You don't need to rebalance more than quarterly, unless there is a big move in the market. In that case, don't get lazy: Failure to rebalance means that your market exposure will get out of whack with your preferences.

> *stickK to Your Goals:* In 2008, Ian co-founded an Internet site which helps people lose weight, quit smoking, even stickK to their financial goals. At stickK.com, you can enter into a binding promise to save $500 a month or to rebalance your portfolio once a quarter—and back up your promise by putting money at risk that will be forfeited if you fail. When you create your savings contract, you can choose who will referee the commitment and you can even choose who gets the money if you fail. As touted at Yahoo Finance, "The idea is that you'll be more likely to stay the course if you stand to lose real bucks (or suffer in other ways) for breaking your resolution."[12] To date, more than 40,000 registered users have risked more than $3 million.

Our theory tells us that you should regularly rebalance your portfolio to take into account changes in the value of your current savings (as well as changes to the present value of your future saving contributions and, potentially, changes to your Samuelson share induced by new expectations about market risk and return). But we're also pragmatists. We realize that most people won't have the mental energy required to rebalance monthly. But quarterly rebalancing is within the realm of reason (we recommend setting up a calendar reminder—and possibly even a commitment contract at stickK.com to make sure you actually follow through). At the very least, you should sit down once a year and make sure that your long-term portfolio is in line with your Samuelson share.

Buying Stock on Margin

The traditional way people obtain leverage (and sometimes get themselves into trouble) is via buying stock on margin. The margin amount is just a loan. An investor with $100 in savings can borrow up to another $100 and thereby purchase up to $200 in stock or stock indices. The broker holds the $200 in stock as security to make sure that the loan is repaid and has the right to require the investor to put up more money if the stock declines in value.

When stockbrokers give margin loans, they in turn borrow from banks at what is known as the "call money" rate. This rate is very close to the risk-free rate. Over the last 138 years, the wholesale cost to brokers of providing this leverage has averaged a mere 34 basis points (about a third of 1 percent) above the average interest on government bonds. While we may think of leveraged investments as risky, leverage does not expose the *lender* to much risk. Indeed, margin interest rates should be lower than mortgage interest rates.

A lender's risk on a margin loan is lower than on a home mortgage because the lender has much more security backing up the loan. A young investor with $6,000 who borrows another $6,000 to buy stock backs up her loan with her $12,000 in stock as security. A home mortgage lender who provides $450,000 for a $500,000 home doesn't have nearly the same security cushion.

Consider the following: Say stocks fall by 25 percent. Then our investor loses $3,000, or half of her money. (Her portfolio is now worth $9,000, leaving her $3,000 after paying off the loan.) The lender has lost nothing and still has $3,000 of equity ahead of him. In contrast, if the home price falls by 25 percent, then the $500,000 house will be down by $125,000. But the borrower only put up $50,000. That means the lender's security is worth $75,000 less than the mortgage owed. If borrower defaults, the lender stands to lose $75,000.

Surprised? Because mortgages are much more leveraged than margin loans, they end up being much riskier for the lender. Moreover, the lender on the margin loan can call the loan if the value of the underlying security starts to decline. If the $12,000 in stocks starts to decline in value, the margin lender has a right to sell the assets long before its price falls below the outstanding loan balance of $6,000. Home mortgage lenders have no comparable right. That's why it should be cheaper to borrow money to buy stock than real estate.

What's really surprising is that many reputable stock brokers charge what seem to be unjustifiably high interest rates for margin loans. For example, on July 22, 2009, Vanguard and Fidelity charged margin rates of 7.75 percent and 8.575 percent, respectively, on small-balance margin loans, even though their cost of funds was only 2 percent. This is closer to the gouging we expect from credit card companies than the low-cost services we usually expect from Vanguard and Fidelity.

Fortunately, much better prices are available if you look around a little. As we write this, Interactive Brokers charges rates as low as 1.65 percent on relatively small loans (and going down to 0.40 percent for larger loans).[13] Their formula is the Fed Funds overnight rate (currently 0.15 percent) plus a premium of 0.25 percent to 1.5 percent depending on the size of the loan. This is almost 7 percent below the rate charged by Fidelity! In our calculations, we assumed investors borrow at the rate that banks offer to brokers (currently 2 percent).[14] This is reasonable for borrowers who shop around for a good rate. It is higher than the rates offered by Interactive Brokers. And it is typically above the implicit interest paid by investors who use options contracts on the S&P index to gain leverage.

Buying Bonds

While our focus is on how to buy stocks with leverage, at some point we expect you will be buying bonds. Alas, even bonds are not entirely without risk. There is a chance of default, which can be minimized by sticking to government bonds. There is also a risk that the return you get won't be worth what you expected because of inflation. In this arena, there is often confusion about which is riskier, a short-term or a long-term bond.

Some think that short-term bonds are riskier because their interest rate fluctuates each time the bond matures and is rolled over. In contrast, a long-term bond locks in the rate. An analogy to mortgages seems appropriate. Investing in short-term bonds is like having a variable-rate mortgage, while investing in long-term bonds is akin to having a fixed-rate mortgage.

While the analogy is apt, the perspective of risk is backward, at least for bonds that aren't inflation adjusted. While a long-term bond does lock in an interest rate, it locks in a nominal rate, not a real one. What you care about is the real interest rate, which is the nominal rate net of inflation. For example, if the bond pays 5 percent nominal interest but inflation is 2 percent, then the real rate for your bond is only 3 percent. If inflation starts up or cools down, the nominal rate will stay put, while the real interest rate you receive will vary, perhaps quite substantially. You care about the real interest rate because ultimately you will be using the bond to pay for part of your retirement. Thus you care about how much stuff you will be able to afford with the proceeds of the bond. If a $100 one-year bond pays 5 percent nominal interest while inflation is 2 percent, then you will only be able to buy 3 percent more stuff when the bond matures. You will get $105, but things will cost 2 percent more.

The interest on short-term bonds fluctuates up and down because of two factors. One is the change in real interest rates, and the second is a change in inflation. Generally speaking, there is more volatility in inflation than in real interest rates. Let's pretend for a moment that real interest rates are constant at 3 percent. If inflation is running at 2 percent, then short-term bonds will offer 5 percent. If inflation rises to 5 percent, then the short-term bond rate will go up to 8 percent. The advantage of short-term bonds is that they mature quickly and so can adjust to changes in inflation.

As for long-term bonds, let's start by going back to the example of a home mortgage. When you take out a thirty-year, fixed-rate mortgage, the "value" of that mortgage varies quite substantially with inflation. If you start out paying 5 percent, and inflation jumps up from 2 percent to 5 percent, then the value of your mortgage (to the holder) will fall by about one-third. You will get to pay back your mortgage with cheaper dollars, and the end result lowers the value of your mortgage. From the lender's perspective, you are still paying 5 percent interest, but that just keeps up with inflation, so it is as if you are paying zero real interest. That is a lot less valuable to the mortgage holder. The holder would have to give someone about a 33 percent discount to take the mortgage off his or her hands.

From the perspective of a homeowner, you tend to think about risk in terms of whether your payments will change or whether you will be able to afford the monthly payment. There is another risk that is more invisible, namely that the economic value of your mortgage will go up or down with inflation. When inflation rises, the economic cost of your mortgage goes down, and when inflation falls, the economic cost of your mortgage goes up. That's why you refinance; when inflation goes down, rates fall, and you can trade your expensive mortgage for a cheaper new one.

Holding a long-term bond is like being on the other side of the equation, except that you can't refinance. If inflation goes up, the long-term bond you hold will shrink in value, and if inflation falls, your bond will appreciate. Short-term bonds don't appreciate or depreciate much with inflation because it is as if they are being refinanced all the time. Thus the rate is adjusting to changes in inflation.

While short-term bonds protect you against inflation, they still expose you to fluctuations in the real interest rate. What you really want is something that locks in a real interest rate. Such an instrument does now exist.

Since 1997, the U.S. Treasury has been selling Inflation Protected Securities or TIPS.[15] The face value of these bonds adjusts with inflation so that it always pays a constant real interest rate.

Consider a $1,000 TIPS bond that promises to pay you 2 percent, or $20 per year (actually $10 paid semiannually). If inflation were 4 percent, the bond could account for it by paying you 6 percent. Instead, what the Treasury does is adjust the principal and say that they now owe you 4 percent more, or $1,040. They pay you interest on that inflated amount, and when the bond matures, you get the extra $40.

The advantage of TIPS is that they lock in a real interest rate. That's why we think the majority of your money in bonds should be in TIPS. The disadvantage is that you owe taxes along the way for the change in principal amount. That's not an issue for a TIPS held in an IRA or 401(k) plan.[16]

In terms of buying TIPS, you have three options. You can purchase TIPS through a mutual fund. For example, the Vanguard Inflation-Protected Securities Fund Admiral Shares (VIPX) has a portfolio of medium-term TIPS and charges only 20 basis points (0.20 percent) in fees. (If you have over $100,000 to invest, the Admiral Shares charge a fee of only 0.12 percent.)

This is the most convenient way to go, as you can buy or sell at anytime. You can also buy or sell any amount. And Vanguard takes care of all the tax accounting, which is surprisingly complicated. (The interest income and principal growth are exempt from state and local income tax.)

A second option is to buy the TIPS directly from the Treasury. This avoids the commission fees and allows you to specialize in one particular maturity length. The downside is that the government only holds four auctions a year, and not all maturities are available every time. The simplest way to proceed is via an online account with the Treasury at www.treasurydirect.gov. You place a bid, specifying the amount of TIPS you want to buy (in $100 increments).[17] The TIPS will be purchased at the next available auction. The Treasury will also facilitate the sale of TIPS in your account. They use the Federal Reserve Bank of Chicago as the sales agent and charge a $45 fee. You can also buy TIPS via your brokerage account, with commission of course.

The Treasury also issues Series E bonds on which the interest rate adjusts with inflation. However, the government limits the amount of these bonds you can buy to $5,000 per Social Security number. And, worse still, the promised real interest rate on these bonds is only 0.10 percent.

In the near future, we hope that new mutual funds will make the leveraged lifecycle approach automatic. In the meantime, we know that the foregoing leveraged approaches can be done, because we've tried them all. We've used OptionsXpress to purchase long-term options on the S&P 500 and Interactive Brokers to buy Vanguard's Extended Market Index on margin. Ian has money in the ProFunds leveraged UltraBull fund. (He has even used LindWaldock to dabble in stock index futures). We're not getting paid to say this, but we're fans of OptionsXpress and Interactive Brokers. Ian's IRA is at OptionsXpress and he likes how easy it is to manage both his options and his mutual fund portfolio in a single account. And as we've already said, Interactive Brokers offers extremely competitive margin rates for those who want to buy stock index products partly with borrowed money.

CHAPTER 9

What If Everyone Did It?

IMAGINE IT IS the year 2020. The stock market has rebounded from the crash of 2008, and investors have seen a decade of steady high returns. And while we're dreaming, imagine that this book has succeeded beyond all imagination. Leveraged lifecycle funds have become the dominant vehicle for retirement savings. Tens of millions of young people have their 401(k) savings invested on a 2:1 basis and have been reaping the rewards of the stock market run-up.

But all is not rosy in this best of all possible worlds. Some analysts claim that the stock market run-up is fueled in large part by the artificial increase in demand from the leveraged funds. And they are even more worried by the escalating cost of leverage, as margin rates have grown with the increased demand for leverage.

And then calamity strikes: On March 23, 2021, a 7.3 earthquake hits California, its epicenter merely eight miles from Los Angeles. "Only" 1,800 people die, but the city is a wasteland and completely immobilized. The next day, the S&P opens down 12 percent. By the afternoon, young investors are receiving margin calls—and lacking cash, they start cashing out their leveraged positions. The market is awash with sell orders, and soon prices are in a free fall (which leads to further waves of margin calls and stock sales). Instead of dropping the 20 percent one might anticipate in response to such a serious natural disaster, the stock market loses a cataclysmic 70 percent of its value.

In retrospect, it all seems so obvious. Leveraged purchase of stock left us vulnerable to massive financial dislocation in 1929. Leveraged purchase of housing and hedge funds left us vulnerable to massive financial dislocation in 2008. And now, just thirteen years later, leveraged purchase of retirement accounts has yet again plunged us into a wholly avoidable meltdown. Is this leveraged-induced Chernobyl a real possibility? And if so, shouldn't Ayres and Nalebuff be stopped before they unleash this disaster on America and the world?

Not so fast. The last two chapters have tried to focus on individual investors. They've been a kind of "how to" analysis of what you should do. Unlike other books, we walked you through reasons why our lifecycle strategy may not be for you. And we provided some tools to help you figure out how your money should be invested. But to answer the Armageddon question, we need to shift the unit of analysis. Instead of asking whether you should follow a lifecycle strategy, we now want to ask what the likely systemic effects are if a large number of people drink our lifecycle Kool-Aid. What are the larger social implications of a big increase in the amount of stock market leverage?

Before we address these issues, we should make two points clear. Current financial markets aren't set up for everyone to employ our strategy. When Andrew bought his call option, he was one of the 171 contracts outstanding in the market. If it turns out that thousands and then tens of thousands of people want to follow our advice, we will see new and more efficient ways of obtaining leverage. The simplest would be for an increase in funds like ProFunds Ultra Bull, which seek to mimic twice the return of the S&P.

The other point to keep clear in your mind is that right now you don't have to ask the question about if everyone did it. There's little danger that our book will instantly lead millions of people to invest with leverage. A simple idea like target-date funds took fifteen years to reach $200 billion in assets.[1] There is a lot of inertia when it comes to investing. Thus when it comes to making up your mind about following our advice, your only question should be whether this will work for you.

We think the leveraged lifecycle approach is a good strategy for individuals as well as for the economy as a whole. Thus we are prepared to defend it as good public policy. We think government regulators should facilitate rather than restrict this option to investors. That's the case we now proceed to make. As a first step, we take a look at how the housing market adapted to a massive increase in leverage in the 1930s created by the Federal Housing Administration.

A History of Housing Leverage

Looking to the future is important. But as we saw with George Bailey in *It's a Wonderful Life*, you can often learn a lot about the future by thinking about the past. Interestingly enough, a core part of that heartwarming movie is a paean to housing leverage. The Bailey Bros. Building & Loan Association does, after all, let people invest money that they don't have—to take leveraged positions in their houses. In a particularly moving interchange, the villainous Mr. Potter (played by Lionel Barrymore) chides George Bailey (played by Jimmy Stewart) for lending money to a cab driver:

> Potter: Now, you take this loan here to Ernie Bishop. . . . You know, that fellow that sits around all day on his brains in his taxi. You know . . . I happen to know the bank turned down this loan, but he comes here and we're building him a house worth five thousand dollars. Why? . . .
>
> George Bailey: What'd you say just a minute ago? They had to wait and save their money before they even thought of a decent home. Wait! Wait for what? Until their children grow up and leave them? Until they're so old and broken-down that they . . . Do you know how long it takes a working man to save five thousand dollars?[2]

Potter's idea that workers should save the price of the house *before* buying seems otherworldly. But it comes close to describing the reality of realty in pre–New Deal America.

Before the Great Depression, homebuyers often had to make down payments of 50 percent or more of the purchase price. This was for the privilege of borrowing the remainder for five or ten years. There was no such thing as a thirty-year mortgage. And what's more, these mortgages had variable interest rates and hefty balloon payments due at the end of the mortgage term. Working stiffs like Bert the cop and Ernie the taxi driver (who gave rise to the characters on *Sesame Street*) would have had to wait and save if they were going to have any chance of buying a house.[3] This was a world that Mr. Potter would have loved.

But all of this changed with the New Deal. Starting in 1933, the Home Owner's Loan Corporation (HOLC) purchased more than a million mortgages that were in default—converting them from short-term, balloon mortgages to twenty-year, amortizing fixed-rate mortgages. Shortly thereafter, the newly created Federal Housing Administration (FHA) followed suit by guaranteeing new home loans that were fully amortizing twenty-year mortgages with fixed interest rates. What's more, these loans only required a 20 percent down payment—meaning that buyers could now buy a house that cost five times more than what they had saved.

Until then, people thought it would be wildly imprudent to make a twenty-year loan with 5:1 leverage. But these long-term, high-leverage loans did not blow up. And make no mistake—FHA loans were a big deal. By 1937, FHA loans underlay almost half of all housing starts.

Academics debate whether or not the loans increased housing prices or the volatility of the housing market, but the bigger picture is one of relative stability in housing for the remainder of the twentieth century.[4] The success of the initial loans was so great that in 1948 the FHA increased the maximum term to thirty years and in 1956 increased the loan-to-value ratio to a whopping 20:1. What's more significant is what didn't happen. From 1935 through 2000 the United States undertook a massive increase in housing leverage, and the world did not come to an end. There was no financial apocalypse. In fact, as emphasized in the introduction to this book, the story of housing leverage underscores the success of temporal diversification. With the help of leverage, young families were able to expose themselves much more substantially to the housing market for many more years. And even though this exposure is badly diversified across assets, it is so well diversified temporally that millions of families in the twentieth century were able to safely invest in their homes on a leveraged basis—transforming the family home into one of Americans' most important retirement assets.

Back to the Future

Of course, the housing market has not been nearly so stable since the turn of the millennium. Housing prices rose 80 percent from 2000 to 2006 but have lost more than a third of their value since then.[5] And with the fall in prices, foreclosures have soared to record highs—rising 27 percent from November 2007 to November 2008.[6] Much of the current crisis is a direct by-product of leverage. Why keep paying on a mortgage when the outstanding principal that you owe is much greater than the value of the house? It seems that the chickens have finally come home to roost. The ongoing housing crisis seems like strong prima facie evidence that leverage is bad for the economy. For the sake of the nation's macroeconomic long-term health, we should take a pass on the leveraged lifecycle strategy.

We disagree. "All good things in moderation" is a popular adage for a reason. The fact that 5:1, 10:1, or even 20:1 leverage worked well for decades on home purchases doesn't mean that we should embrace 50:1 leverage. But that's just what happened during the irrational exuberance of the housing boom.

Ian remembers hearing Harvard Law School professor and bankruptcy guru Elizabeth Warren give a paper back in 2005 that claimed—in a footnote—that the down payments for first-time homeowners were miniscule, just 2 percent.[7] Ian was so sure she was wrong that he (rather obnoxiously) kept pestering her about the footnote, even during the postseminar dinner. Ian thought that there was no way that banks would loan money with virtually no equity cushion. But guess again. According to the *Washington Post*, "4 out of 10 first-time buyers used no-money-down mortgages in 2005 and 2006, according to surveys by the National Association of Realtors."[8] And the median down payment for first-time buyers in those years was just 2 percent. With so little of their own money at risk, it shouldn't be a wonder that many borrowers default when housing prices decline.

Would you want to keep paying on a $200,000 mortgage, when the house is only worth $150,000?[9]

While stratospheric leverage on initial mortgages certainly helped cause the current foreclosure epidemic, it isn't the only culprit. The problem has been exacerbated by the trend for homeowners to remain highly leveraged, even years after they buy. The increased prevalence of "interest-only" loans and the increased tendency to take out second and third mortgages, which pull out any accumulated equity as the first mortgage is being paid off, have increased systematic risk. In the old days, if housing prices dropped 10 percent, most homeowners would keep paying on their mortgages—because they'd have much more to lose if they walked away. But in 2007, a 10 percent drop caused many homeowners with no skin in the game to walk away.

The macroeconomic misery of the current housing crisis is not a reason to give up on the sizeable benefits of temporal diversification in your retirement portfolio. Our leveraged lifecycle does *not* ask people to buy stock at 50:1 leverage. We don't suggest leveraging at the Eisenhower FHA housing standard of 20:1, or even the New Deal standard of 5:1. We only suggest 2:1 leverage, which is equivalent to buying a home mortgage with 50 percent down. In that light, 2:1 leverage seems rather conservative.

What's more, our leveraged lifecycle ramps down. Unlike in the housing crisis, where a large proportion of homeowners remained highly leveraged with the help of second mortgages and interest-only loans, we've proposed a system where fifty- and sixty-year-olds invest decreasing fractions of their savings in stocks. If millions follow our advice, they will be ramping down at different times. Twenty- and thirty-year-olds will be highly leveraged on small amounts, while fifty- and sixty-years-olds will have no leverage on large amounts. The 2008 drop in housing prices sparked a massive sell-off in housing securities. But under our system, an analogous drop in the stock market will not cause a massive sell-off of stocks, since at any point in time the majority of the money invested in the market will not be money that was borrowed with leverage.

This circle of life—with the young investing more than 100 percent of their savings in stock and the old investing less than 100 percent of their savings in stock—also helps explain why this book doesn't imply a massive increase in the population's stock holding at any particular point in time. Sure, the young hold more stock. But our core idea of spreading your market risk more evenly over time means that some investors will be holding less stock when they are in their fifties and sixties. Particularly, those who shift from a constant 75 percent in stock throughout their lives are likely to end up holding less. And older investors, who have less than 100 percent in stock, become an important indirect source of the funds available to lend to younger investors. This produces what economists call "overlapping" generation effects, in which the old, by delevering and investing in bonds, both free up the stock for the young to buy and provide the loans with which they can make the purchase.

We don't want to run away from the fact that there still might be a net increase in the demand for stock. After all, once investors understand that they have a new technology to handle risk, it is natural that some will react by taking on more risk. These investors will still ramp down—but on net they may end up holding more stock over the course of their lives.

At the end of the day, we don't know about how well the stock market could absorb a net increase in the demand for stock. Some academics, like Nobel Prize winner Myron Scholes, have long argued that stock prices will tend to be pinned down by fundamentals.[10] For Scholes, the price of stock should be largely unaffected by changes in demand not related to the fundamental value of the corporation. Other academics, however, have documented price impacts for demand shocks not related to fundamentals. For example, firms are added to the S&P 500 index not because the S&P thinks they're a good investment, but because the firm is thought to be representative of the market. Nonetheless, being added to the index causes an increase in demand for the stock as index funds suddenly need to buy and hold some of the newly included firm's stock.[11] An announcement that a firm is included, contra the Scholes hypothesis, generally increases the firm's stock value by 3 percent. If there is a net increase in the overall demand for stock induced by leveraged lifecycles, there might be a positive impact in the price of stock (and an associated decrease in the subsequent expected returns).

Still, in gauging your reaction to this proposal, keep in mind how powerfully we've been conditioned to fear buying stock on margin. When a popular investment book in 1999 advised thirty-year-olds to increase the proportion of stock in their portfolios to 95 percent (even if they only had "moderate" risk tolerance), no one worried about the untoward macroeconomic consequences of a net increase in the demand for stock.[12] A large part of the reaction to our proposal is caused not by the higher total demand for stock, but by our audacious suggestion that investors break the glass ceiling of a 100 percent stock allocation.

The most important reason not to be concerned about these possible negative system reactions is that our strategy is designed to be self-limiting. If things start to go wrong, people will substitute away from the strategy. This is easiest to see with regard to the cost of borrowing. If massive borrowing (directly or indirectly through the implicit loan of derivatives) drives up the margin rate of interest, the increased rates will naturally turn off the demand for leverage. The cost of borrowing on margin is the real cost of implementing our lifecycle strategy. If the cost of diversifying increases, Economics 101 teaches that people should demand less of it. Thou shalt never borrow at a 10 percent interest rate to buy stock with an 8 percent expected return. We've shown that, historically, it's been dirt cheap to employ 2:1 leverage, either through option contracts or more recently through margin loans at online brokers. Even during the credit crunch, the implicit cost of borrowing through deep-in-the-money calls has remained well below the cost of home mortgages. But if this changes in the future, investors will know it and can reduce their borrowing accordingly.[13]

An analogous dynamic is also true, with regard to changes in the expected risk and return in holding stock. If a sizeable number of shareholders switching to our strategy causes a reduction in the expected return or an increase in the expected volatility of stock, then under our strategy investors would respond by buying less stock. More specifically, investors with more pessimistic expectations about risk and return would lower their Samuelson share, which (along with their present value of current and future savings) crucially determines their investment target.

But how will you know in advance if the world has changed? We only have historical data from the preleveraged world. It is not really self-limiting if you don't know enough to pull away from the table. Or, conversely, it would be a terrible invitation for undisciplined investing if we asked investors to individually assess what they feel the future prospects of the market are. But there are objective factors that can be used to update your expectations about prospective risk and return.

Indeed, Shiller's application of market P/E 10 (described in Chapter 4) provides just such an objective factor. Imagine that the popularity of leveraged investing increases the net demand for stocks and starts artificially driving up the price. Many might think that higher stock prices would be a good thing. But higher prices without higher underlying corporate earnings might mean that stock returns are likely to be lower in the future. That's just what Shiller found. When the price-earnings ratio was unusually high, the future stock return tended to be substantially lower. Investors using a P/E–adjusted lifecycle strategy would naturally reduce their Samuelson share if the price-earnings ratio ballooned. Reducing the Samuelson share is also appropriate if the expected volatility in the market increases. Normally the standard deviation on the return in the S&P 500 is 20 percent, but in late 2008 the Volatility Index (VIX) briefly swelled to more than 80 percent. During periods of such excess volatility, adjusting Samuelson shares downward would be a smart move. While making the appropriate adjustments based on the P/E or the VIX is not for the casual investor, the important point is that the adjustments can be based on objective information and made in a disciplined way that limits the macroeconomic impact when macroeconomic variables—concerning systemic risk or return or margin costs—start turning south.

The most important way in which our proposal is self-limiting is that we've explicitly counseled certain people not to use it. Over 45 percent of American families maintain revolving credit card balances and hence are ill-suited to follow our advice (or at least should only do so after they've gotten their financial act together and paid off their credit cards).[14] Others will be excluded because they don't have the requisite $4,000. We don't have sufficient data to accurately assess the proportion of the population that meet our disparate qualifications. But in a country where fewer than a third of households directly own stock or mutual funds, we're confident that well less than half the population are prime candidates for the leveraged lifecycle strategy.[15] Our strongest response to the "What if everyone did it?" question is that unlike most investment books, we're telling some people, "This idea isn't for you." If everyone started buying stock on margin, many of them wouldn't be following our advice.

So our strategy is self-limiting, not only in that it closes down when objective systematic measures contraindicate buying stock on margin, but also in that it identifies contraindicating factors for individual investors. Taking 50 percent of the population off the table serves to further insulate the system from any untoward impacts of mass migration.

Of course, even if we are advising certain types of people to stay away from the lifecycle strategy, it is possible that they will ignore our advice. The seduction of the ultrahigh returns of leveraged portfolios during bull markets may lure inappropriate adoption of the strategy. We are loath to stand behind the defense: "But that's not what we said." As a matter of policy, it seems appropriate to tailor legal rules to make it harder for the wrong types of investors to pursue leveraged purchases. But it is equally important for the law to make it easier for the right types of investors to take advantage of diversifying time.

Diversification Is Dangerous

Put all your eggs in one basket, and then watch that basket.

Andrew Carnegie[16]

Before diving into the gnarly question of legal reform, let's look back and see what we can learn from the history of the legal regulation of diversification. Of course, we don't have much history on the regulation of temporal diversification—because until this book, nobody had really proposed it. To be sure, people have been buying stock on margin for a long time. But most of these margin investors were short-term speculators trying to make a quick buck on a hoped-for run-up in the price of individual stocks.

No one has advocated buying stock indices on margin as a long-term strategy to diversify temporal risk.

There is, however, a rich legal history concerning asset diversification. Asset diversification is the core message of most of today's investment books. If you're a trustee and you fail to diversify the trust's assets, you have some explaining to do. Everyone knows that it's presumptively wrong to put all your eggs in one basket. But you might be surprised to learn that the law did not always look so kindly on the idea of diversification. It's hard to believe, but there was a time when the trustees could get in trouble for diversifying risk by dividing their portfolio into investments in different kinds of stock. The trouble all started in 1719, when the British Parliament, in response to a generalized joint-stock investment frenzy, permitted trustees to make equity investments in the South Sea Company, which had been granted a monopoly right to trade with Spain's South American colonies.[17] The price of stock in the South Sea Company had been skyrocketing upward, and everyone, including trustees, wanted to get in on the action. But the trouble with bubbles is that they eventually pop. The South Sea bubble popped in 1720, sending the stock price down to less than a tenth of its peak value.

Parliament and the Court of Chancery reacted with a vengeance, shutting off the ability of trustees to invest in stock of any kind. Instead of risky equities, trusts were limited to investing solely in a list of preauthorized types of government bonds. Of course, all this happened in the remote past. But this "safe asset" approach to trust investment has had a long hold on both British and U.S. law. The "legal list" remains in effect in the UK today. Only in 1961 did Parliament reform its trust statute to allow trustees to invest half of trust portfolios in stock. And as late as 1986, Alabama and Montana had constitutional provisions prohibiting trust investment in stock.[18] After the South Sea bubble, the law strongly presumed that capital preservation was the dominant goal of trustees, and opportunities for capital appreciation and diversification were both largely neglected.

How do you make a small fortune?
Give a bank a large one to manage in trust.

Old trust joke[19]

Things began to change in 1830, when the Massachusetts Supreme Judicial Court rejected the legal list approach in a case involving a gift to Harvard College. Upon his death, John McLean left $50,000 under the management of the executors of his will, a portion of which was to be given to Harvard College and Massachusetts General Hospital. As the trustees of his estate, the executors invested some of this money in private securities that declined in value. Though Harvard and Mass General challenged the trustees' ability to invest the trust in stock, the court rejected their claims and established a new standard for determining when trustees could invest in stock: "[Trustees must] observe how men of prudence, discretion and intelligence manage their own affairs, not in regard to speculation, but in regard to the permanent disposition of their funds, considering the probable income, as well as the probable safety of the capital to be invested."[20]

This standard quickly became known as the prudent man rule. And sexism aside, you might have thought that it would open the door to diversified investments in equity. As prudent investors learned the value of diversification over time, trustees "considering the probable income as well as the probable safety" of various investments would be free to buy a broad market basket of stocks.

But the legalization of asset diversification was a long time coming. It took more than a hundred years for a majority of U.S. states to adopt the prudent investor standard. And even under the more flexible prudent man approach, trustees who invested in a diversified portfolio of stocks ran a risk of personal liability. The biggest obstacle to diversification was the tendency of courts to analyze trustee prudence on the basis of individual investments in a portfolio rather than the portfolio as a whole. For example, in 1974 the New York Court of Appeals found: "The fact that this portfolio showed substantial overall increase in total value during the accounting period does not insulate the trustee from responsibility for imprudence with respect to individual investments for which it would otherwise be surcharged."[21]

The unwillingness of many courts to look at the prudence of a portfolio as a whole worked to chill the hearts of trustees who might have considered diversification. After the fact, courts would wonder why a trustee was willing to invest in a company that obviously was going to lose money. It's all too easy for a court to look at a loss after the fact and call the investment "speculative." Understanding this, trustees took the path of least resistance and tended to stick to the legal list of government and corporate bonds.

Indeed, there was still a need in 1976 for two University of Chicago law professors to publish an article calling for the ability of trustees to invest some of the trust's assets in stock index funds. One of these professors was the great Richard Posner, the most prolific and most cited law professor and judge in U.S. history. The other author was John Langbein—the same friend who, as we saw in Chapter 3, has been a persistent skeptic of temporal diversification. One of the great ironies is that while Langbein keeps seeing flaws in our efforts to promote temporal diversification, he himself was one of the most effective champions of asset diversification.

Another irony is that in arguing that trustees should be allowed to invest in index funds—such as the recently created Vanguard 500 index—Langbein and Posner were forced to respond to some of the same skepticism that we face in arguing that trustees should be allowed to invest in temporally diversifying lifecycle funds. Indeed, a major section of their 1976 article is titled "What If Everybody Did It?"

It's hard to imagine that people ever thought of index funds as dangerous. But back then many people argued that merely allowing trust investments in index funds threatened to undermine the stability and efficiency of market pricing. Roger Murray, a distinguished professor from Columbia Law School, published an article providing "five reasons why it is fair to say that the index fund is an idea whose time has passed." Langbein and Posner's critics worried that if everyone bought and held baskets of stocks, there would be no one left to find the efficient price for individual stocks.*

---

*The price of each individual stock should be determined by the price that equates supply and demand for that stock. But if all stocks are bought and sold together regardless of price (because they are all in the index), then there isn't any mechanism to set the price of one stock relative to another. It would be like going out to a restaurant and have everyone point to the person next to him and saying: I'll have what he's having. Without someone actually ordering, the waiter wouldn't know what to bring.

Langbein and Posner responded to this criticism by raising arguments that closely parallel the self-limiting arguments that we raised in the last section:

> Those who argue that the stock market might be rendered inefficient by a pell-mell rush to invest in market funds ignore the inherently self-limiting character of the process whereby investment assets are being shifted into market funds. If the process ever reached the point where it rendered the market inefficient, this would imply the existence of opportunities for investors to increase portfolio performance by research and trading. Some investors (though not necessarily trustees) would increase their search activities to take advantage of these opportunities, and the higher level of such activities would restore market efficiency.

These "if everyone did it" arguments are often specious. If everyone were a professor, we would starve. If everyone were gay, humankind would come to an end. Yes. But in each case, there are natural self-limiting responses to keep the systems away from the extremes. We also think Langbein and Posner's argument concerning ripeness is apt here: "At a time when less than two-tenths of 1 percent of the nation's stockholdings are in [stock index] funds, it is premature to argue against further adoption of the concept—and indeed against the concept itself—on the ground that if 100 percent (or perhaps some lesser fraction) of the nation's investment assets were so managed, the stock market would cease to be efficient." Even if leveraged lifecycles are successful beyond our wildest imaginations, we would be a long way from the point at which we would need to worry about dire systemic effects.

A final parallel between the Langbein/Posner agenda and our proposal is worth exploring. While their article sought merely to grant trustees the option to adopt a buy-the-market investment strategy, another section of their article flirted with the notion of imposing a duty to diversify:

> We think we should conclude our review of the trust law by warning fiduciaries that they cannot "play safe" by ignoring the new learning and

continuing uncritically to put trust money into old-fashioned, managed portfolios. . . . A trustee who declines to procure [diversification] advantages for the beneficiaries of his trust may in the future find his conduct difficult to justify.

We think that analogous arguments will ultimately support a duty to diversify across time. But before turning to our own reform agenda, it is useful to share the good news of the Langbein revolution. You see, John Langbein was not content to simply urge reform from the sideline. He was a major player in the statutory reform movement itself. As reporter (that is, primary author) of the 1994 Uniform Prudent Investor Act, John succeeded in flipping the legal presumption with regard to diversification.[22] Under the proposed model law, trustees had a duty to diversify. Section 3 demands that the "trustee shall diversify the investments of the trust unless the trustee reasonably determines that, because of special circumstances, the purposes of the trust are better served without diversifying." The official comments make clear that a trustee can only avoid the duty if diversification would create special tax obligations or impair a goal of retaining control of a family business. The act is also explicit in rejecting the idea that prudence should be assessed on the basis of individual investments. Under the act, a "trustee's investment and management decisions respecting individual assets must be evaluated not in isolation but in the context of the trust portfolio as a whole." The official Comment says: "An investment that might be imprudent standing alone can become prudent if undertaken in sensible relation to other trust assets, or to other nontrust assets."[23] (Of course, an analogous argument applies to temporal diversification. Buying stock on margin when you're young "might be imprudent standing alone [but] can become prudent if undertaken in sensible relation to other" investments when you are older.) The Uniform Act has seen tremendous legislative success. Forty-six states have adopted John's handiwork (and the remaining four have adopted a nonuniform version that embraces the reasonableness of asset diversification).

The final great irony here is that the same John Langbein, whose skepticism has spurred us on to more exacting proofs of temporal diversification, advanced strikingly similar arguments twenty years ago on behalf of the legal reforms to support asset diversification. It's hard to think that there was a time when the law did not actively encourage asset diversification. But there was such a time, and indeed that time was not so very long ago.

The Future Regulation of Asset Diversification

This history of asset diversification teaches us that we should worry about the costs of overregulation that chills legitimate investment attempts by financial advisors to temporally diversify investor exposure to the market. Just as the prudent investor rule misapplied on an individual asset basis chilled asset diversification, there is a nontrivial chance that the same rule could be misapplied on an individual-year basis to chill temporal diversification.

Indeed, with regard to leveraged positions, this chance of overregulation is even larger because margin transactions have even more preexisting regulation.[24] The Federal Reserve's Regulation T caps the amount of leverage at the time of the original purchase to be no more than 2:1 by requiring that no more than 50 percent of the initial purchase price be funded by borrowing.[25] Stock exchanges as "self-regulating organizations" additionally require that broker-dealers adopt a 25 percent "maintenance margin requirement," which means that subsequent to the initial sale a margin call will be triggered if the outstanding loan balance exceeds 75 percent of the stock's current market value. The SEC also requires broker-dealers to obtain a signed "margin agreement" from investors: "Obtain from such person information concerning his financial situation and needs, reasonably determine that the entire transaction, including the loan arrangement, is suitable for such person, and retain in his files a written statement setting forth the basis upon which the broker or dealer made such determination."[26]

The requirement that brokers and financial advisors determine the "suitability" of leveraged transactions poses hurdles for brokers wanting to help their clients take advantage of the benefits of lifecycle investing. The New York Stock Exchange has a "Know Thy Customer" rule that requires broker-dealers to know the financial situation of their customers.

Members must: "Use due diligence to learn the essential facts relative to every customer, every order, every cash or margin account accepted or carried by such organization and every person holding power of attorney over any account accepted or carried by such organization."[27]

This will be a challenge for young investors looking to follow our strategy. Even if a broker got to know Andrew Verstein, under the current rules he would have trouble certifying Andrew's leveraged strategy to be "suitable." The National Association of Securities Dealers requires that its members "have reasonable grounds for believing that [any] recommendation is suitable" for their customers. Security dealers must "make reasonable efforts to obtain information concerning: (1) the customer's financial status; (2) the customer's tax status; (3) the customer's investment objectives; and (4) such other information used or considered to be reasonable by such member or registered representative in making recommendations to the customer."[28]

To appropriately determine whether a specific stock transaction is suitable for a specific customer, a broker must assess the customer's risk-return objectives and make sure that the risk and return of the stock in question further those objectives.[29] Brokers that recommend stocks that are inconsistent with customers' investment objectives can be disciplined by losing their licenses and by having to make good on losses for ill-advised transactions.[30] Indeed, the SEC has concluded that "as a fiduciary, a broker may only make recommendations that are in the best interests of his customer, even when the recommendations contradict the customer's wishes."[31] For example, in one disciplinary proceeding, the SEC found a broker liable for making recommendations that furthered a client's expressed investment objective of doubling her money: "Even if Wang had desired Pinchas to double her money, that desire would not have relieved Pinchas from his duty to recommend only those trades suitable to her situation."[32] Thus, brokers face some suitability risk even if they are instructed by a client to undertake transactions that a subsequent tribunal deems to be unsuitable for this type of investor.

Brokers have frequently been disciplined for recommending margin trades. Often in these cases the investors state that their primary investment objective is the preservation of capital. The broker, notwithstanding this object, trades the client's account on a leveraged basis and incurs substantial losses after a drop in stock prices.[33] We favor a continuation of suitability requirements and in fact believe that they should be extended explicitly to cover commodity brokers. But just as the prudent investor rule was modernized to take account of advances in asset diversification, both the suitability and prudent investor rules should be modernized to take account of advances in temporal diversification.

This does *not* mean that recommending leveraged transactions is always prudent or suitable. Brokers should still know their customers. If a person is nearing retirement, buying stock on margin is presumptively imprudent. Indeed, Chapter 6 can be reframed as a primer on suitability. If starting out leveraged is contraindicated by any of the six factors in that chapter, it should not withstand suitability analysis. If a person does not have precautionary savings, or has accrued substantial credit card debt that carries a high interest rate, they should not be borrowing to buy stock.

Under a modern view, an investment objective of preserving capital is not inconsistent with a disciplined, ramping-down approach of buying stocks on margin when the client is investing for the long run. Before this book, few regulators would have concluded that buying stock on margin when you are young can reduce risk. Hence a leading book on broker regulation warned: "[A] registered representative could breach his or her suitability obligations by recommending . . . that a customer with an objective of long-term capital appreciation use significant margin loans to purchase securities."[34] But of course the major conclusion of this book is that using margin loans to purchase such securities can be entirely appropriate and "suitable" for young investors.

While tailoring the legal rules of suitability could establish margin sales as a powerful and appropriate way to channel non–tax-deferred investments, the Holy Grail of temporal diversification would be to permit leverage inside defined contribution accounts: the all-important 401(k)s. In 2008, nearly 50 million Americans had approximately $4.5 trillion dollars invested in 401(k) accounts. This is where investors have the greatest potential to take advantage of lifecycle investing.

Dollars contributed to 401(k) plans are quintessentially the kind of savings that are intended to be invested for long-term retirement goals. These plans discourage early withdrawals with a 10 percent penalty (unless the withdrawal is for a narrow set of hardship circumstances, such as death, disability, or medical expenses).[35] A leveraged lifecycle that automatically ramps down from 2:1 leverage when you're young to a fairly conservative 50 percent stock allocation at retirement would make it easy for individuals to implement a disciplined, long-term diversification strategy across both assets and time.

But before we can convince employees to sign up for lifecycle investing in their 401(k) accounts, we first have to convince employers that offering the investment won't blow their safe harbor. You see, ERISA (the Employee Retirement Income Security Act), which governs 401(k) investments, protects employers from any liability for imprudent investment choices made by employees—but only so long as the employer offers a prudent menu of 401(k) investment options. An employer has "an ongoing fiduciary duty to consider the suitability and prudence of all of the selected investment options."[36] To immunize themselves from liability, employers offering employee-directed plans must offer at least three diversified investment alternatives, with "materially different risk and return characteristics."[37]

Under the conventional understandings of leverage, an employer offering a leveraged lifecycle fund would run the risk that a court would hold the employer liable after the fact for failing to "consider the suitability and prudence" of an offering that allows employees to mortgage their retirement savings. To qualify for the safe harbor, an employer's investment alternatives must give employees the opportunity to diversify their investments "so as to minimize the risk of large losses."[38] The court, seeing a sizeable short-term drop in an employee's nominal investment balance caused by the employee's leveraged position, might (mistakenly to our minds) find that the employer was imprudent to offer the leveraged option.

Such a finding would be mistaken, because as we've shown the leveraged lifecycle is an important tool to reduce lifetime investment risk.

The central mistake here is looking at losses on a year-by-year basis. Just as earlier courts erred in judging asset diversification on an asset-by-asset basis, it is wrong to judge temporal diversification by looking at the returns in individual years. The goal of a fiduciary is to produce the right mix of risk and return in the final retirement accumulation. Accordingly, we should judge a leveraged lifecycle by the distribution of likely accumulations it will generate when the employee is likely to withdraw them.

The Department of Labor could be an important player in the development of temporal diversification. A letter ruling or regulation signaling that the DOL does not consider leveraged lifecycles (which start modestly at a 200 percent stock allocation and ramp down to traditional unleveraged allocations) to be per se imprudent or unsuitable would go a long way toward encouraging this type of diversification. We are not so naïve to believe that such a letter will be immediately forthcoming. It may take a decade of experience with an actual fund investing in IRA rollover and non–tax-deferred funds to convince regulators of the prudence of giving employers the option of offering a leveraged lifecycle alternative. But like John Langbein before us, we plan to be in there pitching. In a world where employers are free to offer truly poor long-term investments—low-return bonds that virtually guarantee that you'll do worse in the long run—it's hard to understand why it would be so dangerous to let employers offer a leveraged lifecycle as an additional investment alternative.

We also foresee a time where fiduciaries may not be able to play it safe by ignoring the new learning about temporal diversification. If the results of seasoned leveraged lifecycles bear out the theories that we have propounded, employers will run the risk of being held liable if they do not offer employees the opportunity to better diversify risk. Indeed, under existing law, an employer's investment alternatives must "enable the [employee] to achieve a portfolio with aggregate risk and return characteristics at any point within the range normally appropriate for the [employee]."[39] In the not too distant future, courts may determine that failing to offer employees the option to diversify temporally fails just this test. Tomorrow's normally appropriate risk and return characteristics may look very different when traditional retirement vehicles are compared to life-cycle investing.

It wasn't that long ago that most employees had to opt-in to invest in a company 401(k) plan. Now the default is moving to opt-out. And the default investment option used to be a money market fund—the lowest return option but also almost risk-free. Now the default investment choice is moving toward target-date funds, which put young investors at up to 90 percent in equities. We can see the default shifting so that young investors are put 100 percent in equities and kept there for a longer time. As people see the value of increased equity exposure when young, they will begin to question the artificial 100 percent barrier, especially when they see the results of investors who are following our advice on their own.

The Goal Line

In the end, what are our aspirations in writing this book? In some ways, it's simple. We want to put time diversification on the same footing as asset diversification.

In 1952, Harry Markowitz formalized a theory of asset diversification. He derived the crucial equations that showed how adding an additional asset to a portfolio affected the expected risk and return. The "Markowitz bullet" is possibly the most famous curve in all of finance—mapping out the efficient frontier of investments that trade off risk and return for investors with different risk preferences. But more than just creating a theoretical hypothetical, Markowitz developed a quantitative algorithm for mean-variance optimization that concretely suggests what proportion of portfolios should be placed in different asset classes. The Markowitz approach is still used today by portfolio managers, such as Yale's own David Swensen.[40] When it comes to asset diversification, Markowitz took the prize—literally. He won the Nobel Prize in economics in 1990 for developing precise analytic and quantitative tools for the intuitive idea that you shouldn't put all your eggs in one basket.[41]

John Bogle brought the benefits of Markowitz diversification to the masses. In 1975, as chairman of the Vanguard Group, Bogle launched the first index mutual fund, the Vanguard 500 Index Fund.[42] It was Bogle who created the vehicle by which small investors could cheaply diversify. Because the Vanguard Index funds passively tracked the index stocks, these were cheaper to manage than actively-managed funds. Bogle's decision to have low minimum balances, no-load funds, and razor-thin costs democratized diversification. Suddenly ordinary investors could expose themselves to hundreds of stocks. It's not coincidental that it was 1976 when John Langbein and Richard Posner called for the ability of trustees to invest in passive stock index funds. They published just a year after John Bogle had created the necessary vehicle. Hundreds of thousands of retirees owe Bogle a debt of gratitude. Just this past year, the Vanguard Group passed Fidelity to become the largest mutual fund company in the world.[43] If there were a Nobel Prize for contributions to humanity, John Bogle would be a worthy recipient.

It's a tall order, but we want to follow in the footsteps of Markowitz and Bogle. We'd like to do for temporal diversification what these two giants did for asset diversification. Like Markowitz, we have tried in this book and in our academic writing to develop new tools for diversifying across time. People already intuited that it would be foolhardy to expose themselves to the stock market for just a single year of their life. And target-date funds have long understood that stock portfolios should ramp down as investors got closer to retirement. But as with pre-Markowitz investing, precise techniques for how to ramp down were lacking. Instead of the birthday rule, which was pulled from thin air with little theoretical or empirical justification, we have attempted here to derive and defend a better ramp-down allocation to diversify across time. Ours isn't the last word to be written about improving temporal diversification. It's just a step in the right direction.

In many ways, this book is merely an elaboration of an insight that Paul Samuelson had in 1969: You should allocate your investments based on your lifetime wealth, not just your current savings. A simple idea, and yet its impact is profound. While this is an idea that doesn't seem like it should be controversial, forty years later few have been willing to take it to its logical conclusion: Most young investors should employ leverage. Few even seem willing to meet this insight halfway and advise young investors to start off 100 percent in equities. We take some heart in the fact that views can be changed. Back when we started college, buying index funds was still thought to be imprudent.

Like Bogle, we are also working to bring temporal diversification to the masses. The starting point is to change perceptions. But we also need to make it much easier to follow the leveraged lifecycle path. We have taken the ideas in this book and worked to turn them into a practical investment vehicle. With the help of Yale's Office of Research Development, we've filed a business method patent. We've even started working with a mutual fund provider and hope to create a buy-and-hold vehicle for retirement savings that will automatically diversify investments across time.

And finally, we hope to follow in the footsteps of our beloved critic, John Langbein. We still may not have convinced John about the virtues of temporal diversification. But we want to emulate the actions of his younger self, who was a pivotal player in modernizing the law of asset diversification. It was John Langbein who banged the drum to usher trust law into the twentieth century. It was John Langbein who, as reporter for the Uniform Prudent Investor Act, flipped the presumption in virtually every state to mandate that fiduciaries diversify trust assets. As this chapter has shown, a parallel movement in law reform needs to take place with regard to time diversification. As with asset diversification, trustees and employer fiduciaries need first to have the option of offering these investments without risk of personal liability. And as Langbein suggested in 1976 with regard to asset diversification, we hope ultimately to flip the default. In the end, fiduciaries should have a presumptive duty to diversify across both assets and time.

These are tall orders—to develop the theory, to create real-world investment vehicles, and to change the law. But we hope this book shows that we've made a good start. And with titans like Markowitz, Bogle, Samuelson, and Langbein, we have excellent exemplars to lead the way.

NOTES

Introduction

1. Yale University Office of Public Affairs, "Yale Releases Endowment Figures," 9/22/2009, http://opa.yale.edu/news/article.aspx?id=6899.

2. Ian Ayres & Barry Nalebuff, "Mortgage Your Retirement," *Forbes* 150 (Nov. 14, 2005).

Chapter 1

1. Paul A. Samuelson, "Lifetime Portfolio Selection by Dynamic Stochastic Programming," *Review of Economics and Statistics* 51 (1969): 239–246; Robert Merton, "Lifetime Portfolio Selection Under Uncertainty: The Continuous-Time Case," *Review of Economics and Statistics* 51 (1969): 247–257; and Robert Merton, "Optimum Consumption and Portfolio Rules in a Continuous Time Model," *Journal of Economic Theory* 3 (1971): 373–413.

2. Paul Samuelson, "The Long-Term Case for Equities," *Journal of Portfolio Management* (Fall 1994): 1, 21.

3. Archimedes famously said, "Give me a long enough lever and a place to stand, and I will move the world."

4. See money.cnn.com/2009/01/30/markets/markets_newyork/index.htm.

5. In making this calculation and subsequent calculations, we assume that the pre-fee return on the portfolio is 8 percent. You can try your own fee experiments at https://personal.vanguard.com/us/funds/tools/costcompare.

6. Unfortunately, Templeton is not alone. Consider the Oppenheimer Transition 2030 fund. After paying up to a 5.75 percent fee to join this fund, they take out another 1.93 percent annually in fees. Well, not quite. For the time being they are capping the fees at 1.5 percent. You can avoid the upfront sales charge by buying B shares in the fund. Those shares have annual expenses of 2.81 percent, but for the time being are capped at 2.25 percent. For an investor with $300,000 and a twenty-year horizon, these fees come out to a staggering $511,000, $256,000 in direct fees and another $255,000 in lost profits.

7. Second place goes to Fidelity. Their Freedom Fund 2030 invests in a broad collection of other Fidelity funds. While Fidelity doesn't charge anything for making this allocation, each of the component funds has its own charge, and this averages out to 76 basis points. While 76 basis points might seem like a small amount, for an account with $300,000 over twenty years, this adds up to $198,000 in direct fees and lost profits.

8. Both the Fidelity Freedom Funds and Vanguard's Target retirement funds start with 90 percent in stocks and 10 percent in bonds and gradually move to a fifty-fifty allocation at retirement. The initial ramp-down is slower than linear; for example, Vanguard stays at 90 percent through age forty; see https://flagship.vanguard.com/VGApp/hnw/content/Funds/FundsVanguardFundsTargetOverviewJSP.jsp.

Chapter 3

1. If you are wondering how we ended up with ninety-six cohorts, note that our last cohort starts working in 1966 and retires forty-four years later at the end of 2009, just before turning sixty-seven. Thus we have ninety-six full cohorts of data—people who started working in 1871 through those who started in 1966.

2. For 2009, we use the June 30 data as the end-of-year level.

3. Our model investor's wage profile is based on the "scaled medium earner," as developed by actuaries at the Social Security Administration and used by Robert Shiller in his 2005 paper, "The Life-Cycle Personal Accounts Proposal for Social Security: An Evaluation." All wages are in (estimated) 2011 dollars and income beyond age sixty-four is held constant. Finally, we scale the entire wage profile by 2.35 to make the final income level equal to $100,000.

4. The size of Social Security depends on income. For someone who earns $50,000 at retirement, Social Security will replace roughly 35 percent of his or her income, 10 percent more than for someone with $100,000 earnings at retirement. Because Social Security is a bigger portion of retirement wealth for people with lower incomes, when we don't take it into account, our 200/83 strategy automatically becomes more conservative for investors with lower incomes.

5. See online.wsj.com/article/SB124148722378286001.html.

6. Michael Maiello, "Active Retirement Planning," Forbes.com, April 24, 2009, www.forbes.com/2009/04/23/active-401k-ira-intelligent-investing-stocks.html.

7. Brad M. Barber and Terrance Odean, "Trading Is Hazardous to Your Wealth: The Common Stock Investment Performance of Individual Investors," *Journal of Finance* 55, no. 2 (2000): 773–806; Brad M. Barber and Terrance Odean, "Boys Will Be Boys: Gender, Overconfidence, and Common Stock Investment," *Quarterly Journal of Economics* 116, no. 1 (2001): 261–292.

8. Kenneth R. French, "The Cost of Active Investing," working paper, 2008, http://ssrn.com/abstract=1105775.

Chapter 4

1. James Lindgren, "Telling Fortunes: Challenging the Efficient Markets Hypothesis by Prediction," *Southern California Interdisciplinary Law Journal* 1 (1992): 7–38 (describing a model to test stock market efficiency over a twenty-five-year period).

2. The 10,000 simulations were drawn from a lognormal probability distribution in which we set the mean of the log of return and the log of the standard deviations to the historical average of the log of the returns (6.13 percent) and the standard deviation of those logs (17.31 percent). The lifecycle final allocation of 32.1 percent was chosen to equalize the average returns of the two strategies.

3. Elroy Dimson, Paul Marsh, and Mike Stauton, *Triumph of the Optimists: 101 Years of Global Investment Returns* (Princeton, NJ: Princeton University Press, 2002).

4. The geometric mean of the equity premium for this period is just below 4 percent; the arithmetic mean of the equity premium is 5 percent. The arithmetic mean tells us much stocks outperformed bonds in any one year while the geometric mean tells us how much stocks outperformed bonds on a compounded basis over the whole sample. Our Monte Carlo simulation uses a lognormal distribution and matches the log of returns which, in effect, uses the geometric mean of returns.

5. Malcolm Gladwell, "Blowing Up," *New Yorker*, April 22 and 29, 2002.

6. He recommends that stock forecasters "get another job." Nassim Nicholas Taleb, *The Black Swan* (New York: Random House, 2007), 163.

7. Taleb has suggested that people should invest 85 percent of their investments in super-safe government bonds and reserve just 15 percent of their portfolio for riskier stock plays. He reasons that, no matter what you do, you can't lose more than 15 percent of your investment. Somewhat surprisingly, there is a way to follow both his advice and most of ours, too. With derivatives such as futures and options on stock indexes, it is possible to expose twelve times your investment in the market. Following Taleb, you could invest 85 percent of your portfolio in government bonds, leverage the remaining 15 percent at 12:1, and come close to producing an overall portfolio that implements our 2:1 advice. The problem with this approach is that investing with 12:1 leverage for several years imposes too great a risk of margin calls (or a risk that your options will expire out of the money and be worthless). In other words, it's too great a risk that you will just end up with 85 percent of your portfolio.

8. Just to be extra clear, the all-on/all-off form of investing is in conflict with what we mean by diversifying over time. Holding 100 percent in equities in January and 100 percent bonds in February has both more risk and a lower return than holding 50 percent stocks across both months. Paul Samuelson debunks this schizophrenic strategy in his article "Asset Allocation Could Be Dangerous to Your Health," *Journal of Portfolio Management* 16, No. 3: (1990): 5–8.

9. Because the P/E ratios are based on 10 years of historical earnings, we've lost the first 10 years of our observations and reduced the number of cohorts from 96 to 86.

The accumulation statistics for the unadjusted target strategy, the birthday rule, and the constant % stock strategy are slightly different than in previous tables because of this disparity in the number of cohorts analyzed.

10. Paul Samuelson, "The Long-Term Case for Equities," *Journal of Portfolio Management* 21, no. 1 (1994): 5–24.

Chapter 5

1. His future savings add 50 percent to his current amount. To hit 83 percent of 150 percent, he needs to invest 125 percent of his current amount.

2. We are using the same 138 years of stock data, but now our cohorts are investing from birth to retirement—not just during their working lives. That reduced our number of cohorts down to seventy-three from ninety-six. Our first cohort was born in 1871, started working in 1894, and retired in 1937.

3. Devlin Barrett, "Clinton: $5,000 for Every U.S. Baby," Associated Press, September 28, 2008, www.breitbart.com/article.php?id=d8rulmjo0&show_article=1.

4. Tony Blair, "The Saving Grace of the Baby Bond," *Guardian*, April 10, 2003, www.guardian.co.uk/politics/2003/apr/10/budget2003.policy. The Child Trust Fund website, www.childtrustfund.gov.uk, describes in detail the different account options that have been made available.

5. Bruce Ackerman and Anne Alstott, *The Stakeholder Society* (New Haven, CT: Yale University Press, 1999).

6. Francisco J. Gomes, Laurence J. Kotlikoff, and Luis M. Viceira, "Optimal Life-Cycle Investing with Flexible Labor Supply: A Welfare Analysis of Life-Cycle Funds," *American Economic Review* 98, no. 2 (2008): 297–303.

7. Our 83 percent Samuelson share came from equating the downside risk to the 75/75 strategy. In the next chapter, we show how this share is connected to risk preferences. An 83 percent share is optimal for investors who have a constant relative risk aversion (CRRA) of 2; the Gomez simulation assumes a CRRA of 5. This is discussed more in Chapter 6.

8. To the extent you want to leave a bequest to your kids, if you are invested in stocks, what's leftover will be connected to the market. This indirectly but quite effectively gives your kids and grandkids exposure to the market at an early age.

9. For someone who retires with a $100,000 salary, Social Security will replace some 25 percent of income and slightly more on an after-tax basis given the tax preference of Social Security income. To purchase an inflation-protected annuity that would yield the same payouts would cost something like $500,000. Our average retiree starts out with $1.2 million. But 83 percent of 1.2 million is $1 million, which is only 59 percent of the retiree's total wealth of $1.7 million. For people with incomes below $100,000, Social Security constitutes an even higher fraction of the total wealth, and so the effective percent in the market would be lower still.

10. NGO Monitor, Ford Foundation, www.ngo-monitor.org/article/ford_foundation.

11. Sources for Table 5.3 and text: Ford FY 2008 Financial Statements, www.fordfound .org/pdfs/about/FF_FY_2008_Financial_Statements.pdf; Rockefeller 2007 Annual Report, www.rockfound.org/library/annual_reports/2007rf_ar.pdf; MIT Report of the Treasurer for year ended June 30, 2008, http://vpf.mit.edu/site/content/download/ 4720/23831/file/FY08%20TR%20FINAL%20-%20web%20version.pdf; Yale Financial Report 2007–2008, www.yale.edu/finance/fr/finrep07–08.pdf and The Yale Endowment 2008, www.yale.edu/investments/Yale_Endowment_08.pdf.

12. In a weaker, post–9/11 economy, Yale saw a decrease in alumni giving, resulting in a $30 million budget deficit for 2007. Says Charlie Pagnam, vice president for development, "It is the donor's decision when to make a gift, and when the economy is not strong, that will have a negative effect." Brian Bowen, "Yale Faces Troubling $30m Budget Deficit," *Yale Herald*, January 30, 2004, www.yaleherald.com/article.php? Article=2844.

13. The source for 2008–2009 contributions to Yale is an email dated 9/9/09 from Shirley Chock of Yale's Dept. of Financial Reporting. For MIT, see MIT Annual Fund Annual Report 2008–2009 5-Year History, http://giving.mit.edu/annual_report/results/ five_year_history.php.

14. This logic does not apply to most corporations. Even if corporations can expect profits coming in the future, their shareholders will not want the corporations to engage in temporal or asset diversification because the shareholder can diversify these risks for themselves.

Chapter 6

1. We contacted MT after reading about his experience on Bogleheads.org, a website where disciples of Jack Bogle discuss investment strategy.

2. See www.indexcreditcards.com/creditcardmonitor/.

3. Since the interest you pay on a credit card isn't tax deductible, everything you save is in after-tax dollars. That's why the return is entirely tax-free. In contrast, if you pay off a home mortgage, the interest was tax deductible and so, the two effects cancel out. If you can deduct the interest you pay, then not having to pay the mortgage saves you pretax dollars. Actually, not all mortgage interest ends up being deductible (due to AMT or limits on deductions), in which case paying down the mortgage saves you some post-tax interest.

4. Even this dictum has exceptions. If your employer matches contributions to a 401(k) plan, then the value of that match could outweigh the credit card interest. If you put $10,000 in the plan and your employer matches on a 1:2 basis (or better), then you will be starting with $15,000. That 50 percent head start will justify paying a 14.67 percent rate. And to the extent that your plan permits, you might be able to borrow against your 401(k) account to pay down your credit card debt.

5. For most income levels you won't be able to contribute to *both* a 401(k)/403(b) plan and a traditional IRA. The rules are more liberal for a Roth IRA.

6. As we'll discuss in Chapter 7, it is unlikely that you will find a call option that is so deep in the money as to provide 1.43:1 leverage.

7. www.parentplusloan.com/plus-loans/plus-loan-interest-rate.php.

8. John Heaton and Deborah Lucas, "Portfolio Choice in the Presence of Background Risk," *Economic Journal* 110, no. 460 (2000): 1–26. This is an area of active research; see John Campbell and Luis Viceira's *Strategic Asset Allocation: Portfolio Choice for Long-Term Investors* (Oxford: Oxford University Press, 2002).

9. Vladyslav Kyrychenko, "Optimal Asset Allocation in the Presence of Non-financial Assets," working paper, 2007, www.schulich.yorku.ca/SSB-Extra/NorthernFinance .nsf/Lookup/Vlad%20Kyrychenko/$file/Vlad%20Kyrychenko.pdf.

10. At the other extreme, Benzoni, Collin-Dufresne, and Goldstein provide conditions under which a risk-averse (g=5) young worker may actually want to *short* equities. The reason is the high cointegration of the labor and equity markets. In their model, wages depend on profits, and so the young risk-averse worker is already overinvested in the market through her human capital; see Luca Benzoni, Pierre Collin-Dufresne, and Robert S. Goldstein, "Portfolio Choice over the Life-Cycle When the Stock and Labor Markets Are Cointegrated," *Journal of Finance* 62, no. 5 (2007): 2123–2167.

11. See Moshe Milevsky, *Are You a Stock or a Bond? Create Your Own Pension Plan for a Secure Financial Future* (Upper Saddle River, NJ: FT Press, 2008), and Huaxing Huang, Moshe Milevsky, and Jin Wang, "Portfolio Choice and Life Insurance: The CCRA Case," *Journal of Risk and Insurance* 75 (2008): 847–872.

12. This is very much in line with our thinking, though we cap leverage at 200 percent. How much leverage the actual forty-five year old should employ will also depend on how much he's been saving and how well the market has performed.

13. An example illustrates the effect. Say the market were to fall 10 percent in each of four consecutive months. At the end of the drop, the market would be at 63 percent of its initial level, or down 37 percent, similar to what happened in 2008. A portfolio that rebalances each month would fall by 20 percent each month and thus end up at $0.80^4 = 0.41$, or 59 percent down. The market didn't just fall continuously in 2008 and so rebalancing only reduced the losses to 64 percent.

14. As we'll discuss in Chapter 7, to cover your Social Security gap and buy an inflation-protected annuity that leads to 70 percent replacement income, you will need to have more than seven times your final salary in your retirement account. (The size of the Social Security gap depends on your income level—the 7x corresponds to $75,000.) If your savings only generate a 0.10 percent real return, then over a forty-four-year working life, you would need to save 15.2 percent of your income. This is under the assumption that your income remains constant over your whole life. This is well beyond the reach of most families. To make matters worse,

this is more than what you are allowed to contribute to a 401(k) or an IRA, and so much of this would have to be done on an after-tax basis. In short, this is an impossible dream.

15. One dollar contributed each year and growing at 1.589 percent will accumulate to $65 over forty-four years. With a constant income stream, 1 percent of income contributed each year will accumulate to a retirement pool equal to 65 percent of income. For someone who seeks seven times or 700 percent, that means they will have to contribute 10.8 percent of their income each year. Our calculations line up with the Bodie and Clowes approach, with one exception. In their framework, the retiree sets aside enough money for a fixed number of years, say twenty or twenty-five, and then the money runs out. We have the person buying an annuity that pays out for as long as he lives (and 67 percent thereafter for his partner) and has inflation protection.

16. Of course, were you to follow our strategy and sock away 10.8 percent, then you would have a staggering likelihood of success. On average, you would be retiring with so much money that your savings would equal thirty-three times your final income (instead of around twelve times). That would buy an inflation-protected annuity that offers 175 percent of your final salary, to add to whatever you'll also be getting from Social Security.

17. With these savings, you can buy an inflation-protected annuity that replaces 17.3 percent of your income. For someone with $70,000 final salary, Social Security payments will replace 32.3 percent of your income, and so in total you can replace almost half your income, far below the recommended 70 percent replacement level. If your final income is closer to $100,000, than the 26.8 percent from Social Security will get you to 44.1 percent, only 63 percent of the recommended level.

Chapter 7

1. This survey question was developed by Robert Barsky, F. Thomas Juster, Miles Kimball, and Matthew Shapiro.

2. Robert Barsky, F. Thomas Juster, Miles Kimball, and Matthew Shapiro, "Preference Parameters and Behavioral Heterogeneity: An Experimental Approach in the Health and Retirement Study," *Quarterly Journal of Economics* 112, no. 2 (1997): 537–579.

3. While this equation is an approximation that holds for small amounts of risk, it is an exact answer for the case of constant relative risk aversion and a risky investment that follows Brownian motion. The intrepid can find a derivation of this formula at lifecycleinvesting.net. See Robert Merton, "Lifetime Portfolio Selection Under Uncertainty: The Continuous-Time Case," *Review of Economics and Statistics* 51 (1969): 247–257.

4. These numbers are based on Shiller's annual stock dataset, available on his website: www.econ.yale.edu/~shiller/data/chapt26.xls.

5. Until recently, it was thought that the equity premium was higher post-1926. But once 2008 is factored in, the equity premium ends up lower.

6. Future volatility is no easier to predict than the equity premium. Indeed, uncertainty about the equity premium is a component of long-run volatility. This point was made in recent work by Ľuboš Pástor and Robert Stambaugh. There are two risks we face when investing. The first is that the market may not provide the historical equity premium of 5.04 percent. The second is that the equity premium might not actually be 5.04 percent. The first is a short-term risk in that we expect fluctuations around the mean in any given year. Even if we know that stock will outperform bonds by 5.04 percent on average, in any given year the results could be better or worse. The second risk comes from the fact that we don't really know the value of the equity premium. If the market underperforms for many years, it could be that we were just unlucky, but it could also be that the equity premium is now smaller than we previously thought. As a result of this uncertainty, the long-run variance of stocks may be as much as 50 percent higher than the short-term variance. A counter to this argument is that other factors work to reduce stock volatility. Specifically, stocks have exhibited some amount of negative correlation in returns. After a market crash, the fundamentals look good, and this leads to a recovery in prices. In that sense, stocks are different from a roulette wheel. If you bet on 36 Red and lose, there is no sense in which you are likely to do better next time. But with stocks, there is a real business underlying the stock. Overall, we expect that the value of stocks will reflect the aggregate productivity and profitability of the companies listed. To the extent that the economy falls on hard times, this tends to help firms cut costs and improve productivity. Similarly, hard times lead to reduced entry and capacity, which sets the stage for price increases when the economy turns around. These features help stabilize stock prices over the long run.

7. Over a two-week period, the standard deviation for stocks is about 3.5 percent. The expected movement is then $0.035 \times \sqrt{(2/\pi)}$, or just about 3 percent.

8. Charles J. Cicchetti and Jeffrey A. Dubin, "A Microeconomic Analysis of Risk Aversion and the Decision to Self-Insure," *Journal of Political Economy* 102, no. 1 (1994): 169–186.

9. Most of the time (94 percent) you will end up ahead $5.40, which is worth $5.08. The other 6 percent of the time, you will be down $49.60, which amounts to an expected $2.98 loss. Thus you will be up $2.10 on average.

10. In their scare-tactic letter, the Regional Water Authority (of Connecticut) says that "repairs can easily cost you up to $5,000." At $60 annually, this is a good deal only if the chance of a break is above 1.2 percent, or 1 out of 83. Do you know anyone who has had a water line break in the last year? If you know more than eighty-three people, and none of them did, that suggests the probability is below 1.2 percent.

11. Edi Grgeta, "Estimating Risk Aversion: A Comment on 'A Microeconomic Analysis of Risk Aversion and the Decision to Self-Insure' by Cicchetti and Dubin," working paper, 2003.

12. A combination of a lower tax rate and not having to put money aside for savings allows retirees to maintain similar spending on a lower income. They are also in a better tax position. Social Security payments are entirely tax-free for married couples with outside income below $22,000 and Social Security payments below $20,000. Even in the worst case, only 85 percent of their benefits will be taxable. To the extent that retirees have posttax savings to draw on, those will obviously be tax-free. Money taken out of a 401(k) plan will be taxed, but generally at a lower rate because of their reduced income.

13. Laurence J. Kotlikoff and Scott Burns, *Spend 'til the End: The Revolutionary Guide to Raising Your Living Standard—Today and When You Retire* (New York: Simon & Schuster, 2008).

14. See www.ebri.org/surveys/rcs/2007.

15. We doubt Social Security will go away, but the benefits might all become subject to taxation, and there might be a higher retirement age and lower caps, too.

16. The calculator is available at www.ssa.gov/OACT/quickcalc/index.html. The numbers shown are for someone retiring at age sixty-seven in 2009. This slight delay in retirement age leads to a small increase in benefits today. By 2027 this will be the "normal" retirement age, and so benefits won't be enhanced at that point.

17. If you fund the annuity with the money in your 401(k) plan or your IRA, then the money going in is all pretax (or *qualified* in the lingo). All of the annuity payments will then be taxed as income. In that event, you may find that 70 percent of your preretirement income translates to less than your previous posttax income level. To the extent that you are able to fund the annuity with posttax money, some of the payments you receive will be treated as a return of principal and thus will be untaxed.

18. The pricing of an annuity depends on the expected lifespan of the annuitant(s). Thus the price is higher when payments continue over the lifespan of two people (even with the survivor payment reduced to 66.67 percent). The annuity payments for a single sixty-five year old man are about twenty-five percent higher and this implies that roughly 20 percent less savings are required to finance the same income replacement level of a single man rather than a couple.

19. Strictly speaking, Vanguard is only the retail arm for the annuity. Annuities can only be sold by life insurance companies. The numbers in the text are based on a quote provided by Vanguard on May 22, 2009, on an annuity provided by AIG; see www .aigretirementgold.com/vlip/VLIPController?page=RequestaQuote. As this example makes clear, one of the risks associated with an annuity is that the provider may not outlive you. Fortunately, there are State Guarantee agencies that provide a backup, generally $100,000, though some go to $300,000 and above. You also have the option of splitting your annuity purchase between a few different providers, thereby limiting your exposure to any one firm and taking better advantage of the State Guarantee Agency.

20. The inflation-protected annuity starts out with a 22 percent lower initial payment. Over time, it catches up and surpasses the constant payment option. For example, if inflation runs at a constant 3 percent, it will take roughly nine years for the two payments to be equal and twenty years for the initial losses to be offset. However, if inflation heats up to 5 percent, then the two streams will cross after six years, and after eleven years the inflation-protected product will have provided the higher total payout. The point, however, is not to bet which product is the better deal. Instead, the point of the inflation-protected annuity is insurance—it provides you more money in the event that there is inflation, and thus you need higher payouts to maintain your standard of living.

21. In the case of long-term care needs, it may also be possible to structure an annuity in such a fashion that allows an institutionalized spouse to be eligible for long-term care under Medicaid while leaving the other spouse with income after the death of the institutionalized spouse. If two equal annuities are purchased, one for each spouse, this effectively provides a 50 percent survivor benefit, and if purchased early enough may also insulate half the combined annuity stream should one spouse need long-term care. The rules surrounding a Medicaid-qualified annuity are complex and vary by state; you should consult an elder-law attorney for advice.

22. The numbers also scale up perfectly if you change your rate of savings. If you put aside 5 percent rather than 4 percent, then your numbers will be 125 percent of the above.

Chapter 8

1. You might also be worried about the case where you forget to exercise on the expiration date. Life happens. The good news is that most brokerage houses will automatically exercise any option that is worth some minimum amount. For example, Fidelity automatically exercises all options that are at least 1¢ in the money. You should check to see what rule your broker uses.

2. The "sophistication" requirement could block some young investors from pursuing either the option or margin alternatives—some brokerage houses seem to require savings and prior stock trades to qualify.

3. He is also getting some small amount of benefit from the fact that he can't lose more than $47.70 a share. Were the SPDR price to fall by more than 50 percent over the two-year period, Andrew would come out ahead by not exercising the option. However, the chance of that outcome is quite small, small enough that we will ignore it in our calculation. By ignoring the small value of the option, it will appear that he is paying a higher interest rate (as we are attributing all of the incremental cost as implied interest).

4. The option holder pays $404.50 upfront plus another $500 to exercise for a total of $904.50, which was below the index price of $911.23. There is also a $10 commis-

sion to trade this contract, but the contract is for 100 shares, so this adds just $0.10 to the total cost per share. A screen shot of the index and options prices is available at www.lifecycleinvesting.net.

5. On the third Friday of the contract month, the contract is settled based on what is called the Special Opening Quotation (SOQ) of the S&P 500 Index.

6. A benefit of the futures contracts is that they are traded nearly 24/7; the $975.50 price was the trading price at the 4:00 PM close of the NYSE.

7. Since the SPDR is at 75, that means getting the returns on 13.3 shares, not 20 shares. The ProFunds portfolio responds to the drop in prices by selling 6.7 shares, leaving 13.3 of the initial 20 shares.

8. In a research paper developed for the Chicago Board of Trade, Richard Co shows that the loss grows exponentially at the rate of $2Ts^2$, where T is the number of days and s^2 is the daily variance of the index; see "Leveraged EFTs vs. Futures: Where is the Missing Performance?" available at www.cmegroup.com/trading/equity-index/files/Leveraged_ETFs.pdf.

9. You might think that an answer to this problem is to stop all the extra effort and not rebalance. That would be a fine approach if everyone investing in the fund were to buy their shares all on the same day (and then sell together as well). The problem arises when people buy in at different prices. PF bought in $1,000 when the market was at 1,000, so the fund held 20 shares for him. If the market falls to 75, PF only has $500 of capital left, but, absent rebalancing, the fund still has 20 shares, which is exposure to $1,500 of stock. That means PF is now leveraged at 3:1, not 2:1. If a new investor were to come in, and the fund didn't rebalance, then the new investor would have to invest at 3:1 leverage. Either the fund has to rebalance, or new investors will face a different degree of leverage based on the current stock price.

10. In our simulation, we assumed that the portfolios were rebalanced on a monthly basis. We also did the calculations assuming that the rebalancing took place just once a year and the result were nearly identical.

11. If you are not maximally leveraged, then you increase leverage when stocks fall. For example, if you have total present plus future savings of $400,000 and a Samuelson share of 50 percent, then you would like to be $200,000 in equities. We'll look at the case where you have $150,000 in present savings so you can achieve the goal with 1.33:1 leverage. Now if stocks fall by 10 percent, then your total savings falls by $20,000, to $380,000, leaving you with a desired stock allocation of $190,000. Meanwhile, your current portfolio is only worth $130,000. You can still hit the $190,000 target by increasing your leverage to 46 percent. In essence, it is as if you are buying exposure to another $10,000 of stock.

12. Walter Updegrave, "Fool Yourself into Saving Smarter" (March 11, 2008) http://finance.yahoo.com/retirement/article/104599/Fool-Yourself-Into-Saving-Smarter.

13. One of the ways that Interactive Brokers keeps costs down is by eliminating margin calls. If margin requirements are not met, Interactive Brokers may liquidate

positions in your account without notifying you or allowing you to choose which positions should be sold.

14. The rates are as of July 22, 2009; see www.newyorkfed.org/markets/omo/dmm/fedfundsdata.cfm and http://individuals.interactivebrokers.com/en/accounts/fees/interest.php?ib_entity=llc.

15. Canada has something similar, called Real Return bonds.

16. If you are holding TIPS outside a tax-sheltered account then the advice needs to be modified. Once inflation gets to be above 3 percent, the after-tax real return on TIPS starts to be negative. In that case, short- and medium-term municipal bonds can provide a better inflation hedge. What we'd really like to see is an inflation-adjusted muni bond.

17. Unless you really, really know what you are doing, you should place what is called a noncompetitive bid. This guarantees that you will win at the auction and gives you the average interest rate from the winning competitive bids. If you do choose to place a competitive bid, you will need to specify the interest rate that you require. The government allocates their supply first to the noncompetitive bids and what remains to the competitive bids with the first units going to lowest interest rates.

Chapter 9

1. See www.marketwire.com/press-release/Barclays-Global-Investors-918094.html and http://online.wsj.com/article/SB123549381087960625.html.

2. Wikiquote, *It's a Wonderful Life*, http://en.wikiquote.org/wiki/It's_a_Wonderful_Life.

3. This section is based on the history of mortgage lending that can be found in the following sources: William W. Bartlett, *Mortgage-Backed Securities: Products, Analysis, Trading* (New York: New York Institute of Finance, 1989); Daniel Immergluck, *Credit to the Community: Community Reinvestment and Fair Lending Policy in the United States* (Armonk, NY: M. E. Sharpe, 2004); Raymond A. Jensen, "Mortgage Standardization: History of Interaction of Economics, Consumerism and Governmental Pressure," *Real Property, Probate and Trust Journal* 7 (1972): 397–434; Richard K. Green and Susan M. Wachter, "The American Mortgage in Historical and International Context," *Journal of Economic Perspectives* 19, no. 4 (2005): 93–114.

4. Owen Lamont and Jeremy C. Stein, "Leverage and House-Price Dynamics in U.S. Cities," *Rand Journal of Economics* 30 (1999): 498–514; Jacob L. Vigdor, "Liquidity Constraints and Housing Prices: Theory and Evidence from the VA Mortgage Program," NBER Working Paper No. 10,611, 2004.

5. Wikipedia, Case-Shiller Index, http://en.wikipedia.org/wiki/Case-Shiller_index.

6. RealtyTrac, "The Latest Updated Foreclosure Rates," www.realtytrac.com/foreclosure/foreclosure-rates.html.

7. Elizabeth Warren, "The Over-Consumption Myth and Other Tales of Economics, Law, and Morality," *Washington University Law Quarterly* 82 (2004): 1485–1512. The footnote in question was note 56 on page 1497.

8. Nancy Trejos, "In Pursuit of a Down Payment," *Washington Post*, November 3, 2007.

9. Ian Ayres, "What We Still Don't Know About the Mortgage Crisis," *New York Times*, October 10, 2008, http://freakonomics.blogs.nytimes.com/2008/10/10/what -we-still-dont-know-about-the-mortgage-crisis/.

10. Myron S. Scholes, "The Market for Securities: Substitution Versus Price Pressure and the Effects of Information on Share Prices," *Journal of Business* 45, no. 2 (1972): 179–211.

11. Anthony W. Lynch and Richard R. Mendenhall, "New Evidence on Stock Price Effects Associated with Changes in the S&P 500 Index," *Journal of Business* 70 (1997): 351–383.

12. "Intelligent Investor III," WallStraits.com, June 7, 2006, http://articles.wallstraits .net/articles/1413.

13. More specifically, your Samuelson share declines as the margin rate rises above the risk-free rate. This means that you can have two Samuelson shares—one for the phases of your life when you are leveraged and a second, higher one for periods in your life when you are unleveraged. We've shown formally how our strategy changes with two Samuelson shares, including the appearance of a new lifecycle phase in which investors have a 100 percent stock allocation, in our paper "Life-Cycle Investing and Leverage: Buying Stock on Margin Can Reduce Retirement Risk," NBER (National Bureau of Economic Research) Working Paper No. 14,094, 2008.

14. Brian Bucks et al., "Recent Changes in U.S. Family Finances: Evidence from the 2001 and 2004 Survey of Consumer Finances," *Federal Reserve Bulletin* 2006: A30.

15. Liz Pulliam Weston, "The Big Lie About Credit Card Debt," *MSN Money*, July 30, 2007, http://articles.moneycentral.msn.com/Banking/CreditCardSmarts/TheBig LieAboutCreditCardDebt.aspx.

16. Andrew Carnegie, *The Empire of Business* (Toronto: W. Briggs, 1902), 17: "The concerns which fail are those which have scattered their capital, which means that they have scattered their brains also. . . . 'Don't put all your eggs in one basket' is all wrong. I tell you 'put all your eggs in one basket, and then watch that basket.'"

17. Our discussion of the history of leverage owes a large debt to the work of Langbein and Posner. See John H. Langbein and Richard A. Posner, "Market Funds and Trust-Investment Law," *American Bar Foundation Research Journal* 1 (1976): 1–34; John H. Langbein and Richard A. Posner, "Market Funds and Trust-Investment Law: II," *American Bar Foundation Research Journal* 2 (1977): 1–43; as well as Charles Mackay, *Extraordinary Popular Delusions and the Madness of Crowds* (Radford, VA: Wilder Publications, 2003); Richard S. Dale, "Financial Markets Can Go

Mad: Evidence of Irrational Behaviour During the South Sea Bubble," *Economic History Review* 58 (2005): 233–271; Lawrence M. Friedman, "The Dynastic Trust," *Yale Law Journal* 73, no. 3 (1964): 554; and Peter Temin and Hans-Joachim Voth, "Riding the South Sea Bubble," *American Economic Review* 94 (December 2004): 1654–68. "Historically, trustees were restricted by law to the very safest forms of investments (in many states trustees were limited to certain categories of securities), couldn't delegate to investment specialists the oversight and direction of funds, and were prohibited from diversifying funds in any trust account." Charles H. Breeden and Brian C. Brush, "The Plaintiff as Victim and Investor: Prudent Investing and the Calculation of Economic Damages," *Journal of Legal Economics* 14, no. 3 (2008): 28. See also John Langbein, "The Uniform Prudent Investor Act and the Future of Trust Investing," *Iowa Law Review* 81 (1996): 646 ("Some American jurisdictions had a similar history in the nineteenth and early twentieth centuries, developing so-called legal lists of court-approved or legislatively-approved investments, which were initially restricted to government bonds and first mortgages, but grudgingly expanded in some states to include selected corporate issues."); Marc Gertner, "Trustee Liability Insurance Under ERISA," *William and Mary Law Review* 17, no. 2 (1975): 233–250; J. Fred Kingren, "The Diversification of Trust Investments," *Alabama Law Review* 38 (1986–87): 123–151.

18. Bevis Longstreth, *Modern Investment Management and the Prudent Man Rule* (Oxford: Oxford University Press, 1986).

19. Jesse Dukeminier and James E. Krier, "The Rise of the Perpetual Trust," *UCLA Law Review* 50 (2003): 1335.

20. *Harvard College v. Amory*, 26 Mass. (9 Pick.) 446 (1830).

21. *In re Bank of New York*, 323 N.E. 2d 700, 703 (N.Y. 1974). This scary, antidiversification language was partly softened by the court's simultaneous acknowledgment that diversification was a reasonable strategy for some trust investments:

> The record of any individual investment is not to be viewed exclusively, of course, as though it were in its own water-tight compartment, since to some extent individual investment decisions may properly be affected by considerations of the performance of the fund as an entity, as in the instance, for example, of individual security decisions based in part on considerations of diversification of the fund or of capital transactions to achieve sound tax planning for the fund as a whole. The focus of inquiry, however, is nonetheless on the individual security as such and factors relating to the entire portfolio are to be weighed only along with others in reviewing the prudence of the particular investment decisions.

See also Langbein and Posner, "Market Funds" (1976). As late as 1982 the Supreme Court of Alabama held a bank trustee liable "for 17 disappointing stocks held in the bank's common trust fund." Langbein, "The Uniform Prudent Investor Act," 645 n.

34 (referring to *First Ala. Bank of Montgomery v. Martin*, 425 So. 2d 415, 427 [Ala. 1982]).

22. The reform movement was also impacted by the 1992 *Restatement (Third) of Trusts* sections on prudent trust investment and the earlier 1974 ERISA regulations. Max M. Schanzenbach and Robert H. Sitkoff, "Did Reform of Prudent Trust Investment Laws Change Trust Portfolio Allocation?" *Journal of Law and Economics* 50 (2007): 681–712.

23. 7B U.L.A. 1 (1994). This section relies extensively on Langbein, "The Uniform Prudent Investor Act."

24. This section's description of legal regulation of leverage is largely derived from Jonathan Macey et al., "Helping Law Catch Up to Markets: Applying Broker-Dealer Law to Subprime Mortgages," *Journal of Corporate Law* 33, no. 4 (2009): 789–842.

25. Regulation T, Credit by Brokers and Dealers, *Code of Federal Regulations*, title 12, sec. 220.8.

26. SEC Rule 15c2-5, Rule 10b-16, 34 Fed. Reg. 19,718 (Dec. 16, 1969). See also Charles F. Rechlin, *Securities Credit Regulation*, vol. 22 of *Securities Law* (St. Paul, MN: West, 2001), 3:74 (describing the large amount of disclosure required when customers wish to trade on margin). See also North American Securities Administrators Assoc, *Model Rules*, sec. 1(c), and Joseph C. Long, *Blue Sky Law*, vol. 12A (Eagan, MN: Thomson/West, 2001), sec. 9:108.17.

27. NYSE Rule 405(1), available at http://rules.nyse.com/NYSETools/Exchange Viewer.asp?selectednode=chp_1_5_7_7&manual=%2Fnyse%2Fnyse_rules%2Fnyse -rules%2F.

28. NASD, *NASD Suitability Rules*, NASD Conduct Rule 2310. See also FINRA, *FINRA Manual*, FINRA Rule 2360(b)19: Suitability, http://finra.complinet.com/en/ display/display_main.html?rbid=2403&element_id=6306.

29. See Macey et al., "Helping Law Catch Up."

30. Somewhat surprisingly, commodity brokers are not required to assure "suitability." The Commodities Futures Trading Commission (CFTC) at one time considered promulgating an analogous rule but ultimately chose a different course. See *Dyer v. Merrill Lynch*, 928 F. 2d 238, 241 (7th Cir. 1991); *Bieganek v. Wilson*, 642 F. Supp. 768 (N.D. Ill. 1986); Norman S. Poser, *Broker-Dealer Law and Regulation* (Gaithersburg, MD: Aspen Law and Business, 2000), sec. 3.03. Brokers can also be found liable under Rule 10b-5 if a court finds:

(1) that the securities purchased were unsuited to the buyer's needs; (2) that the defendant knew or reasonably believed the securities were unsuited to the buyer's needs; (3) that the defendant recommended or purchased the unsuitable securities for the buyer anyway; (4) that, with scienter, the defendant made material misrepresentations (or, owing a duty to the buyer, failed to disclose material information) relating

to the suitability of the securities; and (5) that the buyer justifiably relied to its detriment on the defendant's fraudulent conduct.

Brown v. E.F. Hutton Group, Inc., 991 F. 2d 1020, 1031 (2d Cir. 1993).

31. See *In re Stein*, Exchange Act Release No. 47,335, 79 SEC Docket 1777 (February 10, 2003) (also discussed in Macey et al., "Helping Law Catch Up").

32. *In re Pinchas*, Exchange Act Release No. 41,816, 70 SEC Docket 1108 (Sept. 1, 1999).

33. See Macey et al., "Helping Law Catch Up." *DelPorte v. Shearson, Hammill & Co.*, 548 F. 2d 1149, 1153 (5th Cir. 1977); *Troyer v. Karcagi*, 476 F. Supp. 1142, 1152 (S.D.N.Y. 1979); *In re Muth*, Exchange Act Release No. 52,551, 86 SEC Docket 956 (Oct. 3, 2005).

34. See also Charles R. Mills and Ronald A. Holinsky, *Broker-Dealer Regulation*, sec. 6:1.2[B] (2007).

35. James M. Poterba, Steven F. Venti, and David A. Wise, "Saver Behavior and 401(k) Retirement Wealth," *American Economic Review* 90 (2000): 300.

36. Howard Pianko and Orrin Feldman, "Participant Directed Individual Account Plans Under ERISA Section 404(c)," 310 PLI/Tax 165 (1991). See also Final Regulation Regarding Participant Directed Individual Account Plans (ERISA Section 404(c) Plans), 57 Fed. Reg. 46,906 (Oct. 13, 1992) (codified at *Code of Federal Regulations*, title 29 sec. 2550, Rules and Regulations for Fiduciary Responsibility): "All of the fiduciary provisions of ERISA remain applicable to both the initial designation of investment alternatives and investment managers and the ongoing determination that such alternatives and managers remain suitable and prudent investment alternatives for the plan."

37. *Code of Federal Regulations*, title 29 sec. 2550.404c-1(b)(3)(i)(B).

38. *Code of Federal Regulations*, title 29 sec. 2550.404c-1(b)(3)(i)(C). An employer is also not eligible for safe harbor if an investment alternative plan "could result in a loss in excess of a participant's or beneficiary's account balance." *Code of Federal Regulations*, title 29 sec. 2550.404c-1(d)(2)(ii)(D). But this prohibition does not pose an impediment to leveraged lifecycles, deep-in-the-money call index purchases, or even traditional margin purchases of stock—because none of these exposes the employee to a risk of losing more than his or her account balance.

39. *Code of Federal Regulations*, title 29 sec. 2550.404c-1(b)(3)(i)(B)(3).

40. David Swensen, *Pioneering Portfolio Management: An Unconventional Approach to Institutional Investment*, rev. and updated ed. (New York: Free Press, 2009).

41. Harry Markowitz, "Portfolio Selection," *Journal of Finance* 7, no. 1 (1952): 77–91; Randall H. Borkus, "A Trust Fiduciary's Duty to Implement Capital Preservation Strategies Using Financial Derivative Techniques," *Real Property, Probate and Trust Journal* 36, no. 1 (2001): 134–135 ("Markowitz set himself apart from other economists by developing specific quantitative models to measure a portfolio's composite risk and

expected return. Through the use of his quantitative models, Markowitz showed the world of finance how diversification worked to reduce portfolio risk while maximizing return").

42. John C. Bogle, *The Little Book of Common Sense Investing: The Only Way to Guarantee Your Fair Share of Market Returns* (Hoboken, NJ: Wiley & Sons, 2007); Robert Slater, *John Bogle and the Vanguard Experiment: One Man's Quest to Transform the Mutual Fund Industry* (Chicago: Irwin Professional, 1997).

43. John Wagonner, "Bear Market Alters Mutual Fund Landscape," *USA Today*, December 12, 2008.

ACKNOWLEDGMENTS

This book got its start in 2005 when Bill Baldwin, the editor-in-chief at *Forbes* magazine, rejected one of our regular column submissions. This was the first time that had happened, and we were a little taken aback, but Bill gently pointed out that *Forbes* had previously published similar analyses of target-date funds. He challenged us to go back to the drawing board and come up with something new. This prodding led us to propose an early version of the lifecycle strategy in the article "Mortgage Your Retirement," which appeared in that year's November 14 issue and became the impetus for this book. We've never been so grateful for a rejection.

When it comes seeking help, we're well diversified. Thank you Nick Barberis, Bill Barnett, Charley Ellis, Frank Fabozzi, Larry Hilibrand, Lydia Marshall, Andrew Metrick, Jim Poterba, and Robert Shiller, along with seminar participants at Yale University, Harvard University, Columbia University, the University of Chicago, the University of Missouri, and Stanford University. This book has greatly leveraged the wisdom of these friends and colleagues.

We also thank Andrew Verstein and Market Timer for letting us share their stories, and Shirley Chock for helping us interpret Yale's data. Lynn Chu and Glen Hartley, our agents at Writers' Representatives, pushed back on our proposal, making sure you didn't need a Ph.D. to understand our ideas. Beth Wright of Trio Bookworks deftly served as our copyeditor. And Tim Sullivan, our editor at Basic Books, has gently and gracefully continued the process.

Isra Bhatty, Jonathan Borowsky, Ben Gross, Alice Shih, Heidee Stoller, Anthony Vitarelli, Dan Winnick, and David Zhou provided much of the programming and research assistance. And special thanks go to Katie Pichotta, who not only helped us crunch numbers but also painstakingly read and reread the manuscript, ferreting out errors. On top of that, she did the book's illustrations and built our website! Katie has improved our lives immeasurably. We promise never to ask you to read a patent application again.

INDEX